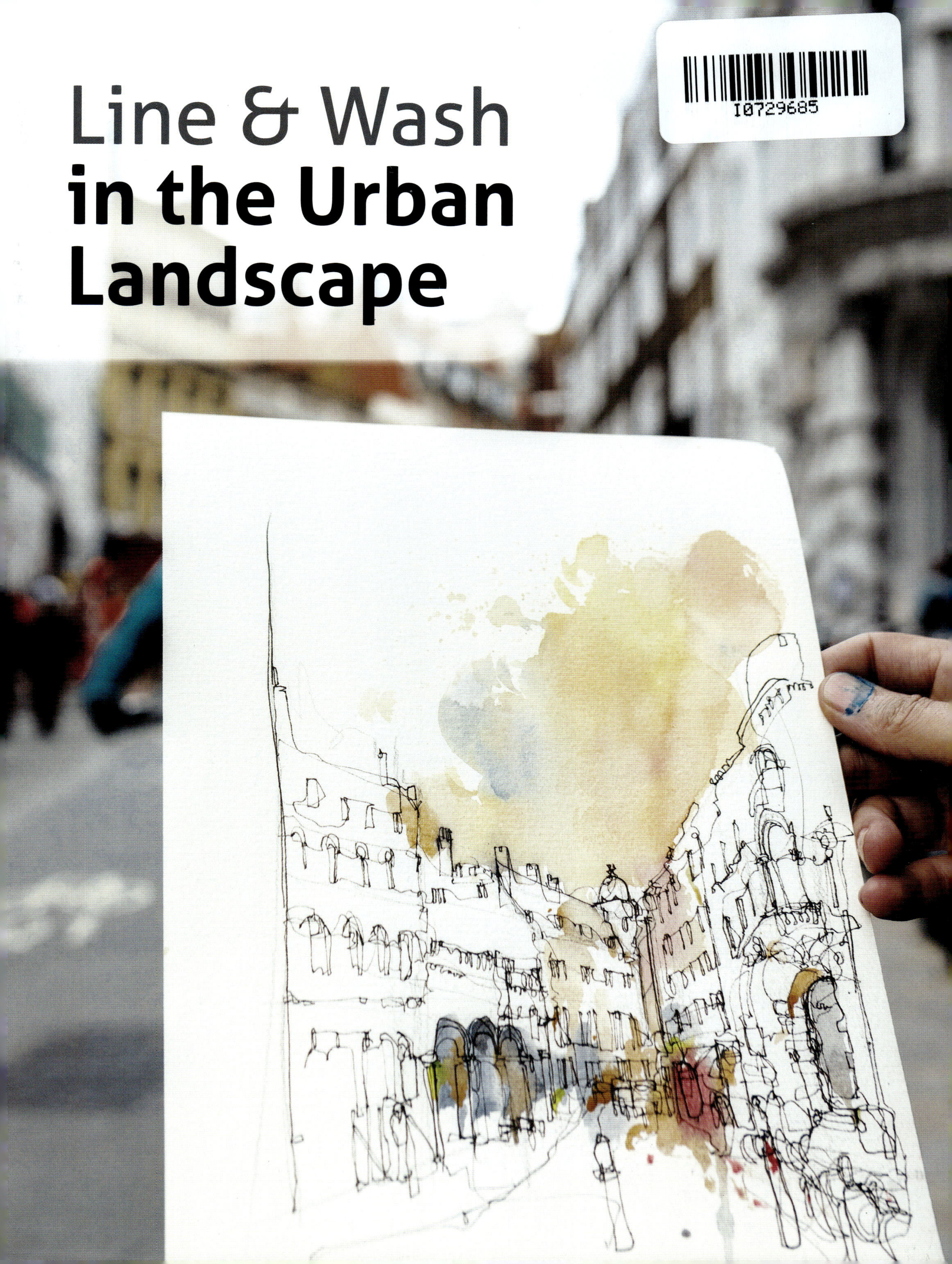

Line & Wash
in the Urban
Landscape
I0729685

Dedication

To Mum and Dad.

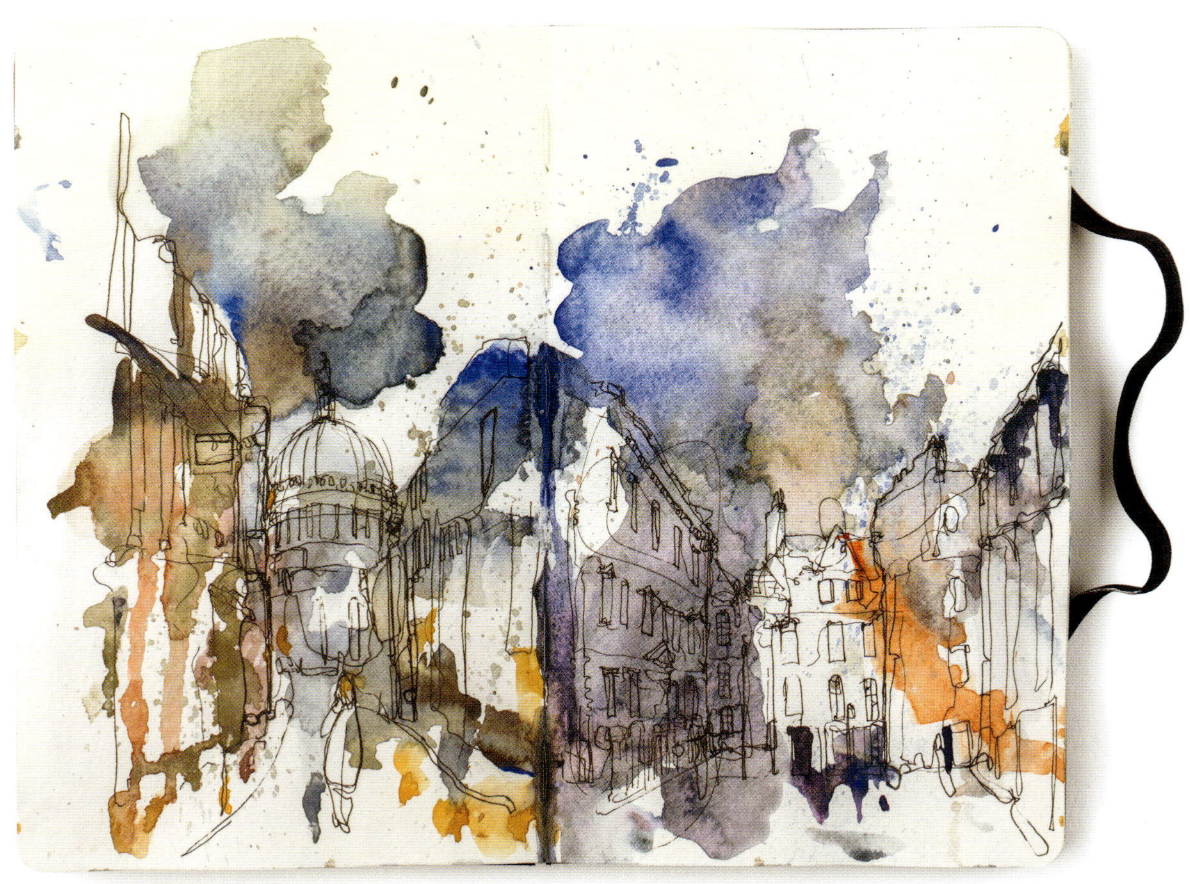

Line & Wash in the Urban Landscape

Sketching with watercolour and ink

NEIL WHITEHEAD

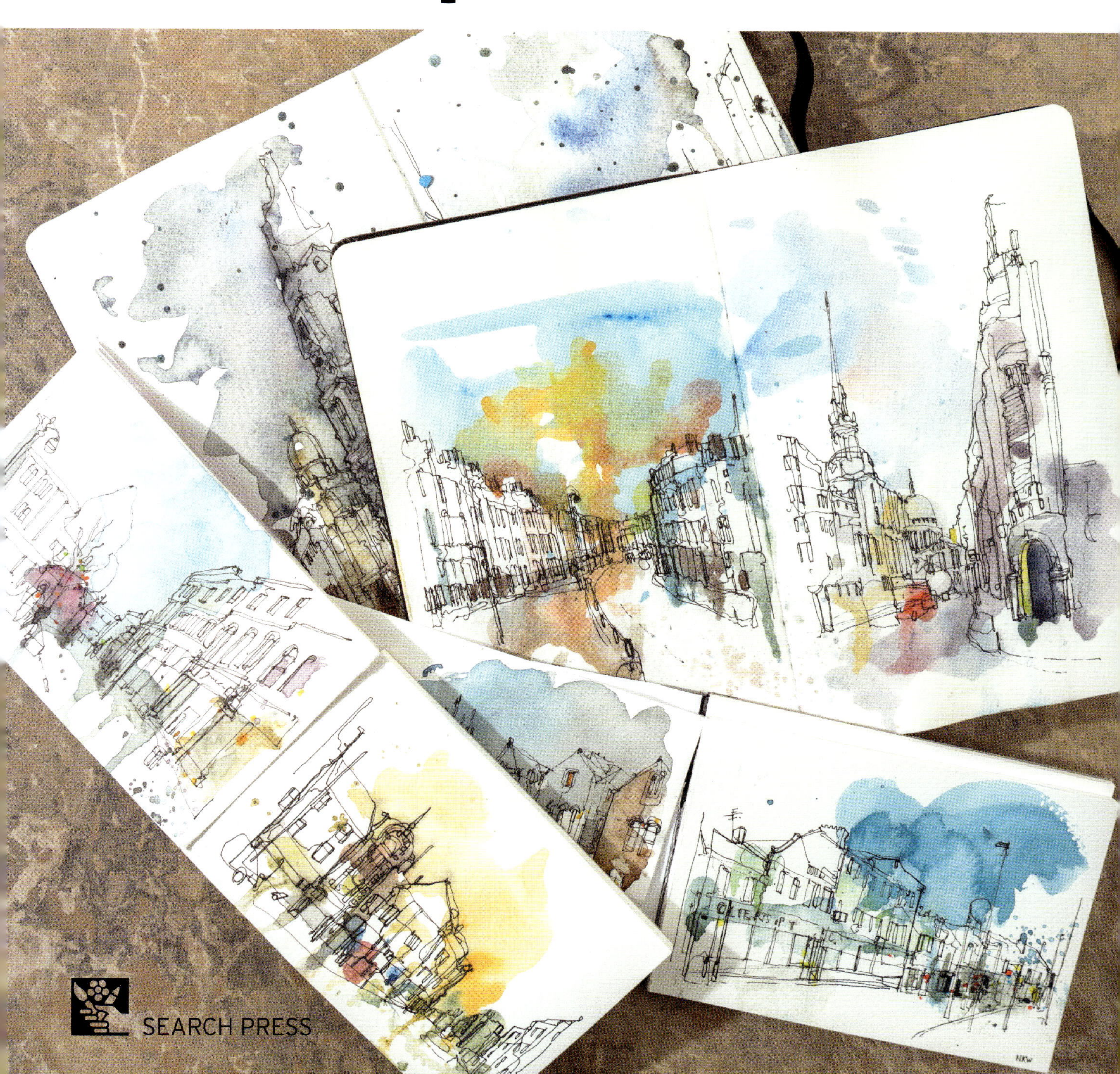

First published in 2025
Search Press Limited
Wellwood, North Farm Road,
Tunbridge Wells, Kent TN2 3DR

Text copyright © Search Press, 2025

Photographs by Mark Davison at Search Press Studios
and on location

Photographs and design copyright © Search Press Ltd. 2025

ISBN: 978-1-80092-195-5
ebook ISBN: 978-1-80093-180-0

The Publishers and author can accept no responsibility
for any consequences arising from the information,
advice or instructions given in this publication.

Suppliers

If you have difficulty in obtaining any of the materials
and equipment mentioned in this book, then please
visit the Search Press website for details of suppliers:
www.searchpress.com

You are invited to see more from the author:
www.neilwhitehead.co.uk
Instagram: @ennkaydraw
Pinterest: neilwhiteheadartist
YouTube: neilwhiteheadartist
TikTok: @neilwhitehead

Bookmarked Hub

For further ideas and inspiration, and to join our free
online community, visit www.bookmarkedhub.com
Search for this book by title or ISBN. Membership of
the Bookmarked online community is free.

Acknowledgements

Who'd have thought it – I've been bowled over by
the support for my art over the years!

Thanks date back to my Art teacher, Miss Gabner,
who gave me so much confidence in my ability. And
to my Mum, Dad and sister for putting up with me
constantly drawing them through the 1990s.

More recently the love, encouragement and patience
of my wife, Viki, has given me the belief to make this
happen. To my son and daughter, Ollie and Grace –
this is proof that if you set your sights on something
wildly unachievable you can achieve it.

There are so many brilliant sketchers and artists
who've directly or indeed unknowingly inspired
and supported me with their precision, expression,
artistry and inspirational use of colour, including
Simone Ridyard, Alex Hillkurtz, Martin Lachmair,
Felix Scheinberger, Teoh Kim Seah, Uta Polster and
so many more.

Big thanks go to those who've given me a huge leap
in my artistic journey and the confidence to push
through my own comfort zones: Rocket and Bird,
Artist Talk Magazine, The Holt Gallery, Bath
Contemporary Art Fair, Urban Sketchers Latvia,
Urban Sketchers London and Urban Sketchers
Switzerland – Zurich 2023 was just the best!

Final thanks go to Derwent Art, for the materials
and encouragement they provide me as a
Brand Ambassador.

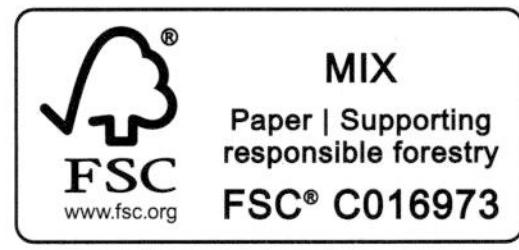

Contents

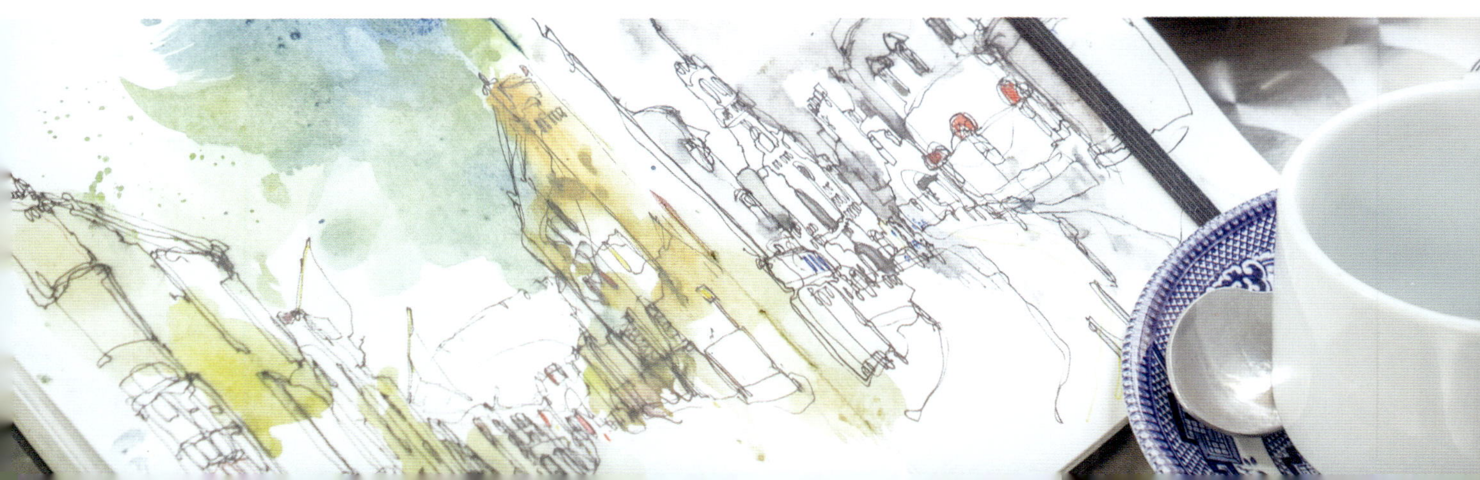

Introduction

Line & Wash in the Urban Landscape is a book created to help
you learn some new sketching techniques, brush up on your
current skills or take the plunge and begin to embrace drawing
a new kind of subject – all with a very healthy dose of fast and
fluid rhythmic expression. I'll take you through my typical kit,
my usual set-up arrangement, and studying a scene to find the
composition that will deliver the most interest for both the
artist and the viewer. I'll advise where to start with suitable
pens, sketchbooks and watercolour paints.

Like so many, I grew up drawing and colouring – my
sketchbooks were never far away. I'd draw my Mum, Dad,
sister and dog while relaxing in the living room, and draw
what I saw out of my bedroom window. I'd sketch on the bus
in a small notebook and I'd draw on my travels. Art was my
first love and I left secondary school for art school; constantly
experimenting, trying new subjects, new mediums and
immersing myself among brilliantly talented people. During
my years at university in Portsmouth in the late 1990s I found
my love of sketching the city. I would sit for hours drawing
Portsmouth Guidhall and observing the constant passage of
time. I was fortunate during my time as a student to visit Paris
and New York, where the architecture was on another level and
I knew that the urban landscape was special to me.

Working in central London after university was a goal, and
I was fortunate to work just minutes from St Paul's Cathedral.
To this day, St Paul's is by far the most sketched building in
my portfolio.

My artistic style has evolved over the years, but a small
constant remains – speed and fluid lines. I've always had a
somewhat urban style and I love to create a sense of tension.
It's as if each sketch could align itself to a piece of music – no
surprise, perhaps, that I had dreams as a boy of being an album
cover designer.

Being loose and free is a very distinct characteristic of my
style which is why I have found real enjoyment in the 'line and
wash' technique – flowing bold colours mixed with clear dark
pen lines.

Architecture inspires – I've always liked drawing buildings.
Spoilt for choice, growing up near London, the history of the
urban landscape has always fascinated me. The hustle and
bustle of crowds, the history that runs through an ancient
church spire, the majesty of medieval domed roofs, modern
shops framed with Victorian architecture, to the sleek modern
feats of engineering that outline the ever-changing urban
skyline. This mesh of architectural styles, angles and materials
seen around our cities and towns deeply satisfies my artistic
motivation and is my artistic happy place. Mix this with people,
movement, traffic and nature and you will find a multitude of
sketching targets whether you are in the most exciting cities on
Earth, or the quietest rural towns.

Why urban sketching?

The meteoric rise in urban sketching over the past few years has also brought about a huge community with a common goal – sketching on location and sharing the love for the places we live and travel. Sketching in a group is a great experience and good for building confidence (often the nemesis of those starting out). It helps dilute the stress of the general public peering over your shoulder when sketching!

Solitary sketching can also be a very satisfying experience. Whatever the circumstances or the output, it's important to keep hold of your early works and full sketchbooks as a future reference, as you will noticeably improve and, in time, develop your own style. Seeing this progression is something that never stops.

Sketching the urban landscape can serve as a form of visual diary of a town or city's history and its progression – over time witnessing a city's growth and development.

I'm a fast sketcher and painter, I like to simplify complex scenes to bring about new artistic interpretations. My lines are quick, smooth and often continuous, and my colour use is rapid – lots of water and no holding back with pigment and contrast. This may seem somewhat unconventional to most watercolourists, who will build up with three or four layers of darks and lights, but I like to paint once and leave big chunks of the page white to allow the work to breathe. Negative (white) space will become one of your greatest tools.

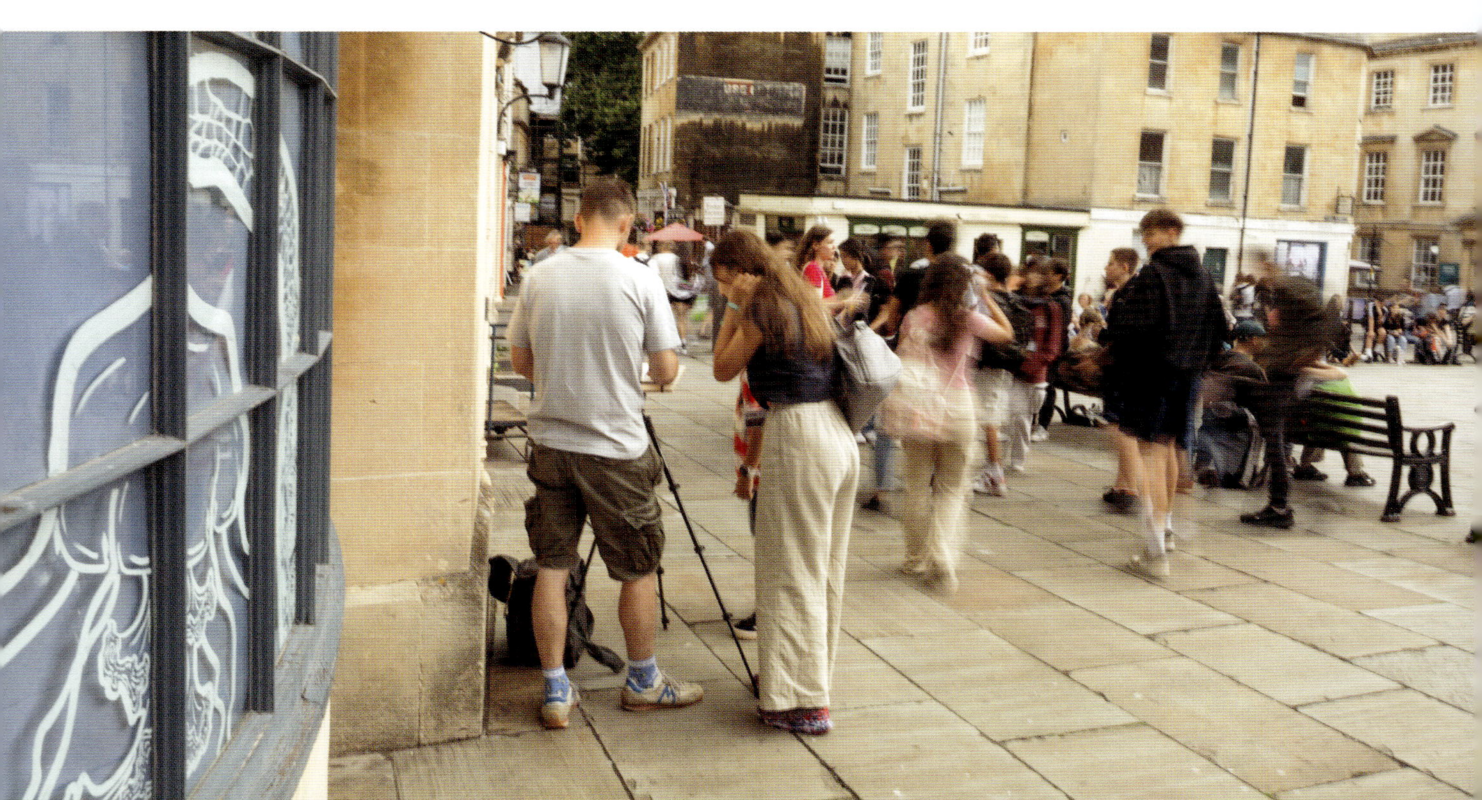

Line and wash in the urban
landscape is about:

▸ Fast and fluid work
▸ Capturing emotions
▸ Imperfections
▸ Having fun and being expressive

These days everyone has a brilliant camera in their pocket. I don't aspire to recreate what the camera can do – I want to create something unique that has energy and individual interpretation. The commissions I complete for clients worldwide are for people who have deep memories around a city or favourite location and who crave an artistic version to make it unique to them.

I've had the pleasure of exhibiting at some tremendous galleries and running workshops across the UK and abroad – something I never thought possible when I started drawing buildings as a teenager.

When starting out, I struggled to read instructional art books as they often made it seem too hard to get started, had lots of overwhelming theory, or contained pages of recommended kit that I couldn't afford or didn't understand how to use – there are hundreds of pens and paint types that all do a very similar job. This book is deliberately lighter in theory and is designed to inspire and appeal to those who like the discipline of line and wash and want to fill their sketchbook and hear it creak under the weight of pigment and water.

Whatever the basis of your work and whatever kit you have, enjoying doing it is the key. I'll give you an overview of how I start out. We'll touch on perspective, what I look for in a scene and how to add that spark with a dynamic line and wash technique.

I hope this book offers you a reason to loosen up your drawing, gives you the confidence to be a little different in your approach to watercolours, and ultimately encourages you to enjoy the process.

Expect some challenging aspects and exercises to free up both the hand and the mind. There will be lots of fun, plenty of water and many pages of expressive sketching.

Sketching tools and materials

There is no right or wrong answer as to what kit you should use or which brand to align with. I would encourage simplicity; keep it basic to begin with and don't get consumed by the wide range of materials available. Like anyone with an interest in drawing, I began sketching surroundings with a humble 2B pencil, which provides enough tonal range to add some depth and interest. As we'll discover later, a variance in line weight and tone is key.

My typcial set-up when sketching out and about.

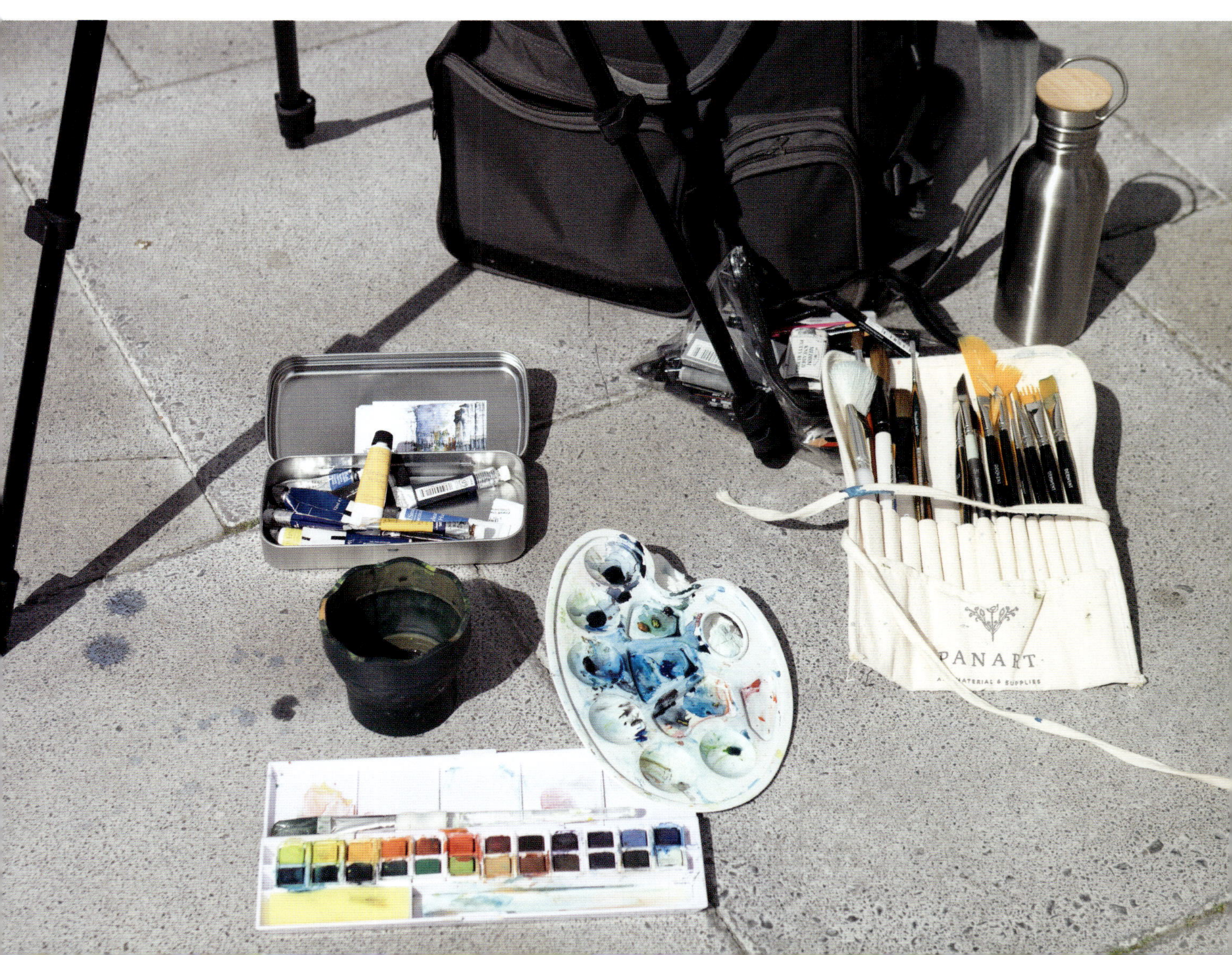

Pencils

Sketching in pencil is a good way to kick-start a sketchbook and can help build your confidence before you move on to begin future sketches with a pen. Working in pencil also means the lines can be worked over later on to create the strong visible lines on your finished sketch. I might occasionally use a pencil to plot some key scale elements of the scene. I try to avoid a standard HB pencil, as I find this too bland, and instead suggest a 2B as a minimum.

Mechanical pencils

These offer a great deal of control and are relatively affordable. They lend themselves to accuracy and architectural detail, but I tend to find them rather too exact for my style. They do, however, offer the same benefits as traditional pencil in that they can help build sketching confidence.

Eraser

I carry a kneadable eraser or putty rubber – these are essential if working on textured paper, they won't damage the surface or leave residue behind.

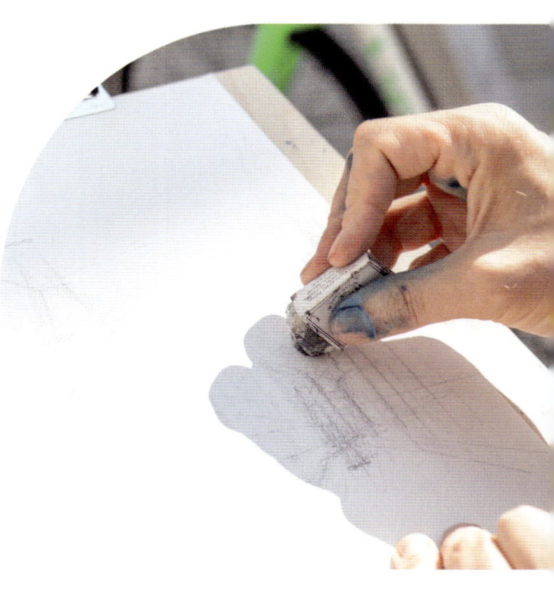

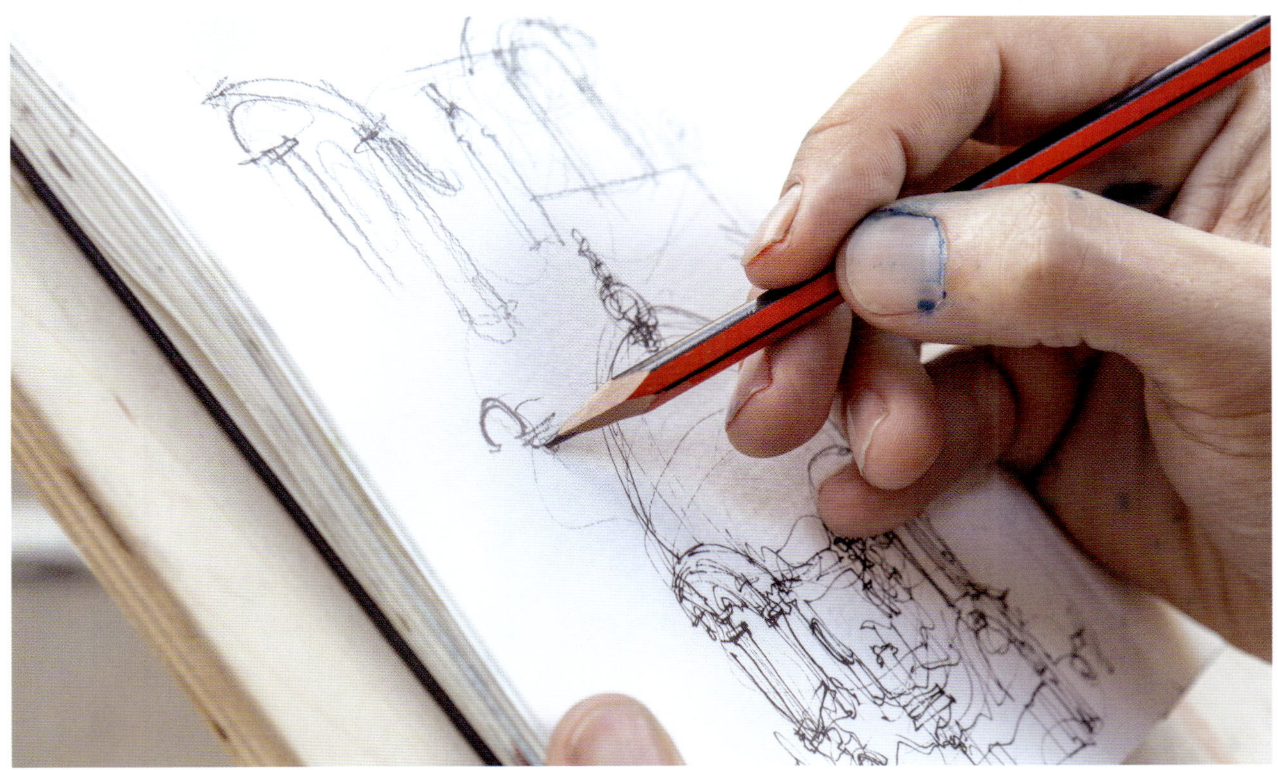

Pens

The mighty pen! Pen work feeds off confidence and a personal connection – this can take time, but the beauty of diving straight in with pen is that it can help cultivate a sense of action and decisiveness, whereas pencil work always offers the safety net of editing and 'perfecting'. You'll see throughout this book that my lines are rarely perfect.

Fineliners

My preferred method of sketching is with a fineliner pen. The Derwent range is my preferred all-round option, but I would encourage a little exploring to find what is most comfortable for you. I carry a wide range in my toolkit, varying in thickness from 0.1 to 0.8. I prefer fineliner nibs that protrude slightly to avoid scratching the paper when held at an angle.

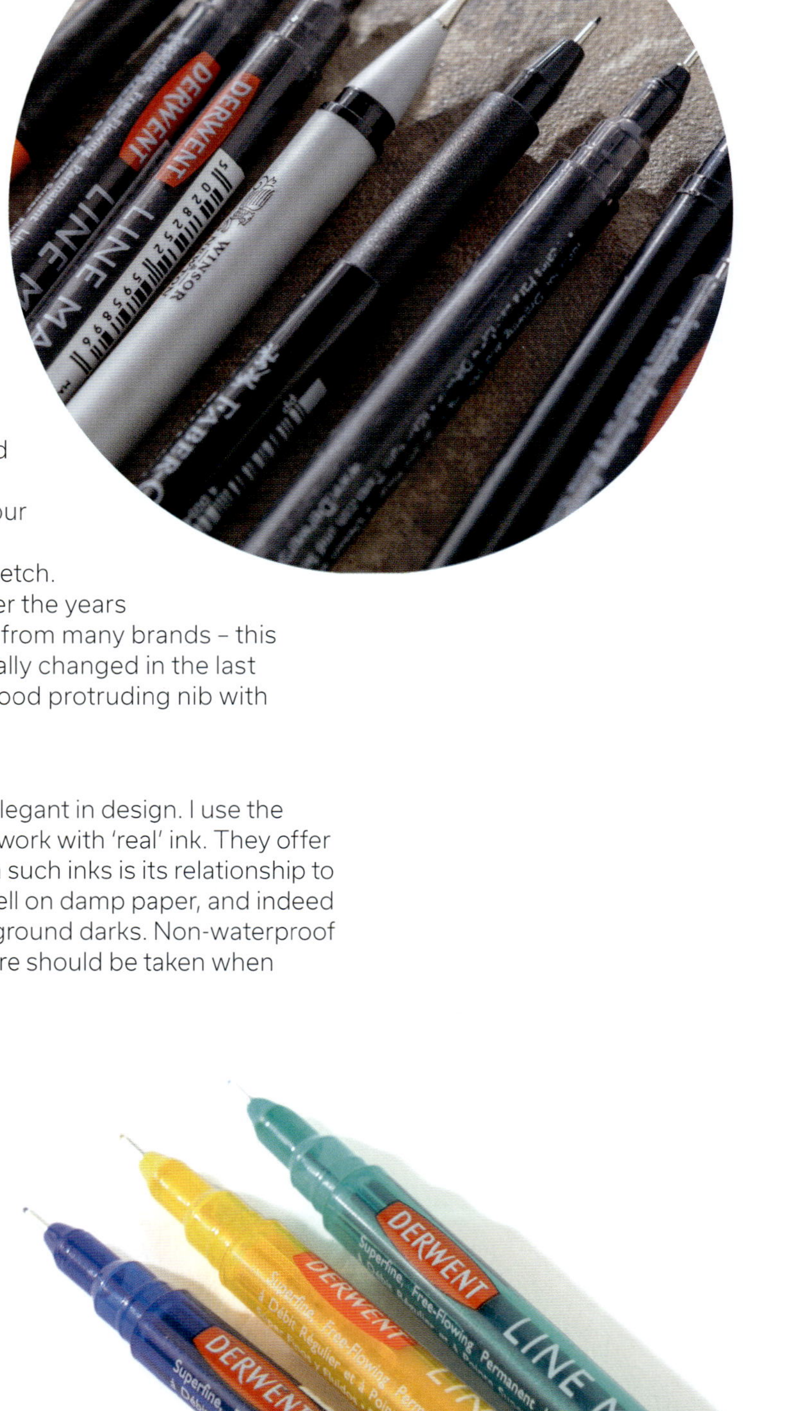

The rest of my pen toolkit is made up of colour fineliners and felt tips: red, green, yellow and blue. These are great for small detailing in a sketch. I've collected various other bits and pieces over the years and had the opportunity to try out many pens from many brands – this is always fun – but my essentials kit has not really changed in the last decade. The golden rule for pens remains: a good protruding nib with permanent ink.

Fountain pens

An alternative to the fineliner and always very elegant in design. I use the Safari range from Lamy when I feel the urge to work with 'real' ink. They offer brilliant control over line variance. The caveat in such inks is its relationship to water – of which I use plenty. Fineliners work well on damp paper, and indeed I encourage reworking to further enhance foreground darks. Non-waterproof fountain pen ink will move with the water, so care should be taken when applying watercolours or working in the rain.

Coloured fineliners make a great addition to your toolkit (used in Out & About 4, pages 92–97).

Sketchbooks and paper

What to look for in a sketchbook? My preferred sketchbook, which works well both in the studio and on location, is the A5 (148 x 210mm/5¾ x 8¼in) range of Moleskine Art Watercolour sketchbooks. These have around 100 thick, super absorbent pages and are very capable of handling lots of pen, water and pigment. The compact size is perfect for urban sketching and, once finished, they are nice and easy to keep on your bookshelf.

It's important to keep your work to provide a running commentary on your progress. No matter how experienced you are, it's healthy to chart your progress and have a personal reference guide to techniques and styles that worked well or didn't work.

If I'm working on larger pieces in the studio on a commission or upscaling a smaller sketchbook entry, I tend to use Derwent Inktense cotton papers as they offer superb colour blending properties, typically seen in some of my bold skies. Larger paper tends to be a little more expensive so don't rush into investing straight away. Alternatives to Derwent Inktense include Bockingford, Arches and Winsor & Newton papers, these all work well with my heavy water use and don't ripple too much.

Watercolour paper can be confusing! I generally recommend working with paper that is around 200gsm (90lb) (this is a measure of thickness) when working at A5 (148 x 210mm/5¾ x 8¼in) size, and around 400gsm (200lb) for A4 (210 x 297mm/8¼ x 11½in) and larger.

Papers can also be listed as 'cold-pressed' or 'hot-pressed'. Generally I opt for cold-pressed as they tend to me more textured and more absorbent. Hot-pressed papers have more of a shiny, smooth texture. Paper is also sometime listed at 'Not', which basically means that it is not hot-pressed, and therefore is cold-pressed.

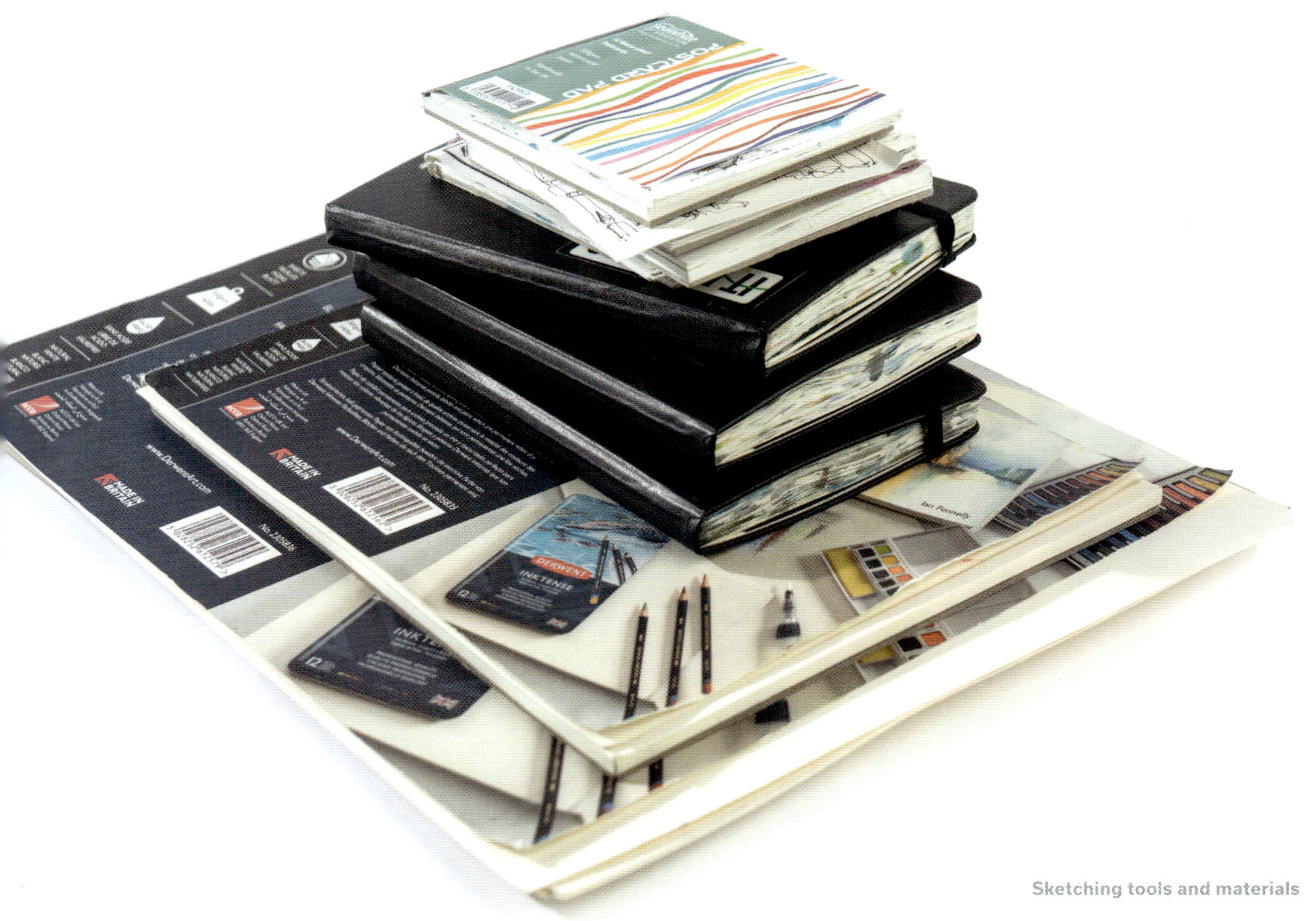

Sketching with rhythm

How to begin – loosening up

When it comes to capturing the urban landscape in a sketch, many people are drawn to the idea of capturing a perfect likeness. Striving for perfection is a common aim. This can often result in hours spent trying to capture every detail with precision and accuracy. While there is absolutely nothing wrong with wanting to do this, I prefer to add a twist, with some artistic licence to make the scene pop and create work that has personality and rhythm.

What is rhythm in sketching? Rhythm traditionally sits with music but equally forms a vitally important part of art and sketching, and refers to the dynamic flow and movement of the lines and shapes – rhythm is what truly brings a sketch to life. Rhythm is movement.

Rhythm over perfection

There can be real delight in capturing the hustle and bustle of a busy street, the calm of a quiet park, or the majesty of a dramatic city skyline. It can convey the sense of motion and energy that is at the heart of urban life.

Creating a sketch that has a strong sense of rhythm helps draw the viewer into the movement and flow of the lines and shapes. We can almost feel the energy of the city pulsing through the sketch. This sense of movement is what makes a sketch feel alive and dynamic. When sketching the urban landscape, try not to focus on just capturing the physical buildings and structures of the city – try also to capture the essence of the city: its energy, its vibe, its character. Rhythm is a powerful tool.

Sketching fast

Working fast requires focus and concentration, which can help to clear the mind. Sketching fast is a key aspect to my work and a great way to improve your observational technique. By capturing the details of a scene quickly, you must pay close attention to their surroundings. This heightened awareness of the environment can lead to a deeper appreciation of the city and its unique characteristics.

Working fast really helps train the eye to capture the essential details or features of urban scene observation, to help loosen any tension and also to help you focus on the elements that speak to you personally. I don't use a stopwatch as that's perhaps a little too pressured, but feel free to introduce some sort of basic time limit.

Tip

Hold your pen/pencil lightly so it glides easily.

Methods to help loosen and speed up your sketches

1 Quick pencil sketch before the pen
Hold the pencil nice and loosely and fill the page with lots of views, breaking the tension of the white page. I like to warm up my technique with a quick pencil sketch, such as the one to the right.

2 Pure contour loosener
The ultimate sketching loosener and yet something that never loses its effect – pure contour drawing requires 100 per cent focus on the subject. Pure contour specifically focuses on capturing the outlines or contours of a scene without looking at the paper while it is in progress. This is all about freeing up the technique and diving into pure observation, which can also help kick-start a new range of line quality.

It's an odd feeling, most definitely, but it serves as an immediate attack on our perceptions, or more accurately it stops any reliance on what we think we know as opposed to what we might see. No matter what the subject, urban scenes, portraits or general sketching, we all have our preconceived ideas of what something looks like. Think of it as tricking the brain to step out of your subconscious for few moments. Have you ever tried copying another drawing by simply turning the subject upside down? You'll be amazed at how well you start to observe when you barely recognize the subject.

Pure contour needn't be a huge scene. You might want to concentrate only on a smaller section – the key to this technique is to loosen up.

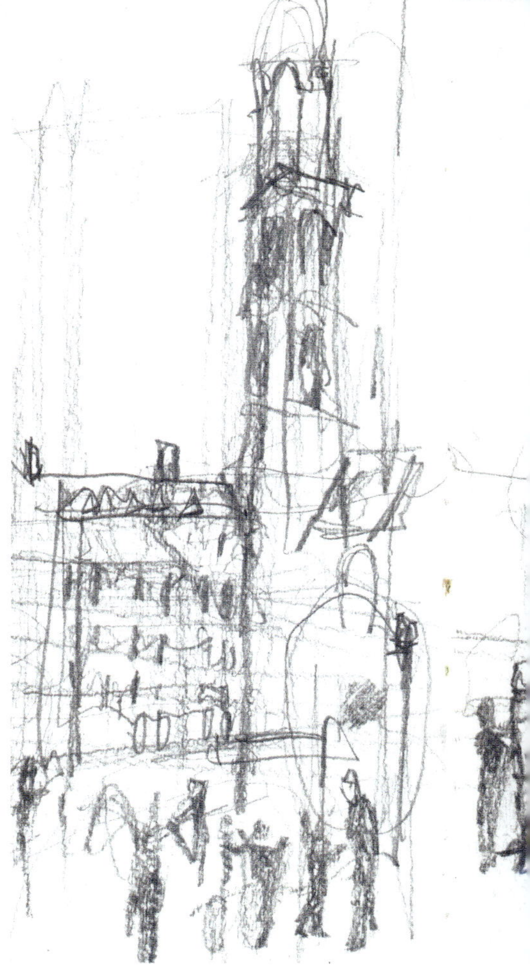

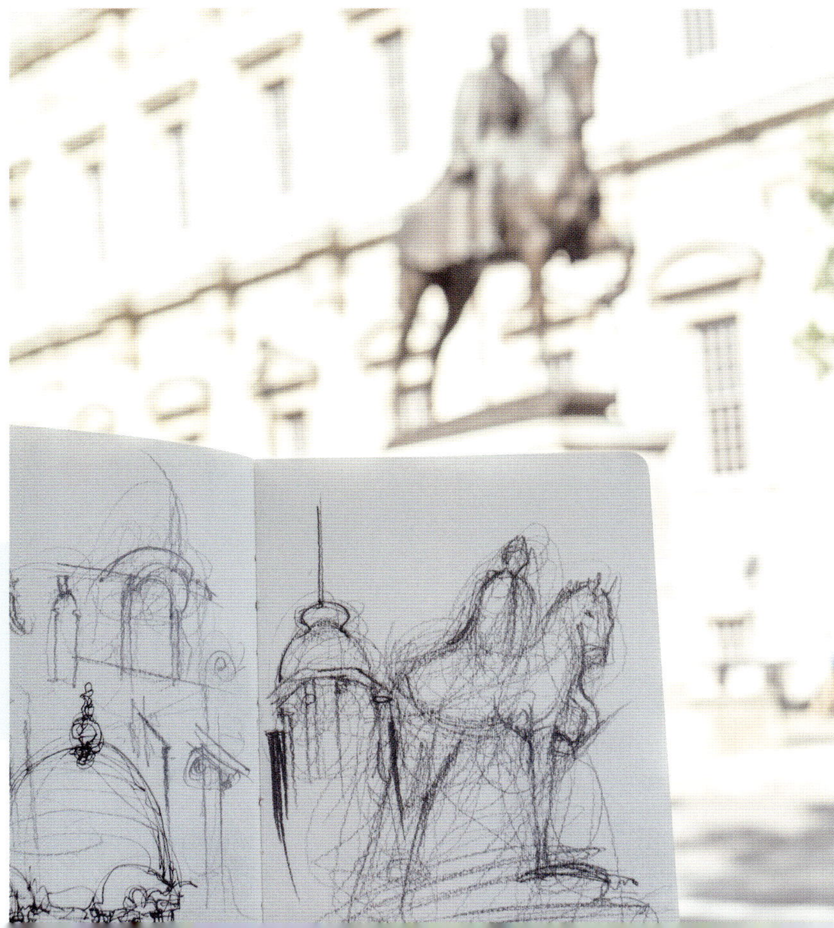

3 Continuous line sketch

As with the pure contour sketch, before you dive in, reassure yourself that
the result will not be perfect – but you might surprise yourself with a line
that oozes rhythm and character. It's those deeper connections that we're
looking for.

To get started with continuous line sketching, all you need is a pen
or pencil and a blank sheet of paper. Begin by choosing a subject that
interests you, and then try to depict it using a single, unbroken line. Don't
worry about making mistakes or getting every detail right – the goal of
continuous line sketching is to capture the essence of your subject in a
flowing and expressive way. As you work, try to keep your line as smooth
and continuous as possible. Use varying weights to glide across the page,
don't get consumed by the detail in the windows, just give an impression.

How do we encourage a fast, loose sketch? The challenge is to keep
the pen in constant contact with the paper. One of the main benefits of
continuous line sketching is that it encourages focus on the overall form
and structure of the subject, rather than getting bogged down in the
details. It's a technique I use when urban sketching or in the studio to 'free
up' my arm and to kick-start rhythm in my artwork. By eliminating the need
to lift the pen or pencil off the page, continuous line sketching allows you
to capture the essence of the subject in a more intuitive and expressive
way. Continuous line sketching can help to improve hand–eye coordination
and develop spatial awareness, because you must keep the line moving
and flowing while also navigating around the contours and details of the
subject. Don't be afraid to loop your line back and forth, mimicking some
of the less obvious shapes: car wheels, trees, road signs and so on all form
part of the matrix. This is the beginning of searching for shapes – covered
later in the book.

Over the years, I've adopted
the continuous line method
as more than a loosener and it
has become the backbone to
my regular sketching style. The
fluidity that comes from this
method sits well with me. Typically
I would now sketch loosely like
this, with connected lines but not
100 per cent continuous. If I take a
break to re-observe or adjust I will,
however, consciously look to rejoin
my old line and keep the same flow
as before.

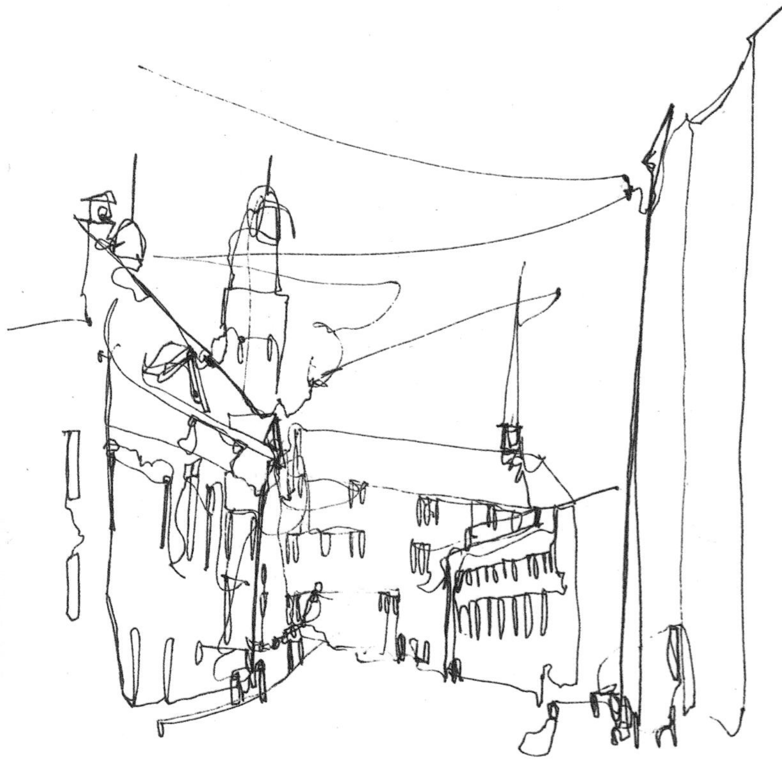

4 Line weight variance

A huge part of my sketching relies on a very considered
variance of my line work. This is where I start to bring depth
into the scene and isolate areas of interest. A sketch with
every line of a uniform thickness will struggle to come alive
by itself – it is the variance in line weight and thickness
that helps generate visual clues and interest. Much like
a highlighter, it gives emphasis to a particular structure
or detail. A mix of thick and thin lines is commonplace in
architectural drawings and is used to show perimeters and
areas of space.

   Consider having three levels of contact between pen
and paper:

Light

Often used in the continuous line as the pen or pencil
glides arounds the page (great for distance detail).

Normal

Your most natural sketching weight.

Heavy

More pressure, and potentially a line that gets a second
layer of ink after the painting process (great for foreground
detail or specific points of focus). This can be a great tactic
to define a dominant foreground edge.

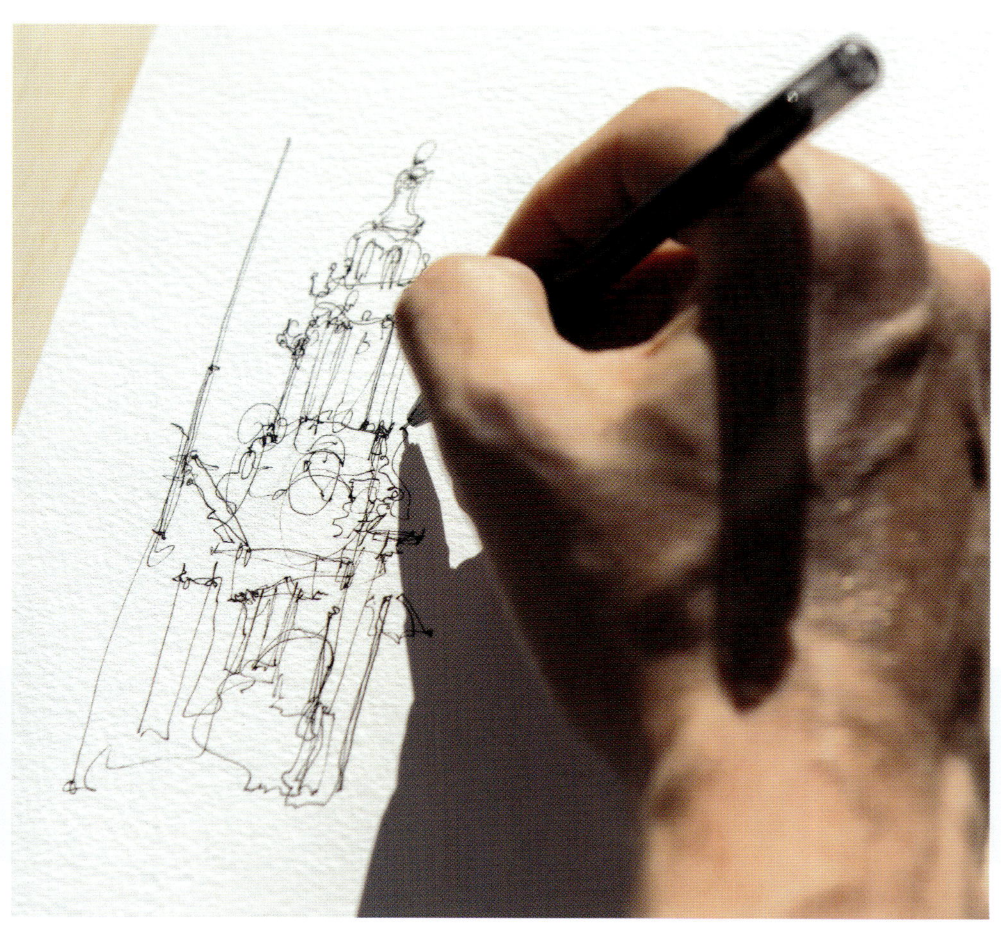

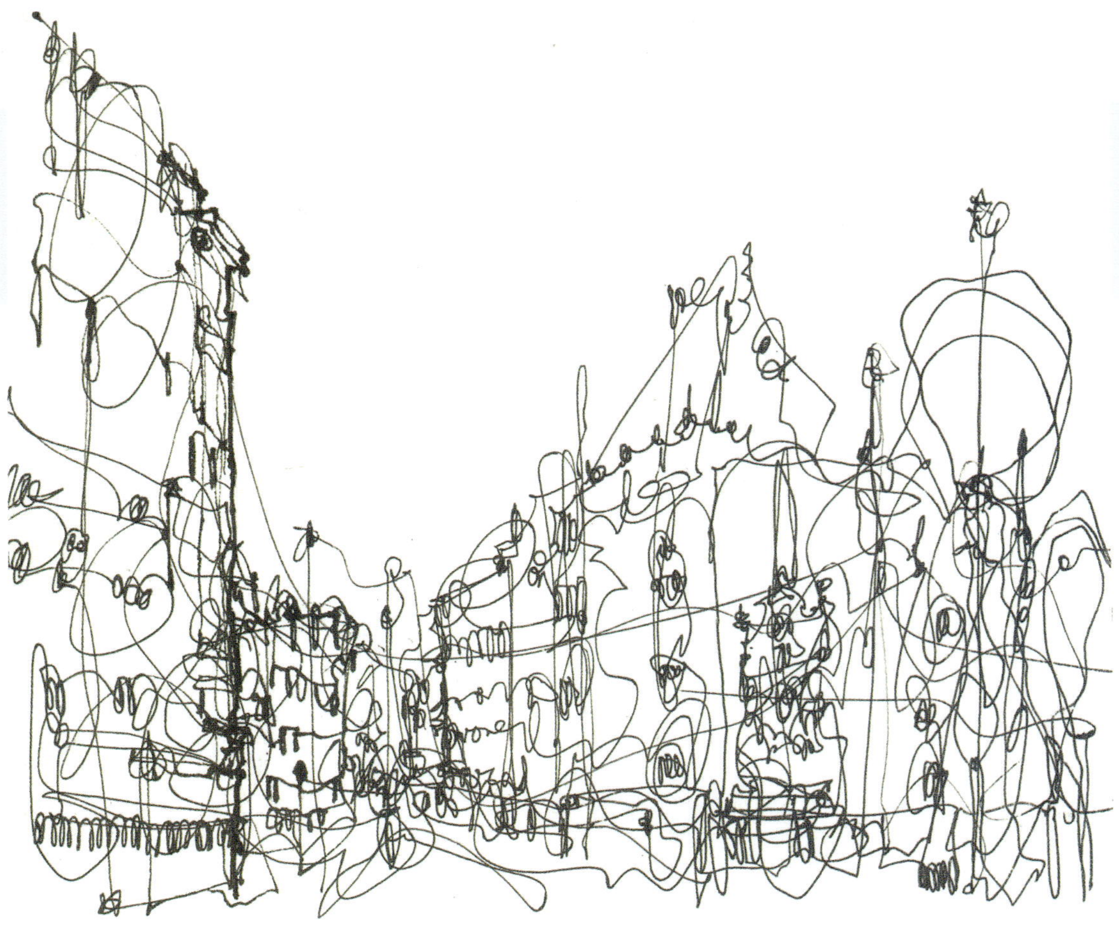

▲ A balanced sketch of varying line weights naturally starts to spark some visual interest and bring about visual hierarchy and depth that is so important to create artistic interest.

Throughout my work you'll see how I capture background movement with the gentlest of lines: like a spider's web, they help knit the core features together and bring about harmony in the sketch.

Tip

I don't tend to mix pen thicknesses on a single sketch unless I am working much larger. When working on larger peices, around A3 (297 x 420mm/11¾ x 16½in) to A2 (420 x 594mm/16½ x 23½in), I might use up to six different line weights which requires a more considered balance of white space to sit together.

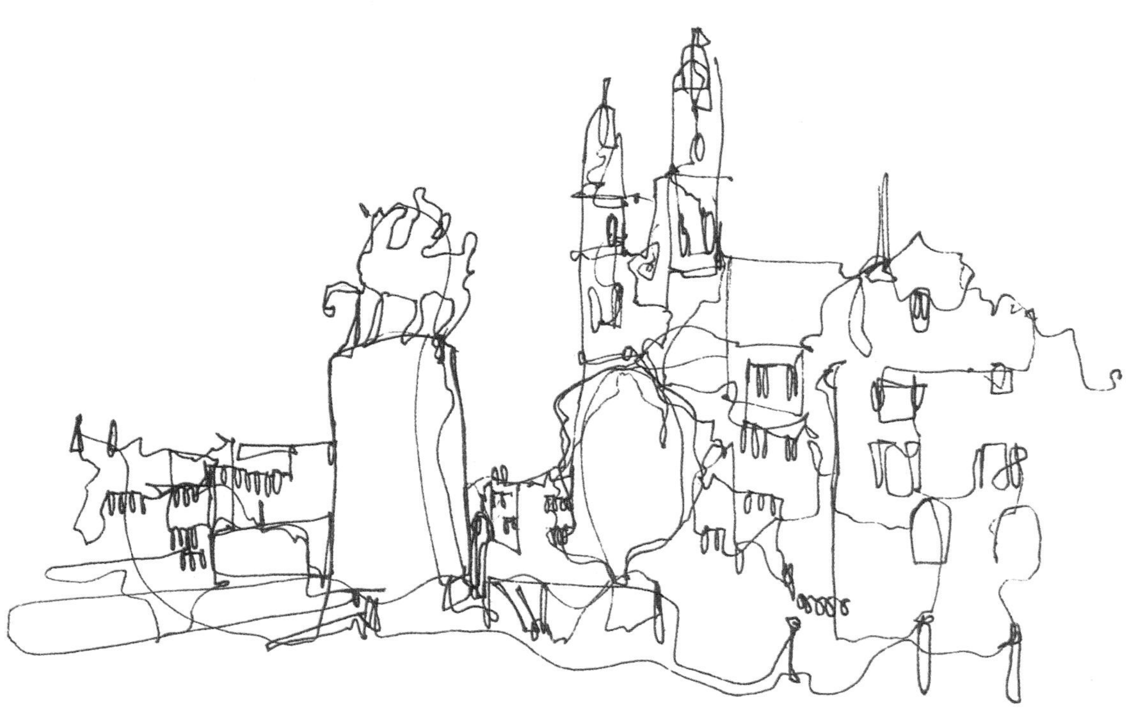

▲ Hold your pen with a little less pressure – just as mentioned in the section on pure contour loosener (page 15) and continuous line sketching (page 16) – I can't emphasize enough how easily tension can travel down to the paper. Also try holding the pen a little further away from the nib. As the sketch builds you might naturally see certain elements become denser in line work – seek this – treat your line work as you would your shading. The dense lines of activity help offer up the balance of hustle and calm in the scene.

Exercise

Pure contour

Take a moment to challenge your comfort zone and free up your sketching. A pure contour line sketch will help you focus on the key parts of the scene.

This is an exercise I do regularly to break up any tension in my sketching and to reset my observation. In all the workshops I've done this remains a favourite to break down tight sketching.

Find your subject
Choose a simple object with interesting contours or shapes. This doesn't have to be an urban landscape at this stage – it could be a plant, a chair, a mug, a person or any object with clear outlines. The goal is all about line quality and observation.

Take your time
Draw the outline of the object very slowly and deliberately. This is not a race. Keep your eyes fixed on the object. Scan every outline and shape and try to keep your pen or pencil on the paper constantly until you've drawn the shape. The focus is purely on the contours, not the detail and shapes within. Don't worry about fixing any perceived mistakes – any imperfections will make this unique to you.

Observe the results
Once you've finished capturing all the outlines, lift your pen and observe. It's likely that your lines don't meet or that your drawing has become almost an abstracted version of the scene. The main aim of this exercise is to loosen up and reset your observation.

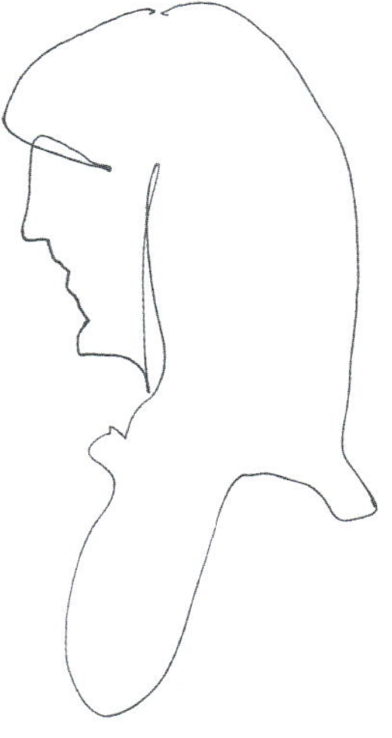

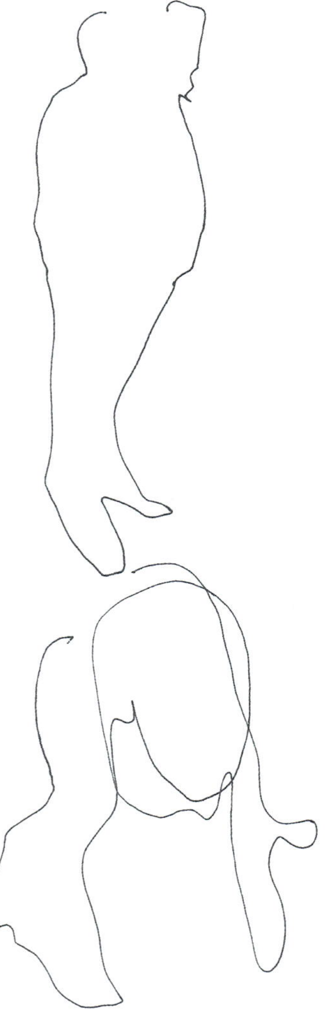

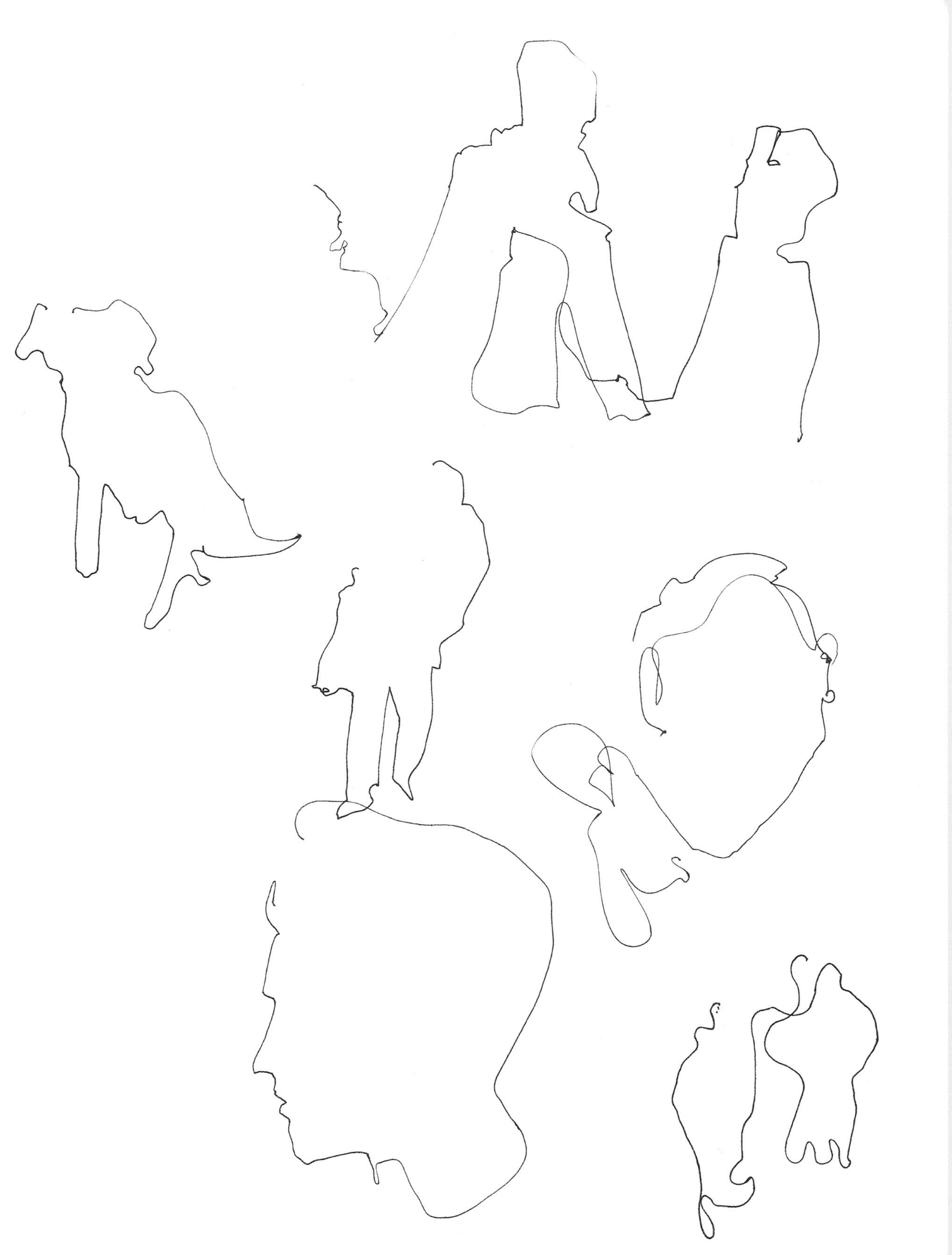

The watercolour wash

I love the creative freedom available as an urban landscape artist. We're not here to recreate exactly what the camera sees; we're creating art. Colour use is very subjective and I encourage it in any form. I can be influenced by a certain palette I'm working with, perhaps I have only my darks and greys with me, or I can be influenced by my mood.

Urban scenes under examination will contain hundreds of colours: the sky, the street signs, the road, the cars, the people and so much more. The exercises with paint that come later will help free your colour use. Pigment and tone can bring the most average sketch to life.

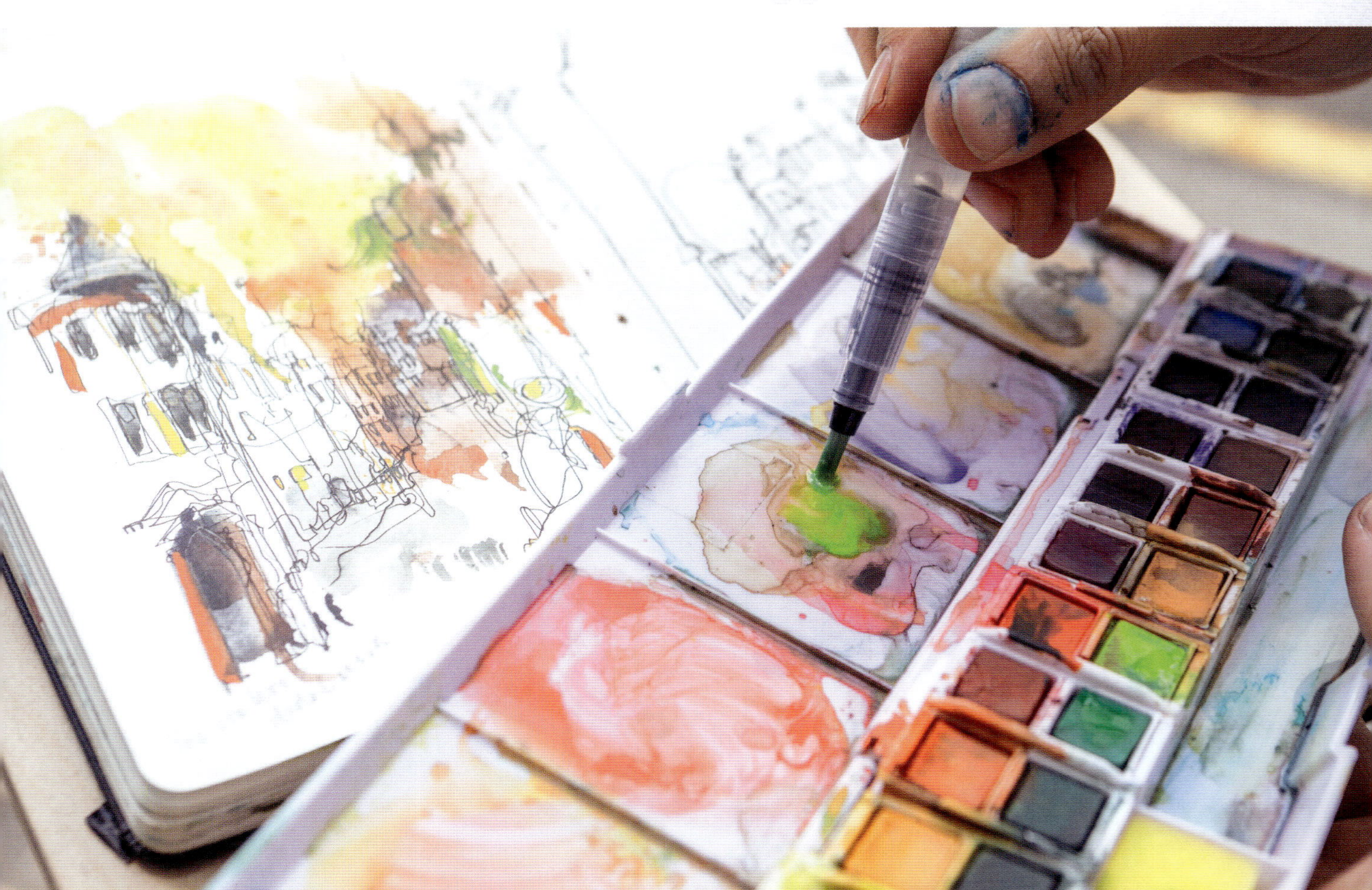

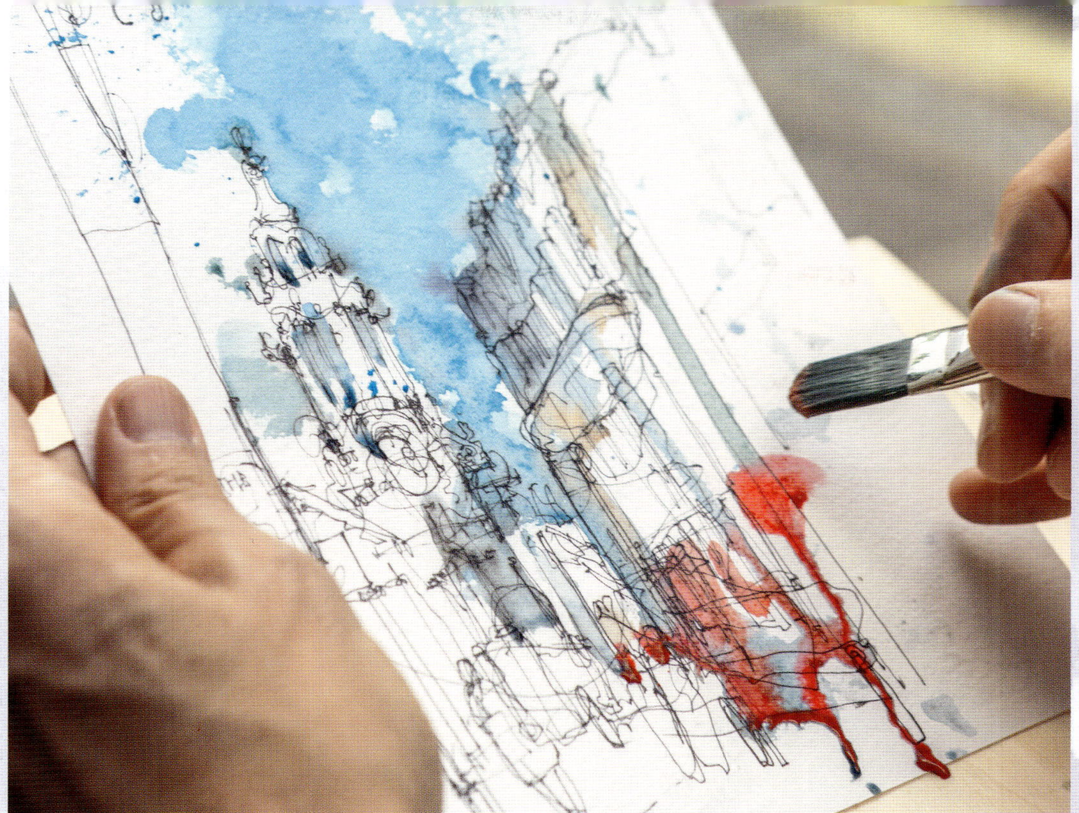

Adding watercolour

Once the sketch is done, we can unleash the colour and give our pages a wash of life and interest. This is the chance to deliver some further artistic licence on the scene which, for me, is born through a few key factors. The scene itself and the immediate colours we see are key to understanding the overall general mood. Focus on the weather, the building make-up, the brickwork, the contrasts – where are the dark and light areas of the scene? Where are the details we want to show?

Sometimes I like to squint my eyes when studying a potential scene. This can help you identify the contrast by reducing the amount of visible detail. When the amount of light entering your eyes is reduced, it eliminates some of the finer details, making it easier to identify the underlying shapes, tones and values in the scene. I find I can then better judge the overall composition of the scene and the relationships between the different elements within it. Focusing on the areas of the scene that are lightest and darkest in contrast can help to add further dynamics to the painting, which is crucial for creating a sense of depth and atmosphere when you add washes.

What you need: painting tools and materials

Paint brushes

Brushes can also come in a mesmerizing range of options and varying degrees in quality. I have dozens of brushes but often choose to work with a small range of traditional paint brushes, however tempting the art shop is with shiny new models!

I'd be lost without my large filbert style brush. It's relatively inexpensive, and the attribute that makes the filbert my favourite and most-used brush is the volume of water it holds. A key and very obvious aspect to my expressive works are the drips and bold water use. To complement the filbert I also have a traditional mop brush which holds good volumes of water, as well as a dagger, which offers supreme control and has an obvious and manicured point or nib.

I opt for synthetic brushes that can hold plenty of water and aren't too dainty. Steer clear of the beginner brushes with a spiky and sparse collection of bristles that simply sprout out from the handle in exclamation, and which lack any density for rigid water tension.

My travel paints and top three go-to brushes: large filbert, dagger and mop (left to right).

Brush pens

In addition to the traditional brushes, I also always have a portable watercolour brush pen in my kit (shown to the right). These are super helpful tools that contain a reservoir of water. As you'd expect, these are perfect for on location sketching and can work well as a backup brush.

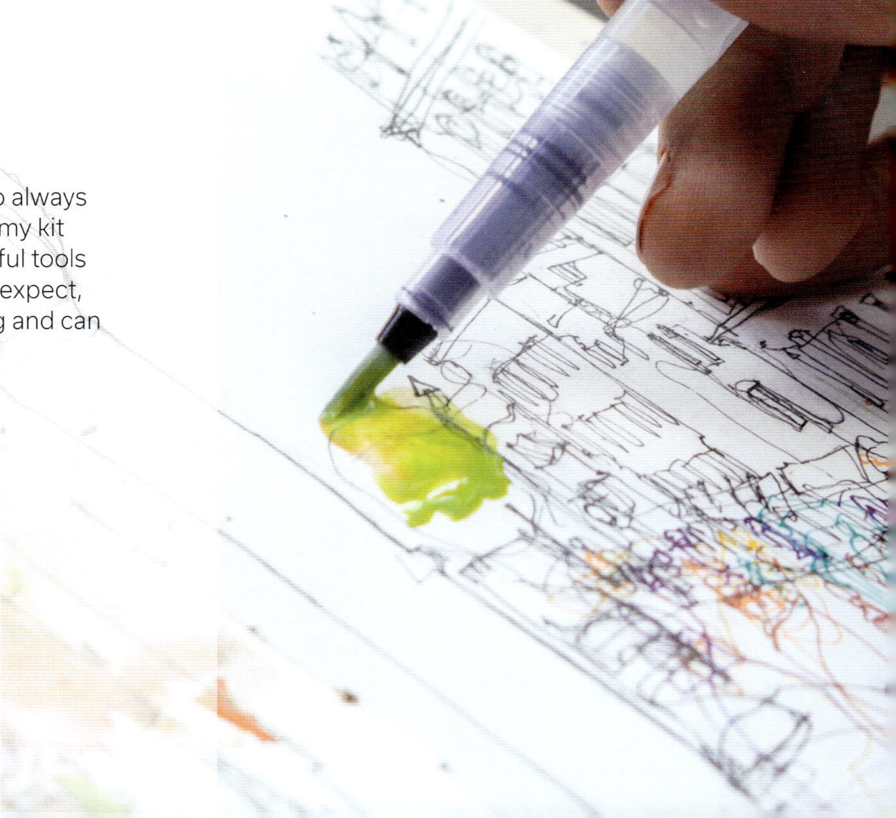

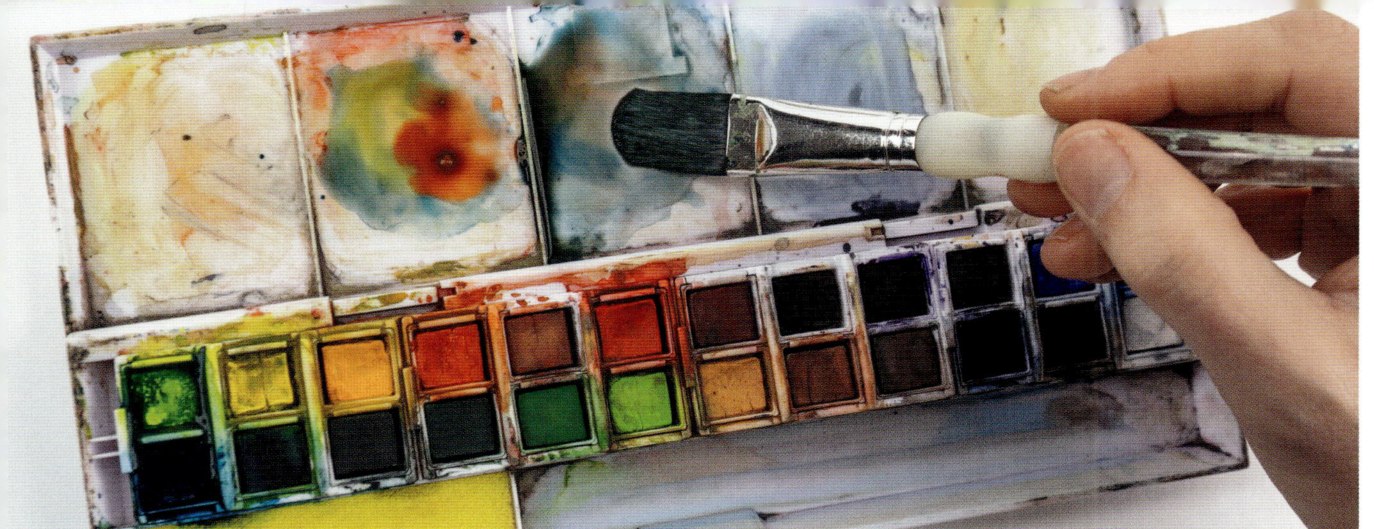

Watercolour paints

Watercolour paint is ultimately what brings the sketch to life and is the tool to deliver artful expression, drama, subtlety and rhythm. There is little opportunity to edit and start again. No 'undo' exists here. But adding colour is where the world of line and wash can offer a new way of working with watercolours.

Watercolours were the first paints I grew up with as a child; washable and unlikely to stain the best clothes. Childhood sets were often poor quality and the paint pans rather mucky and garish. Given our early experiences of watercolour and the nature of such a delicate medium, they can be hard to return to.

As discussed earlier, all the kit available – the wealth of pens and paints – can seem overwhelming. In the simplest form, watercolour paints are usually supplied in dry blocks or 'pans', or supplied in a more liquid form via a tube. I use both types as they allow me to add simple washes or heavy work where the paint is thick and bold.

Watercolours are often classified as students' or artists' range. In my experience, the professional artists' sets tend to have slightly stronger pigments and fade less when dry (though all watercolour fades somewhat when dry). Derwent Inktense pans (pictured above) are ink-based, staining watercolours that give a super-vibrant finish.

I sketch, work and produce commissions using both student- and artist-quality paints. There is no right answer, and I would suggest buying a modest set to get comfortable before investing more.

Portable or travel paint sets like the ones shown here are great for working on location and also at home. These can fit in your bag and, when the sketch is complete, they can be easily dabbed dry with kitchen paper. The concise range of colours helps to capture scenes quickly.

Watercolour from a tube requires an external palette and can be a little messier to pack away when you're finished on location. I typically have a handful of colour tubes that are always with me when working on pieces.

My expressive skies are quite a signature giveaway, and I am never without phthalo or cerulean blue as my go-to for a vibrant sky hue. In addition, I often use yellow ochre as it provides a great base for typical brick and stonework tones while being the catalyst for a warm green when mixed with the phthalo blue. Lastly, I keep yellow and red tubes to act as my highlighter tones. The message remains, however – keep it simple, and don't be tempted to buy too much when you visit your local art store!

Water pot

I use a collapsible water pot and carry clean water in a drinking flask or bottle. Be sure to get in the habit of refreshing your water so it doesnt muddy the colours as you work.

Palette

A separate watercololour palette is essential when working with tubes. A simple plastic palette is lightweight, relatively inexpensive and easily available in art shops and online. As a general rule, the larger the brush, the larger the palette needed. Watercolour pan sets usually come with a built in area for mixing. Both types should be easy to clean with a wet cloth. I have on occasion put my palette through the dishwasher!

Start with the sky

There's a good chance that the top third of your page will be dedicated to the sky, and in urban scenes we often have a natural 'V' shape, where the lowest point of the sky is impacting a key intersection of our rule of thirds (see Composition, page 82). The colours I use in my work are always open to interpretation and I prefer not to restrict my palette to exactly what I see, particulary with the sky. Instead, the watercolour wash is a chance to unload the day's emotion and exaggerate the tones of the scene. It's a deeply personal moment and offers you the chance to further add your personal artist licence into the work. Don't force it, lead with what is comfortable and enjoy it.

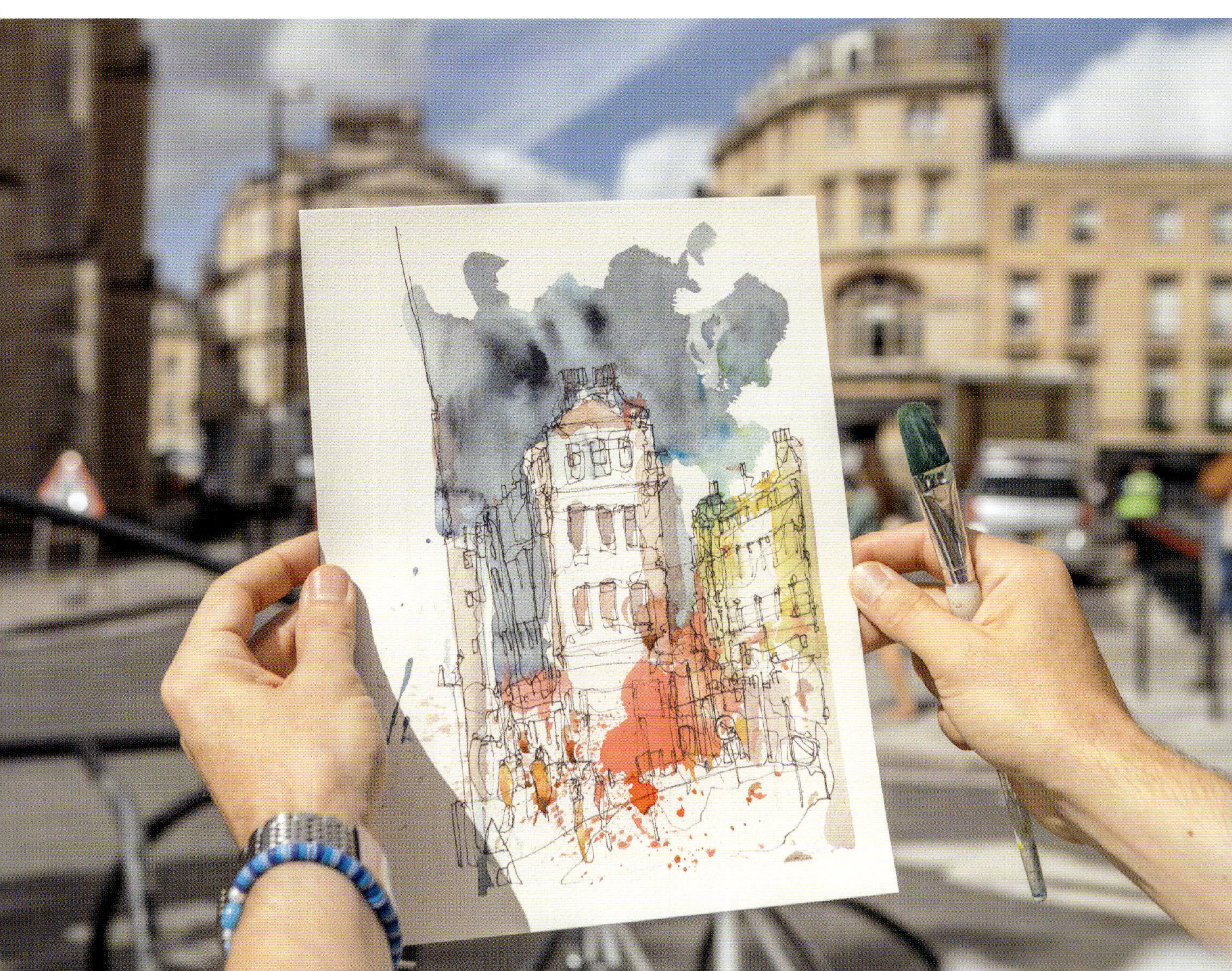

Let the paint flow

I load my brush with paint, have my sketchbook tilted to encourage a natural vertical movement, and push my brush into the page – sometimes it feels as though I'm feeding the page so the brush might push through the page. Apply enough pressure so that the brush fans out and dominates the surface.

Encourage the drips: quite often I will lift my sketchbook and tilt it further to really encourage the drips. There's little control here but this is the magic of the unknown! You'll find the paint will naturally travel along some of the pen lines and pool together. If you have a little too much water here and it needs some intervention, simply grab some kitchen paper to mop up. It's most certainly a good idea to have something handy to catch the drips.

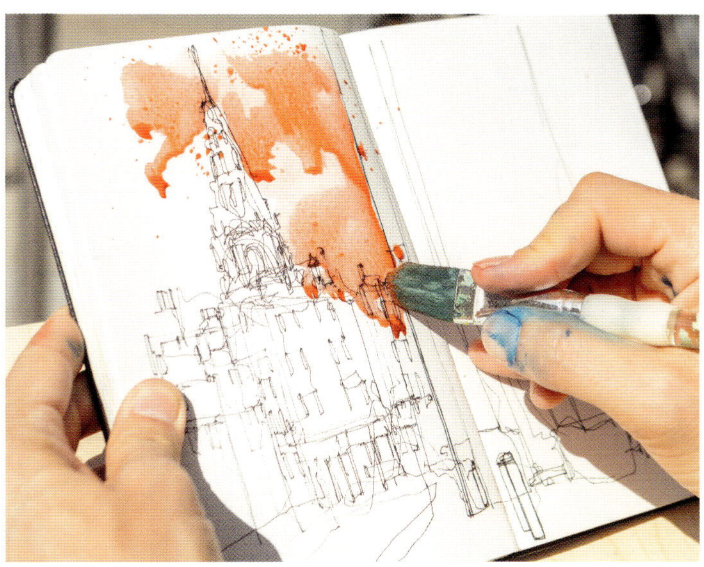

Left: Red buses dominated this sketch so much that I gave up trying to draw the bus and simply protested by unleashing a bold red splatter to depict the constant movement and commotion of the scene. This is where we deliver our social commentary and full expressive nature as artists. If you're facing challenges then show it in your art – deep stories like this are always more interesting than sketching perfection.

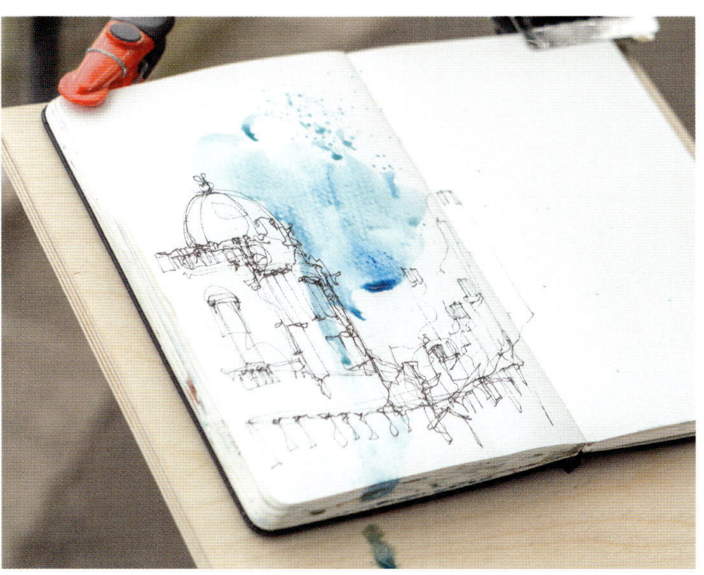

Adding depth with paint

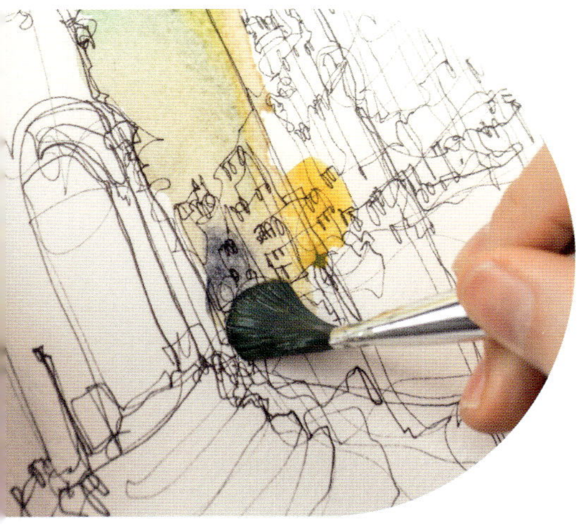

To break up the texture of the wash, I add a few splatters – this again adds some further personalization and immediately starts to create a sense of depth. They work well to give the impression of air movement, birds in the sky, dappled sunlight or moving shadows.

The chunky filbert brush (below) lends itself to the splatters. Hold the brush above the paper and simply flick your finger into the bristles at a good rhythm. Vary your distance from the surface, and enjoy! Be careful not to overload the splatters, they're a complementary addition and are not meant to dominate the work.

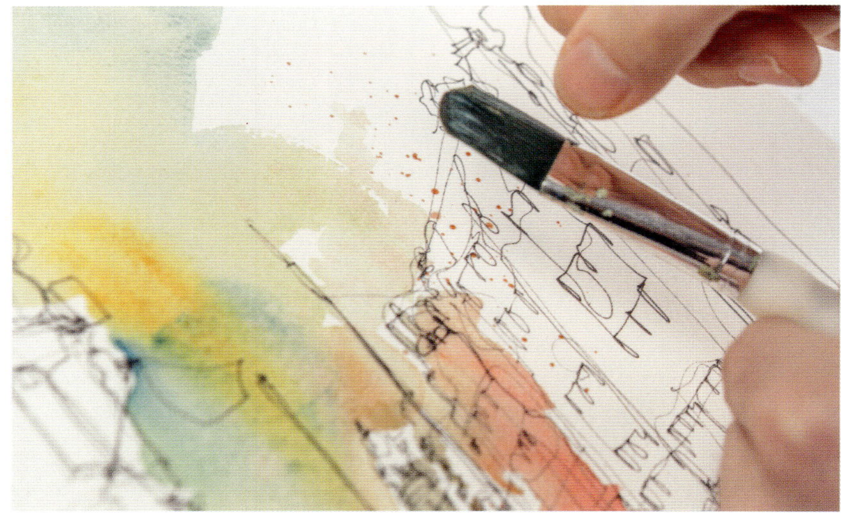

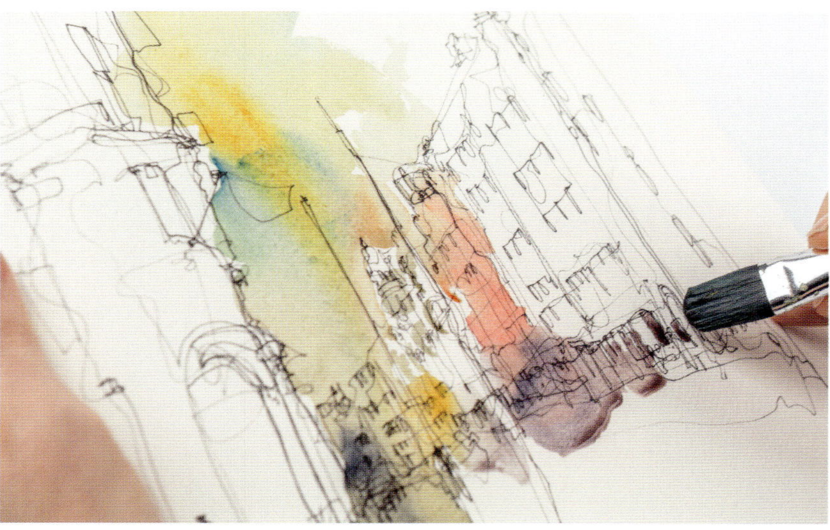

Don't fear merging colours, I tend to paint as quickly as I sketch and keep the brush loaded for smooth gradients.

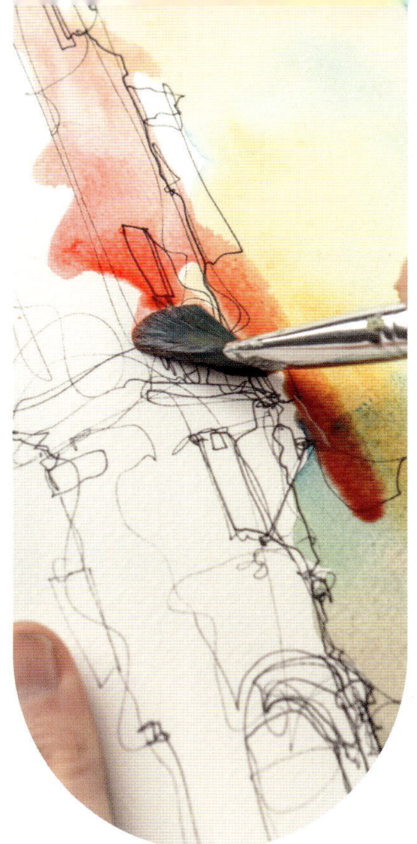 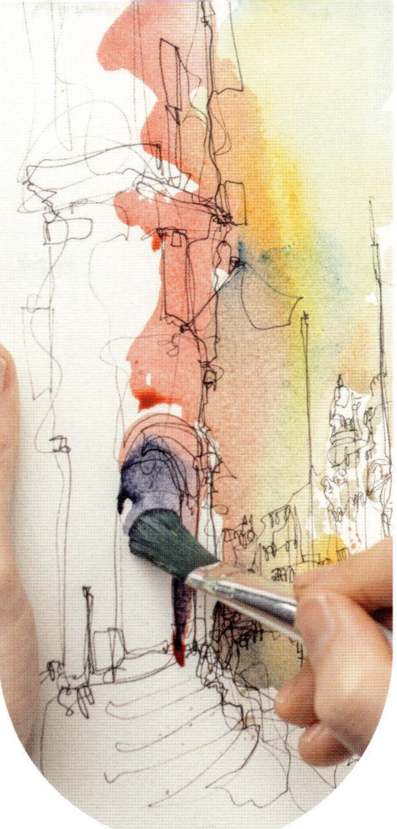 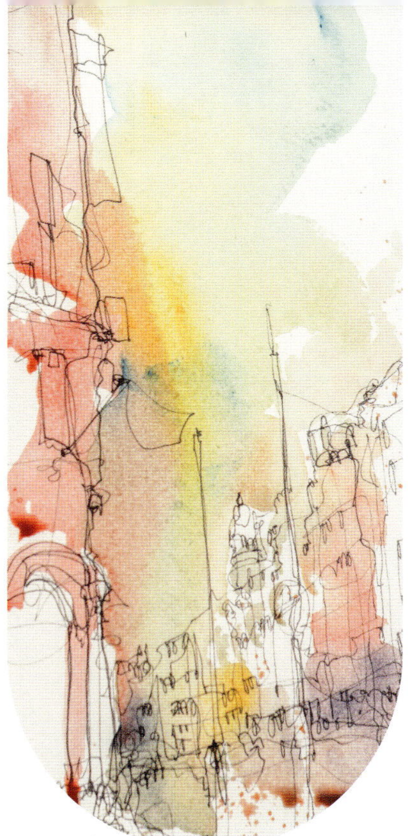

In this sketch, which is full of tall vertical lines and shapes, my sky is also painted with vertical strokes very deliberately. I leave some sections white so the sky takes on an almost rectangular shape. This helps create a tall, dominant artwork, making the architectural elements appear tall and very obviously buildings.

I continue this technique by using the brush vertically. Holding it at 90 degrees to the paper, I make sure to add little canals of paint that drip and have few obvious brush strokes.

With the brush fully loaded, all it takes is a gentle touch to the surface to trigger the release of the paint into the paper. This is where you see the benefit of good-quality, thick, absorbent watercolour paper. The examples here use Derwent Inktense cotton paper, a slightly off-white paper that almost comes across as thirsty. It wants to be fed. Working this way on a glossy, smooth surface is more challenging as there are fewer chances for the paint to rest and blend.

Tip

The texture of cold-pressed or rough watercolour paper is great for holding pigment and water in tight pools. Hot-pressed paper can cause the paint to run over the page, due to the smoother surface.

Exercise

Working with watercolour

Sketches come alive with colour, and my washes are quite recognizable. This exercise can help you master the wash over the buildings.

Urban landscape scene
Sketch a quick urban landscape scene at around A5 (148 x 210mm/ 5¾ x 8¼in) or A4 (210 x 297mm/8¼ x 11½in) size. I then want you to nominate three colours that speak to you from the original scene. A dark tone, a mid-tone and a light tone. Get your kit set up and make sure you're comfortable and in a well-lit place.

Brush ready
With a chunky filbert brush loaded with your mid-tone colour and pressing into the paper, apply the wash with a dominant stroke to the main structure of the sketch and let the watery paint flow downwards. Don't worry about going over your lines – hopefully now you have lots of loose lines that soften the sketch.

Water time
Make sure that you have a good amount of water on the page as this encourages a good deep flow and creates nice drips. Let the watercolour flow and blend on the paper, embracing any unexpected outcomes as part of the creative process. Remember that imperfections and spontaneity can add character and charm to your urban landscape paintings.

Dark tones
Once you're happy with the first wash (remembering to leave some negative space), add some dark tones to the more densely packed areas of the sketch – these are often in doorways and archways. This is where we want to turn up the contrast dramatically as the watercolour will fade once dry. Embrace the mixing of mid-tones and darks, and perhaps tap the sketchbook to encourage more vertical mixing.

Add the highlights
With the first two washes down and the paper slightly drier, clean your brush and load it with your lighter tone. I usually have yellow or orange ready for this stage. Recall the days of colouring books and look for shapes to fill. This is the very simple advice I have. With your loose sketch you probably have a few interesting shapes. Adding this light colour just helps lift the scene.

Add the movement
Adding movement is the last thing to do. Hold your brush close to the paper and simply flick the bristles onto the page.

Opposite: Phthalo blue, yellow ochre and a pinch of red blend to create greens and purples.

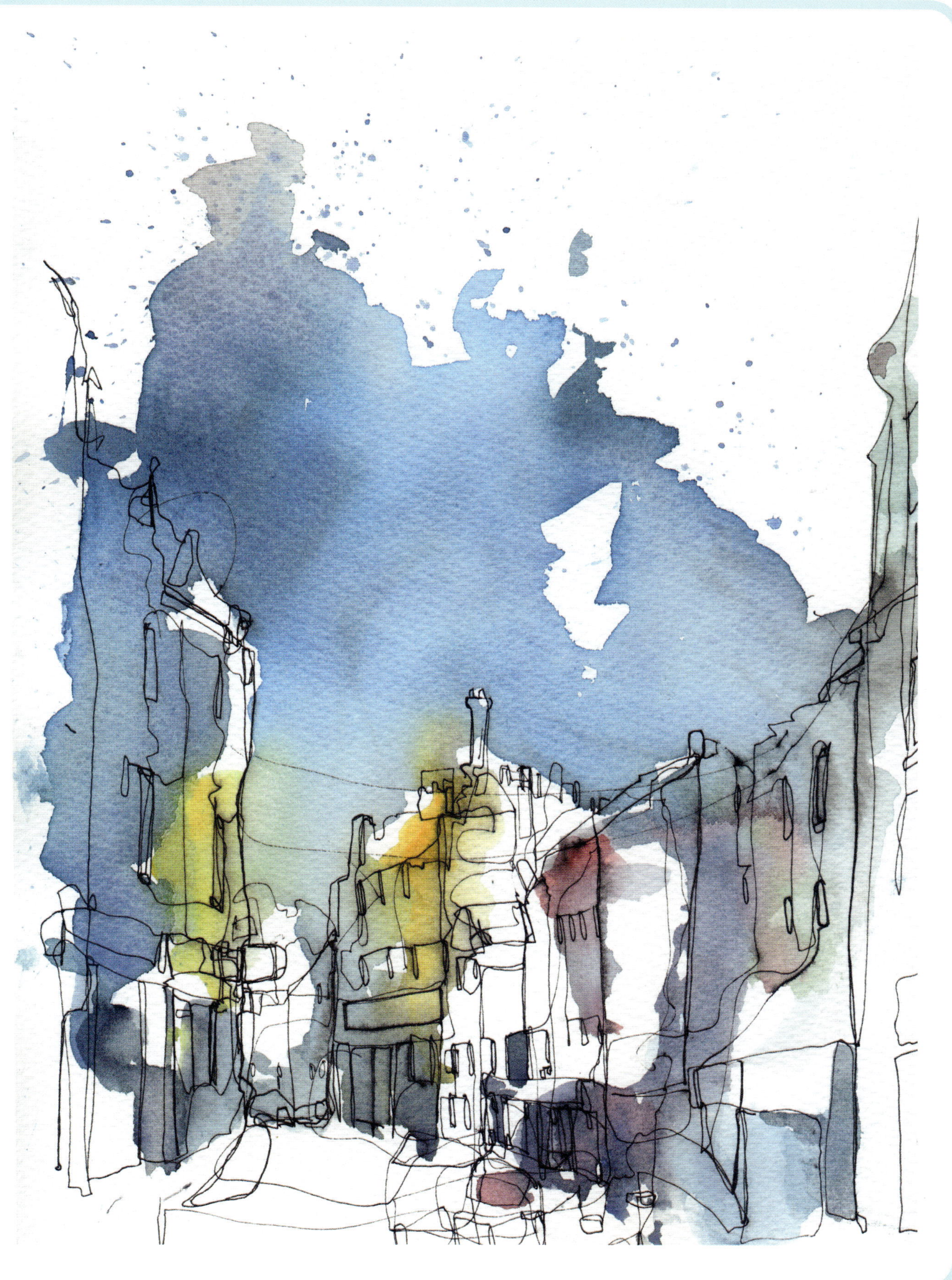

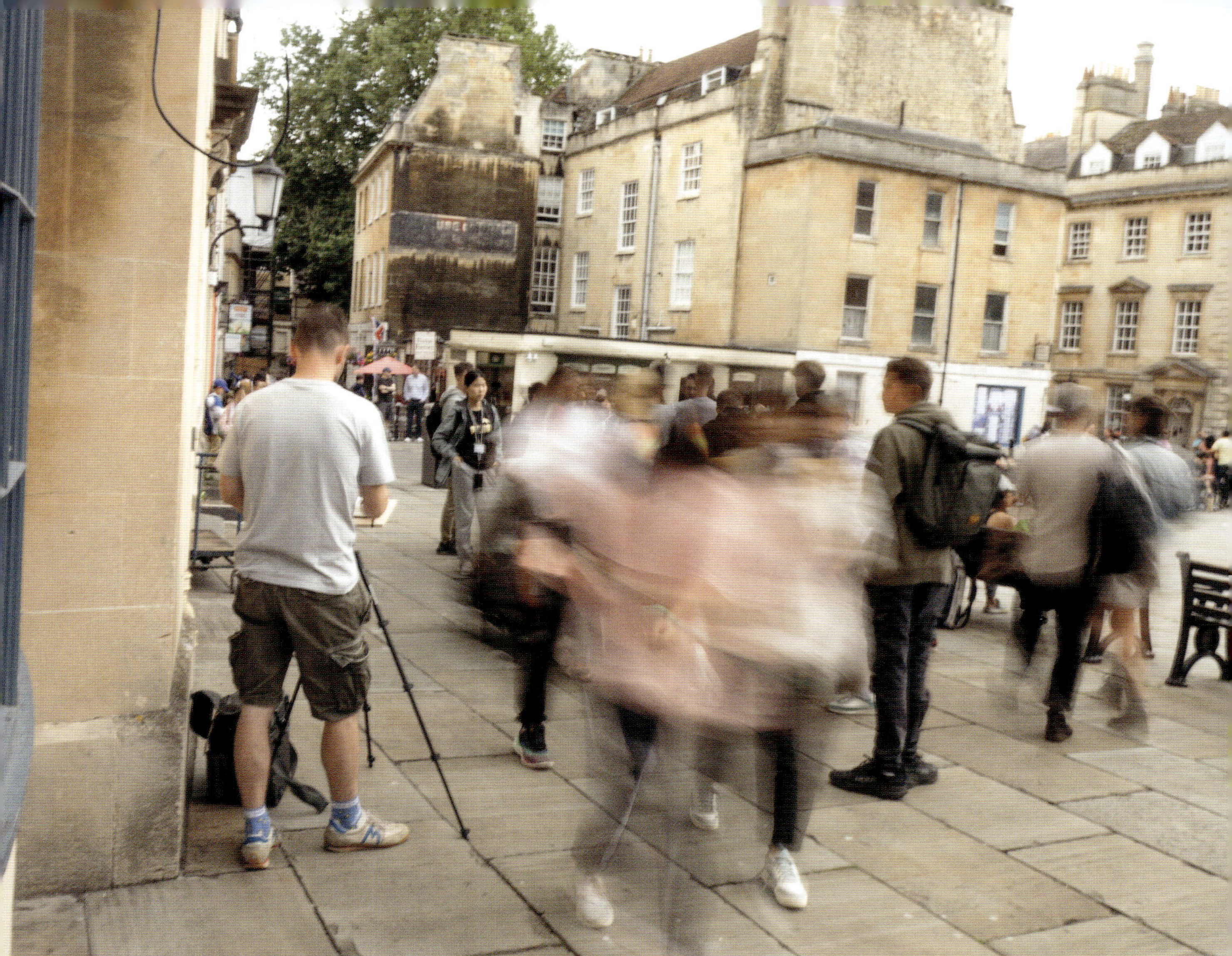

Working outdoors or in?

Capturing the urban landscape on paper, in a sketchbook or even on canvas is all about enjoyment. This is best done on location, known as 'urban sketching' – a fully immersive form of artistic commentary, personal expression and social immersion. It needn't be complex – it's just about sketching.

Working on location

Sketching on location in a group can be a wonderful experience, and the varying abilities and confidence levels can be a boost. There's a real camaraderie that exists when you have the chance to sit, chat and draw with others. It's always remarkable what others can see in a scene and hugely comforting to see that everyone has a slightly different approach. Usually after a session is finished the sketchers will have a throwdown – everyone's book is laid out to see. There are plenty of urban sketching groups globally, and many have dedicated pages on social media, so I recommend having a search, either for inspiration or for making plans to join a sketching group or meet-up. It's not always possible to get every sketch painted on a meet, and I tend to get as many sketches done as possible with a view to adding paint later in the studio from a reference photo, or even on the train ride back.

When you're out on location, get used to people having a peer over your shoulder, and don't be afraid of reaction – people enjoy looking at art and are complimentary, and genuinely envious of someone with the confidence to sketch in public. Where you position yourself is key: sitting or standing with a wall behind you limits the interaction you'll attract.

Of course, we can't all jump on a plane to set up in central London or in a back-street Tokyo suburb to sketch on location, so when the desire to sketch and paint hits you, I wouldn't hesitate. Remember, as artists, we are creating a new form from observation and artistic inspiration.

If urban sketching is not possible due to physical constraints or accessibility, then working from pictures is also a good option (see pages 36–39).

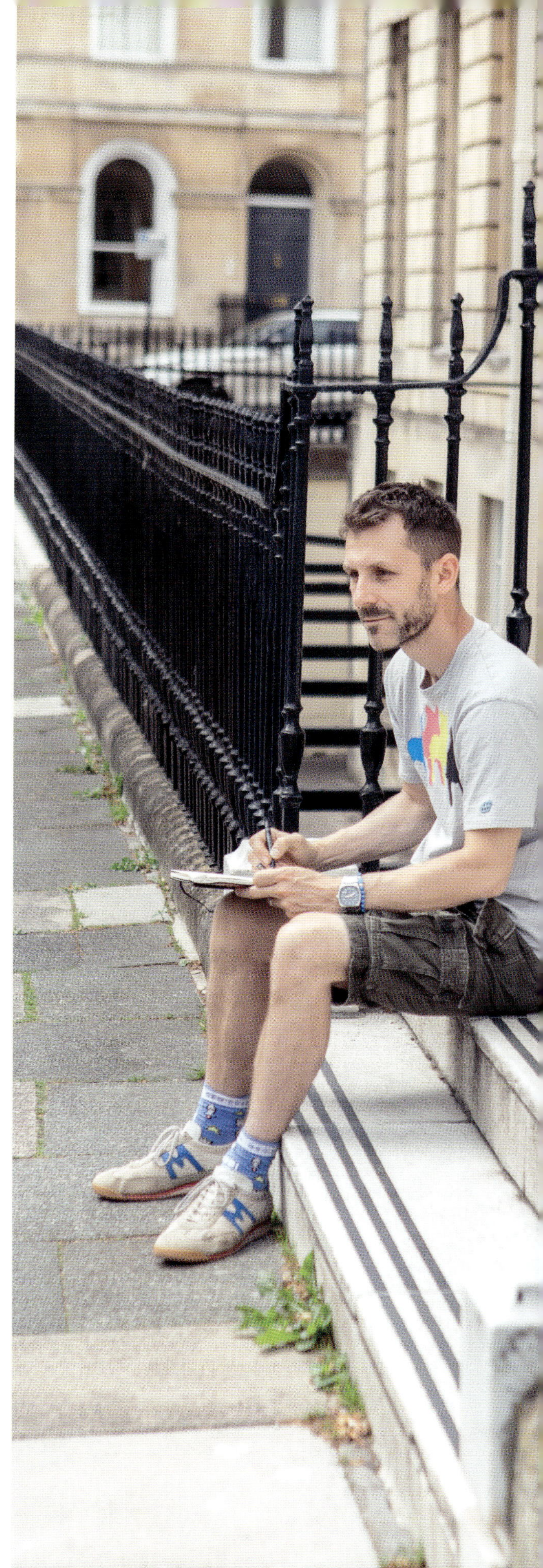

Your sketching set-up

Whether sketching on location or
working at home, your set-up is a very
important consideration. Sketching while
uncomfortable will rarely deliver a fluid and
relaxed result. I have customized a tripod to work
well as a field easel that can be adjusted to sit flat or
at an angle. This was done by attaching a piece of
birch plywood to a 1cm (½in) screw that connected
to my tripod's locking nut. There are tutorials online
and plenty of second-hand tripods available to buy
too. This is a relatively inexpensive set-up – the lighter
the tripod the better! In time I might look to attach
some elastic to help keep my sketchbook firmly
planted. For now, I tend to use chunky clips to keep
the page flat. Sketching when it's windy is no fun if
the paper is flapping.

For moments of real satisfaction, place tape around
the perimeter of your page and when the work is
complete you can enjoy peeling it away to reveal the
crisp edges. I've tried many different masking tapes,
and often they can be too adhesive and damage
the paper. More recently I've used electrical tape
and found that this works best! Experiment in your
sketchbook first and take notes to find what works
best for you.

Other items to pack

I always keep some kitchen paper handy, which is
useful for mopping up drips or drying off brushes
when sketching outdoors.

You might like to take a portable stool when you're
sketching out and about, but it isn't essential.

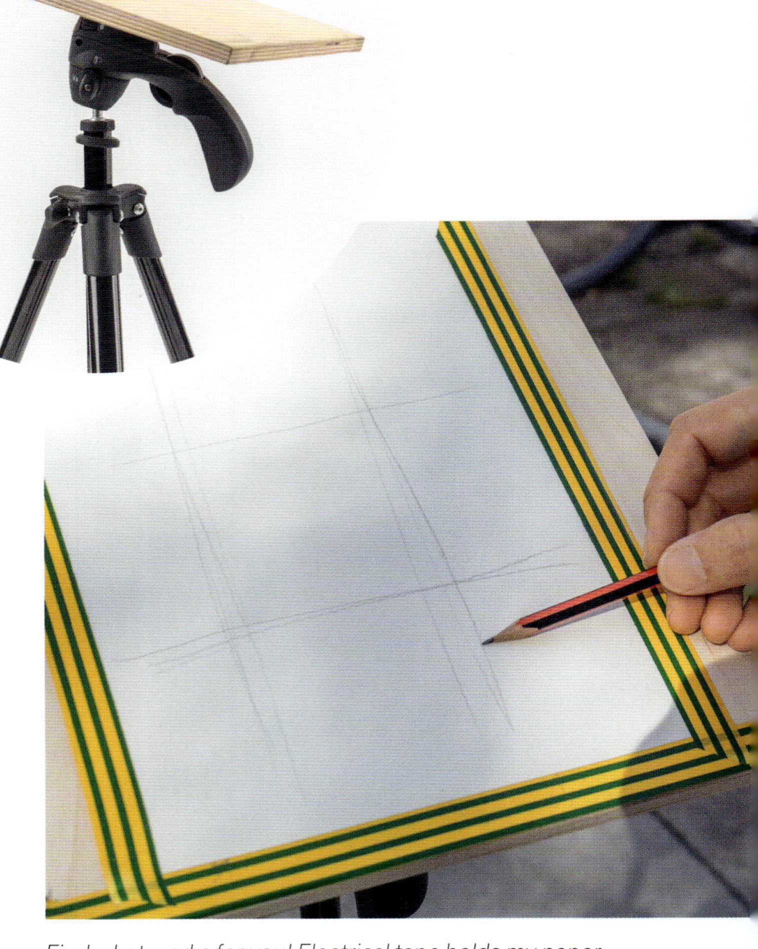

*Find what works for you! Electrical tape holds my paper
down perfectly without tearing when it's removed.*

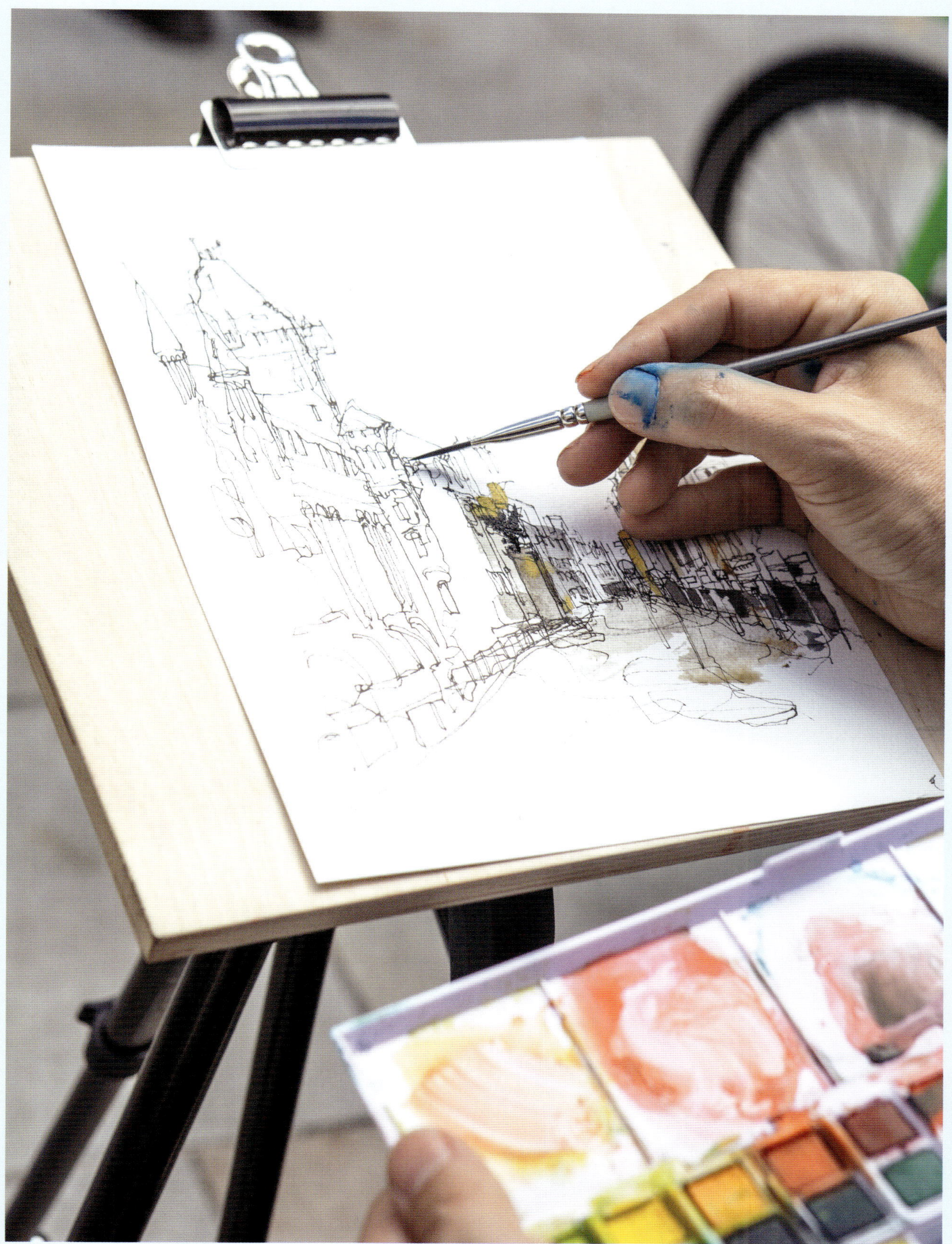

Working from pictures

The overall flavour of this book is about being artistic and loose rather than photographic, and this is true whether working from pictures or outside. Every scene is open to interpretation, cropping, simplifying and colour use.

Getting started is often the biggest challenge, building confidence in a new subject always requires some practice and working from source pictures is a great way to get started drawing and painting the urban landscape. Start looking for areas of perspective and vanishing points in photos you own or those available online. There are plenty of brilliant photographers posting great images on social media daily. Over the years I have reworked dozens of original shots with the photographer's permission – this provides a crisp and interesting shot and offers great exposure for both should you be looking to share your work online.

The overall goal here is to start drawing and painting and to build confidence to fill your sketchbook with expressive artful interpretations.

The days of the 2020 lockdowns saw the sketching community jump online. I ran workshops online with a library of scenes to choose from. There was also a hugely popular movement to sketch at home and there were hundreds of sketchers simply drawing the view outside their window.

Sketching from pictures allows you to:

- control the environment
- create a diverse scene
- sketch anywhere in the world
- experiment with different techniques quickly
- gain confidence in your ability
- get familiar with new kit
- explore the fundamentals of drawing
- find what you like to do and what suits your style
- have some privacy to learn specific techniques, and avoid public scrutiny!

In the following example the vantage point was in the road, so sketching from a picture was certainly the best method. The oddity about working from pictures as opposed to urban sketching is the change of scale. When working from a printed picture or from your phone, you're likely to be sketching larger than your subject – a complete reversal from when you're on location and observing from life. This can present a challenge, but can also help develop your editing skills and the ability to remove or add detail.

Some key points when sketching from pictures

Perspective Remember that the camera lens will flatten the image and this can make it harder to perceive depth and perspective angles.

Lighting This won't move in a photo (a help and hindrance!). Light and shadows and colour changes won't journey with you as you sketch and this can sometimes eliminate some of the spontaneity.

Detail The camera captures every detail, but we're all about simplification; resist the photographic lure to draw everything.

Artistic licence Working from a static scene can inhibit the creative process; we don't want to create another photo.

Practice Photos are brilliant to try out techniques and build confidence. I started out copying other artists' sketching styles – this is a great way to develop a new way of sketching and painting.

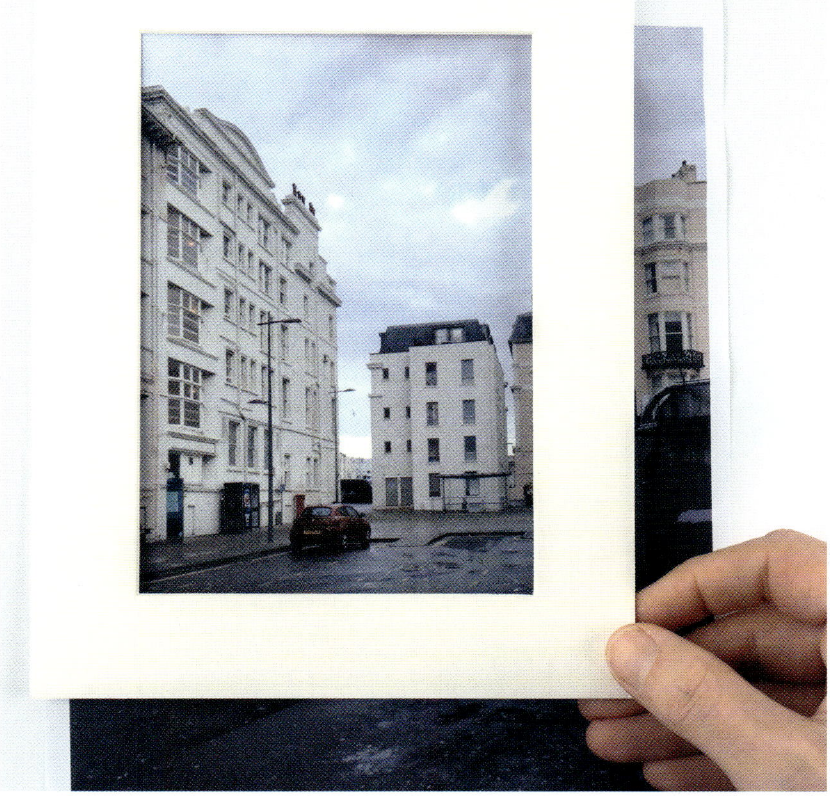

◀ A printed photo gets a crop with my trusty cardboard frame. You can move the frame around to change the focal point and find an interesting angle. Remember to think about the sky and the rule of thirds (see page 82).

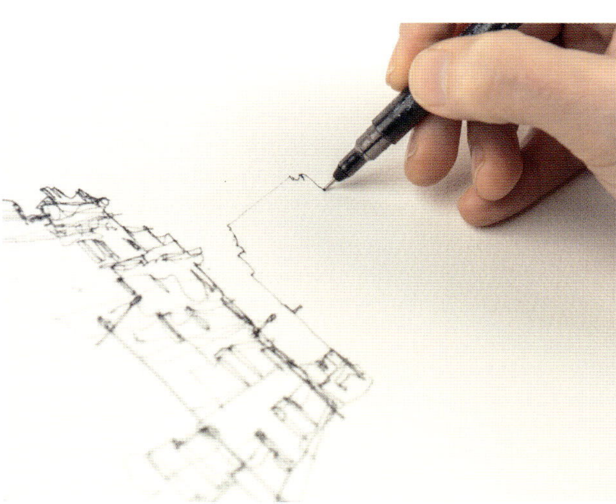

▲ Capturing the outline of the dominant left-hand building was a priority. The more I look, the more windows I can see. The very real mental struggle here can be the temptation to draw too much detail when your subject is perfectly still in front of you.

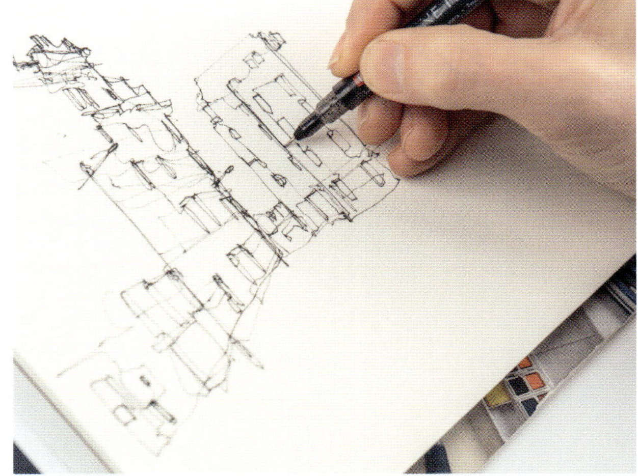

▲ The windows are hugely simplified here; my concentration is set on the space between the two buildings and allowing space for the sketch to breathe. The scene is quite bland in regard to colour, so I'm already thinking about making the sky the dominant part of this painting.

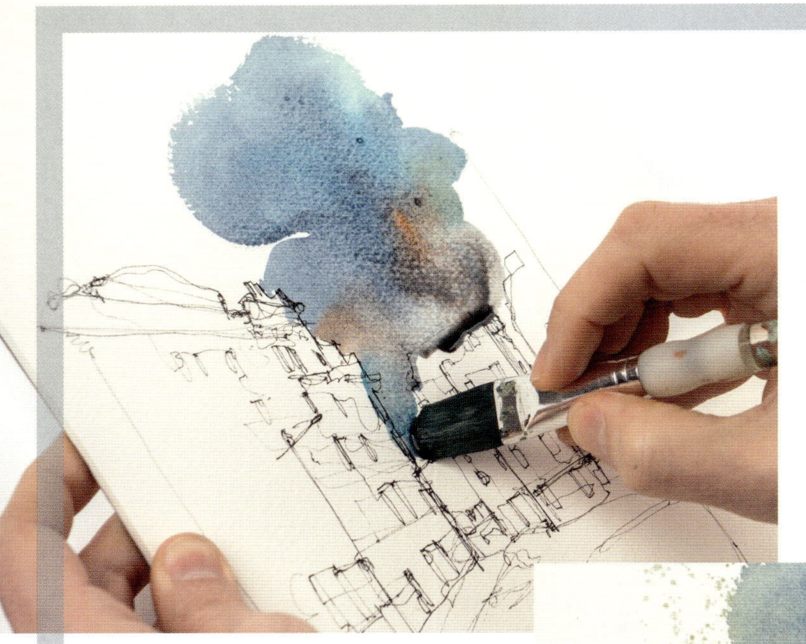

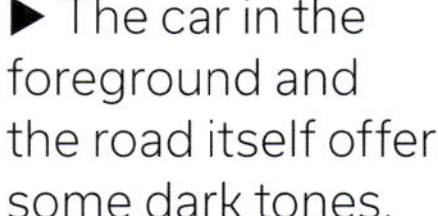

► The car in the foreground and the road itself offer some dark tones.

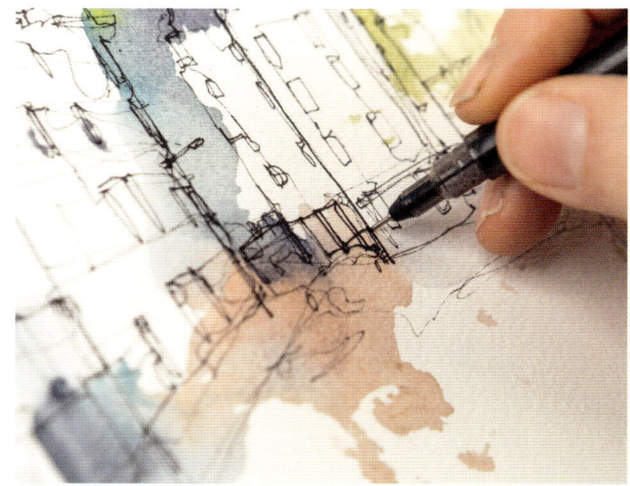

◄ I add some final secondary lines onto the damp paper. These darken the blacks and help define some parts of the background detail.

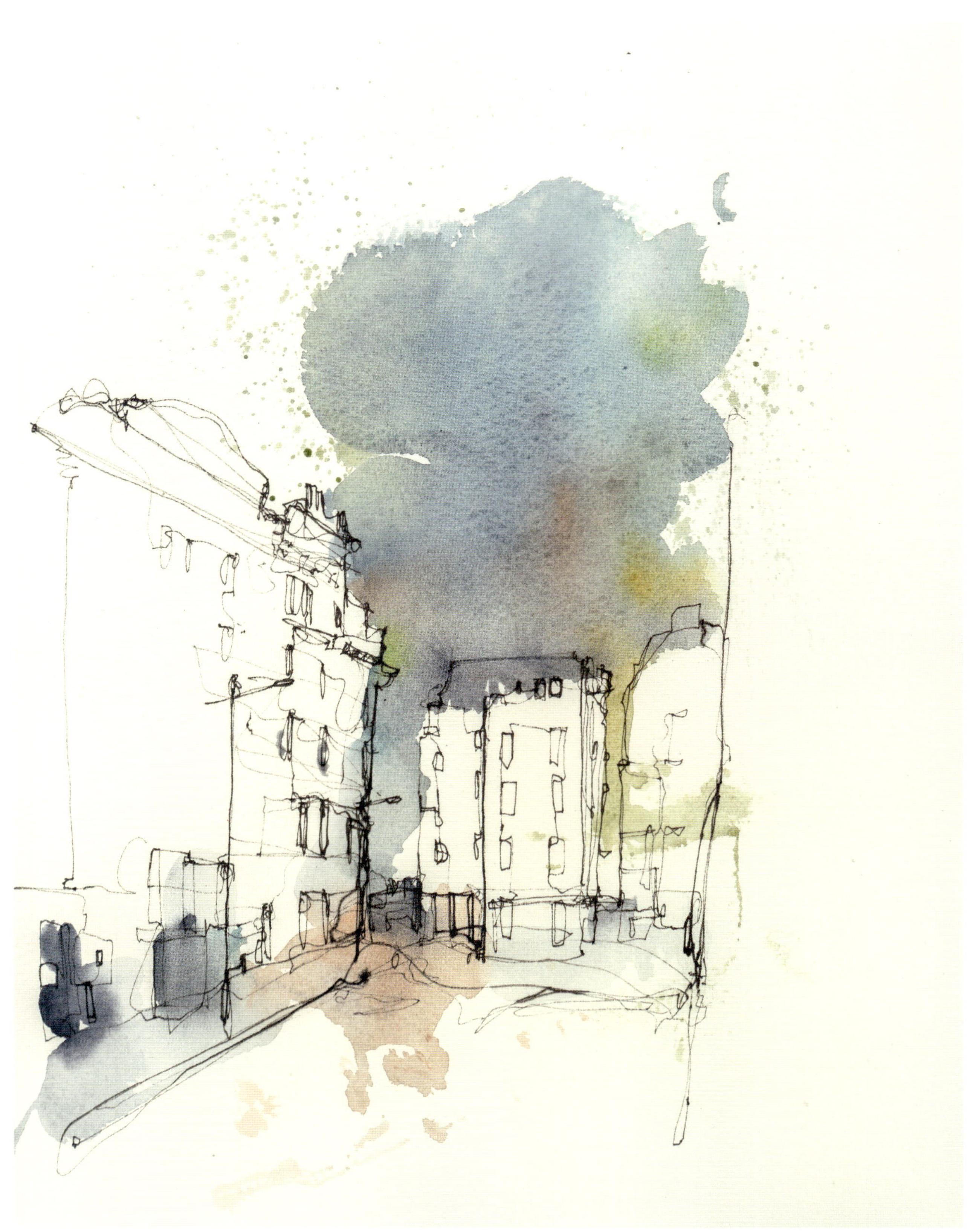

The finished painting.

OUT & ABOUT 1

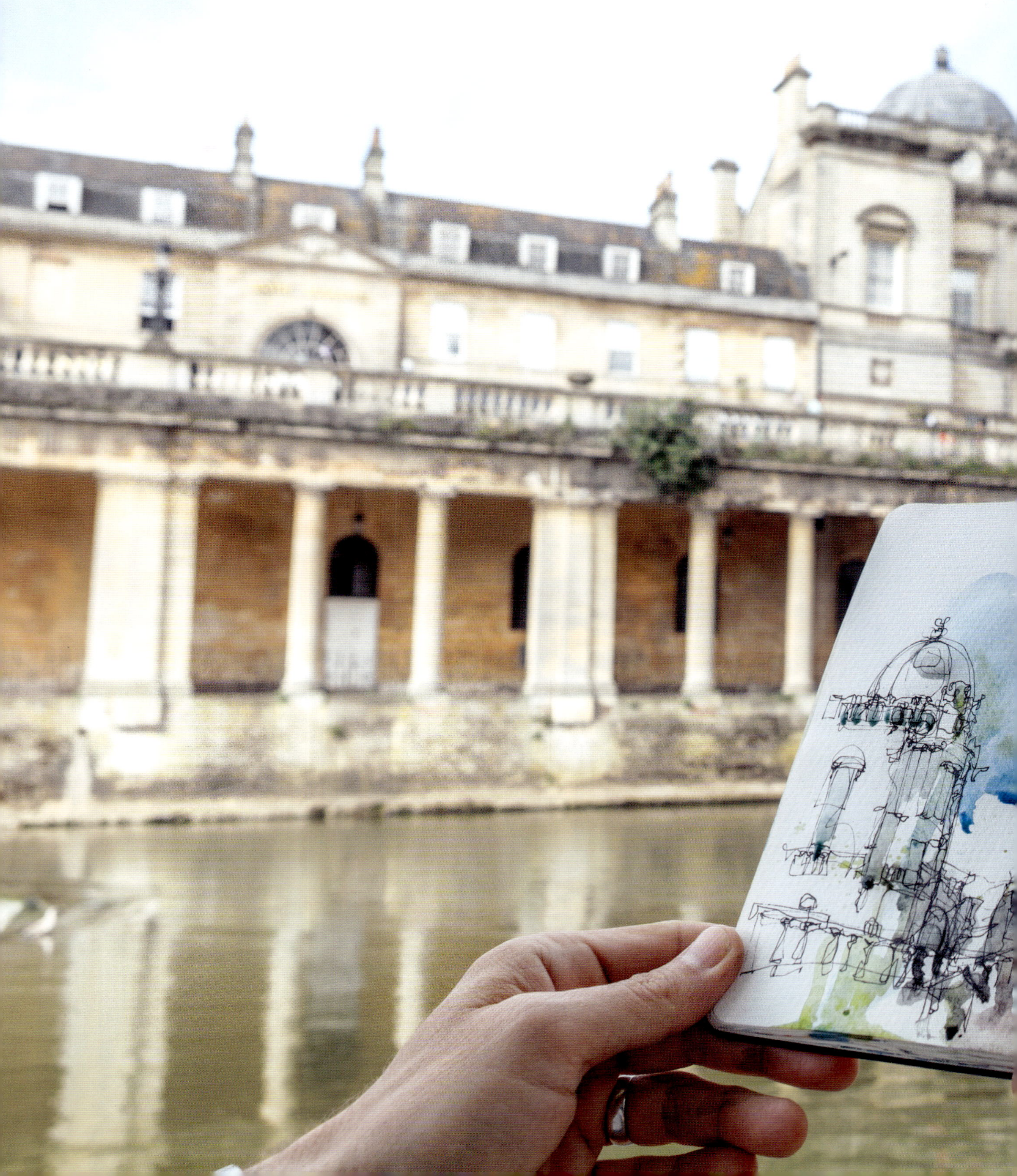

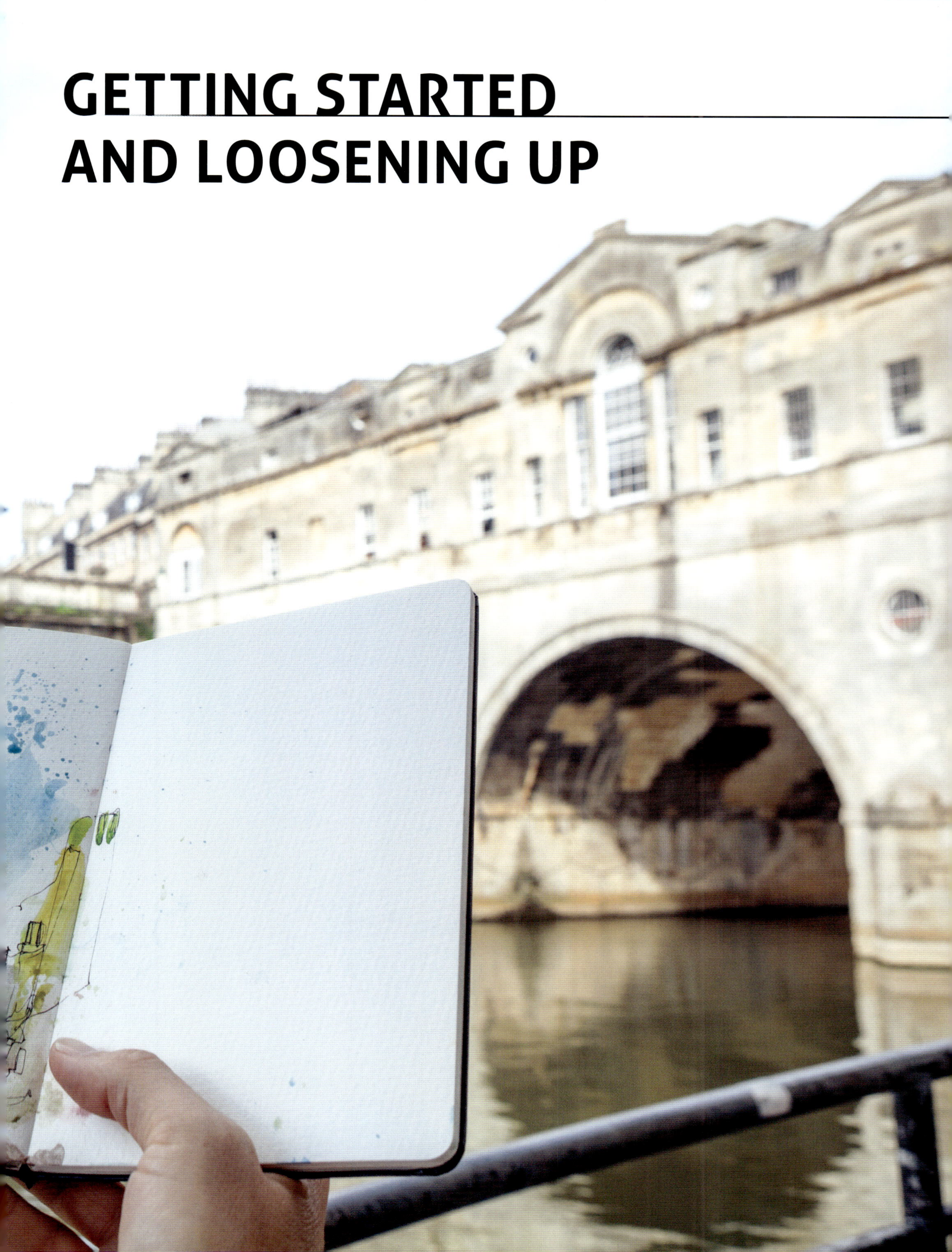

GETTING STARTED AND LOOSENING UP

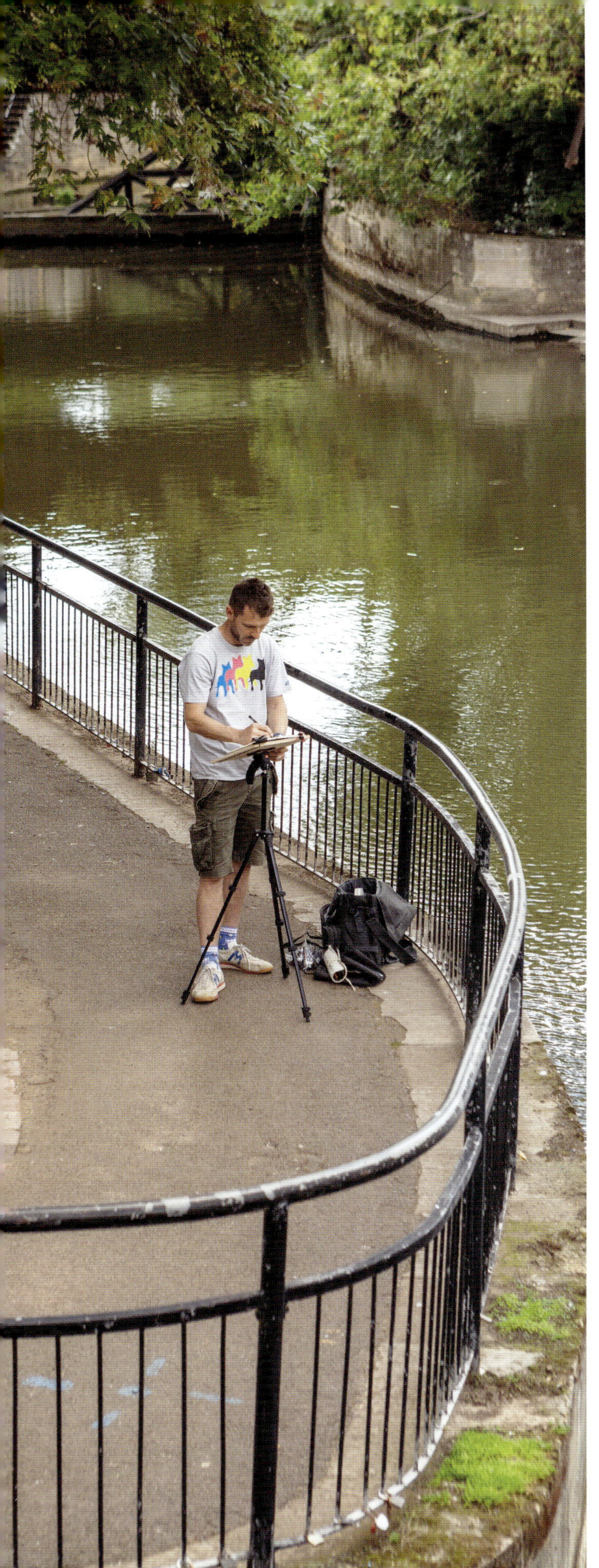

Getting started when on location

Getting out and about, soaking up the feel and atmosphere of the location, and then putting into practice all the theoretical parts of sketching is the real treat.

Find a quiet spot

Early morning sketching before the crowds appear is a good tactic to build your confidence when sketching on location.

Select the area of interest

Take your time. I tend to wander a little off the beaten track to get a different view from the obvious first options. The scene shown opposite jumped out at me for the light of the morning, the domed roof, the summer sky, the strong verticals and the intricacies of the railings.

This scene presents itself as a landscape piece, but don't be afraid to change the view. Could this be more interesting in portrait format? Observe and feel the scene. Don't be afraid of the detail – we will simplify it.

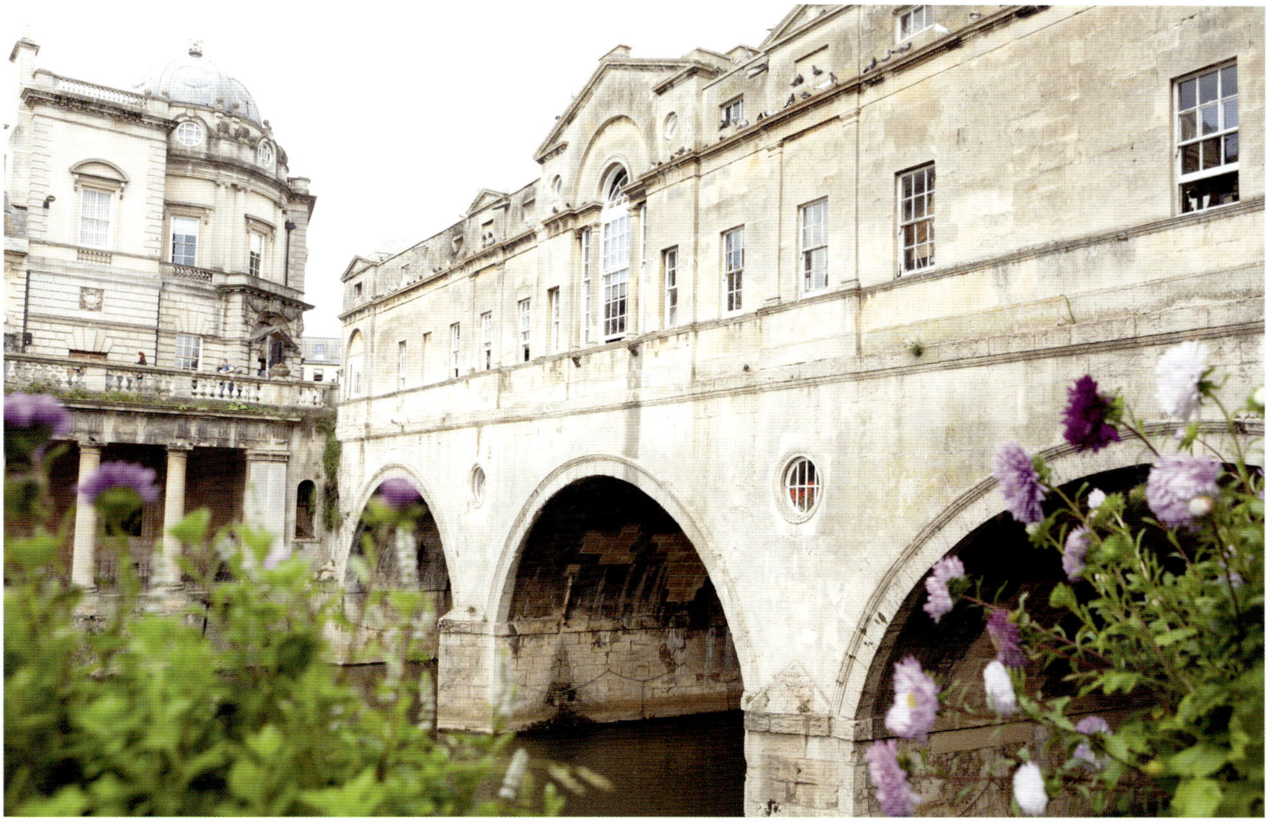

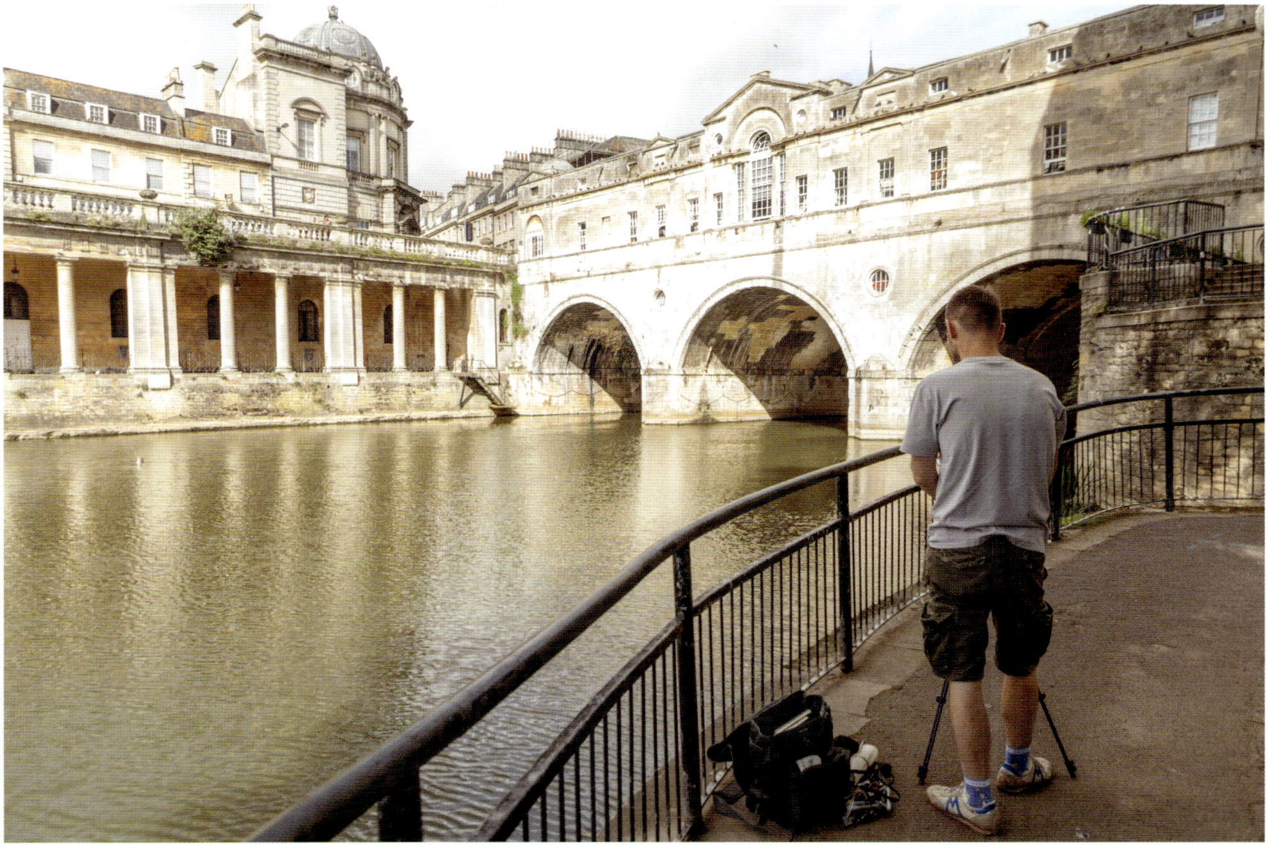

Set out your kit

I like to claim my space – this helps
me relax and mark out where I'm
working. This is my sketching
territory and my easel is my flag!
I like to stand while I sketch as it
feels more agile and I'm not relying
on balancing a sketchbook on my
knee. A solid surface helps me
keep a consistent line throughout.

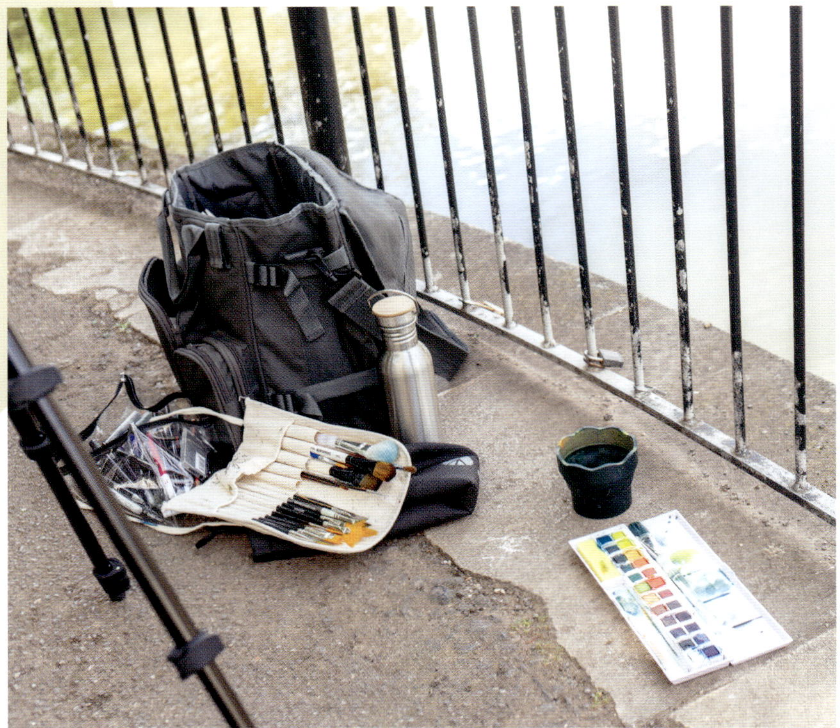

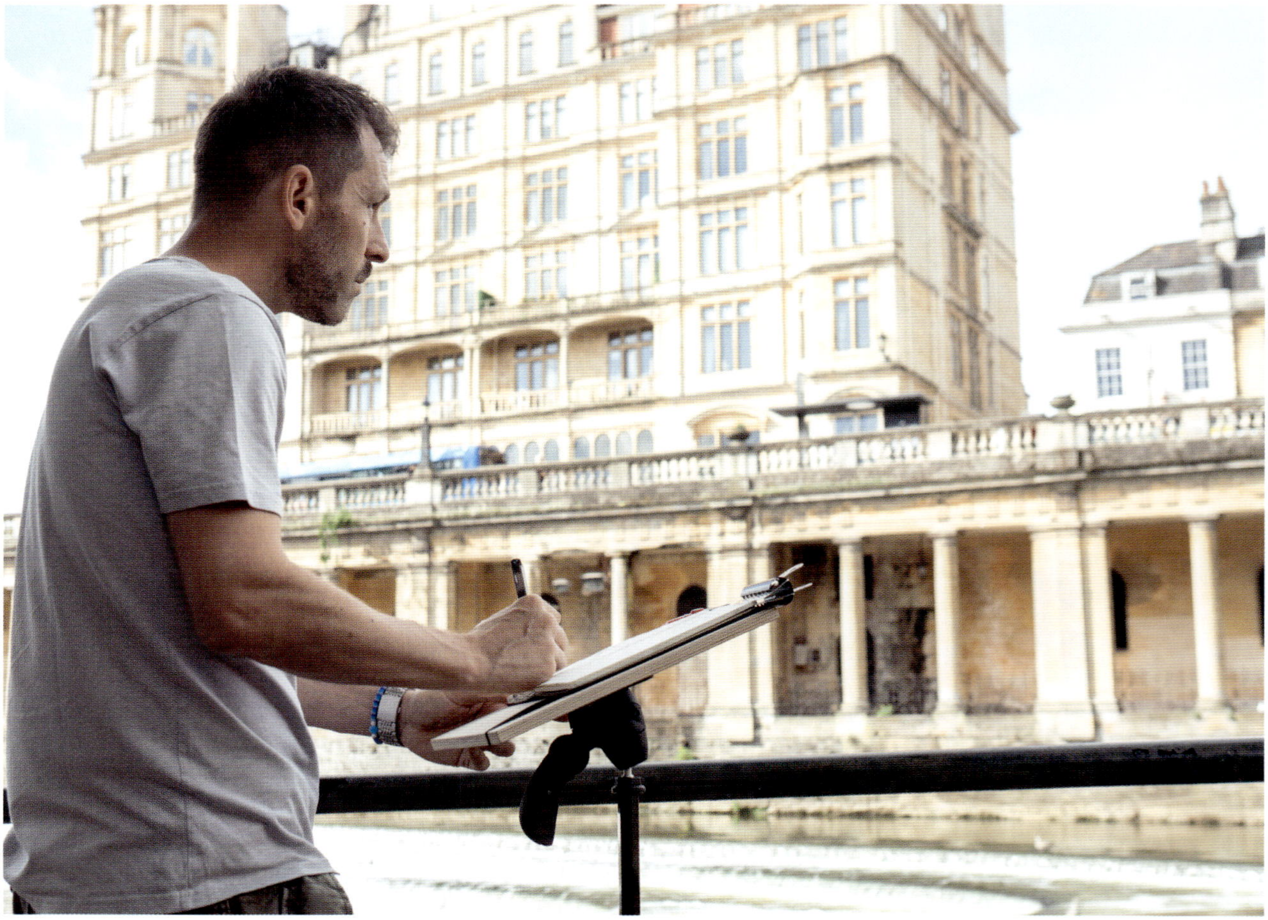

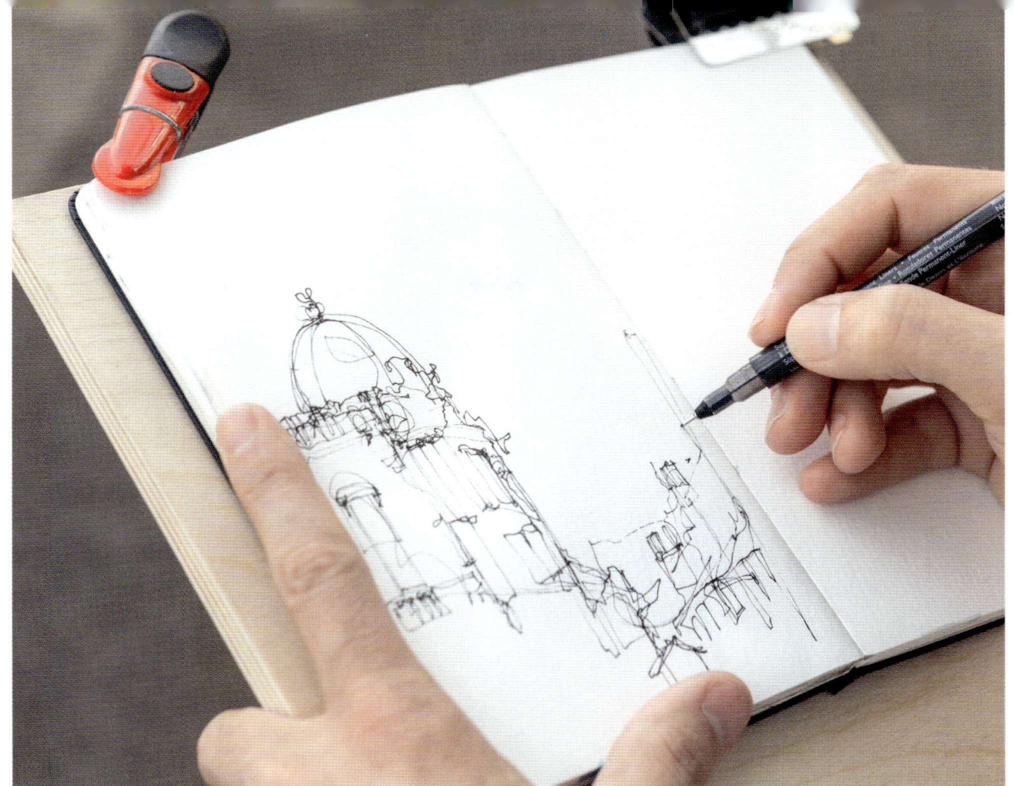

▲ Typically, I'll loosen up with a one-line sketch – warming up the hand and the sketchbook itself. We're not after perfection – we want simplification and rhythm.

I effectively cropped the scene so much that my horizon line is set to a high point in the sketch. I didn't want to capture the water as this would make the sketch much smaller. Don't feel you have to include everything – it's perfectly fine to remove detail and elements that distract from the overall composition. Part of sketching and art is exercising the skill of removal.

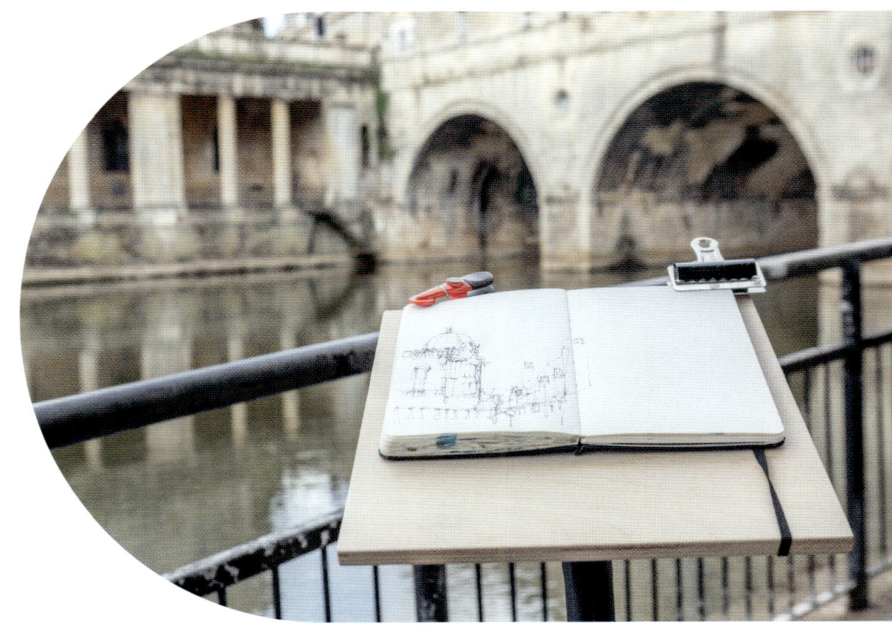

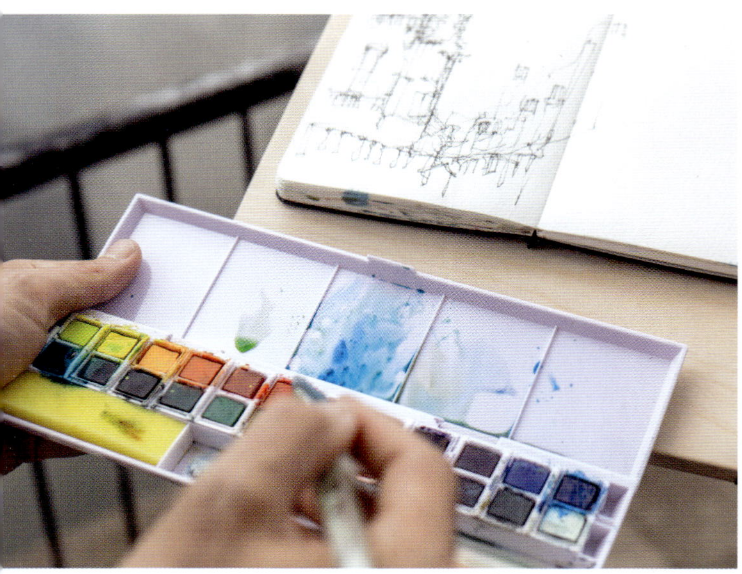

▲ With the quick loosening sketch down, I swap to my paints. I use just two colours initially, using the Derwent Inktense pans. I'm using a turquoise blue and a mango orange – these work well independently and together – to create the green that reflects off the water's surface.

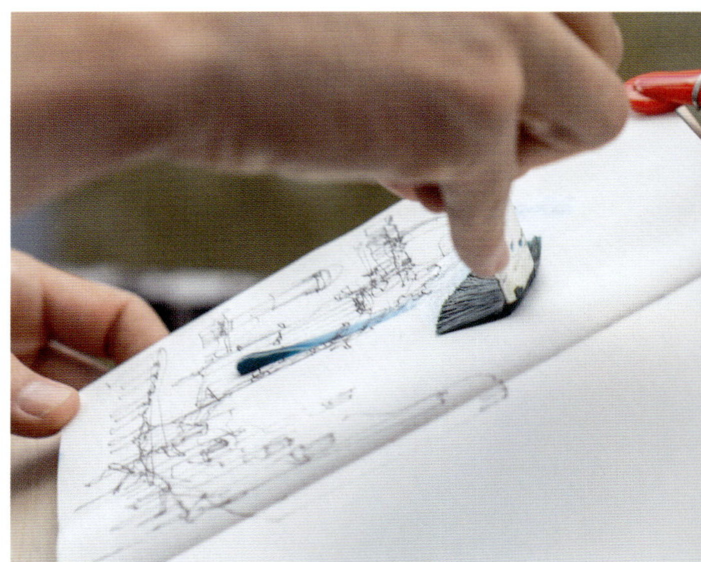

▲ Using loose and fluid brush strokes with the easel set to a slight gradient, I feed the brush into the paper and let gravity guide the paints vertically. I focus on the sky first and look to define the domed roof. The fineliner ink is not yet 100 per cent dry, so I take advantage of this and let the water bleed into the line work, creating a natural darker wash – nothing too heavy, but just enough to bring another colour into the sketch.

▶ A good chunk of the scene remains unpainted – this acts to further develop depth in the sketch. The white space next to the domed roof immediately helps transport the viewer to this high contrast, and then I gently follow the journey down (with the help of the watery drips) into the narrow gap between both left- and right-hand structures.

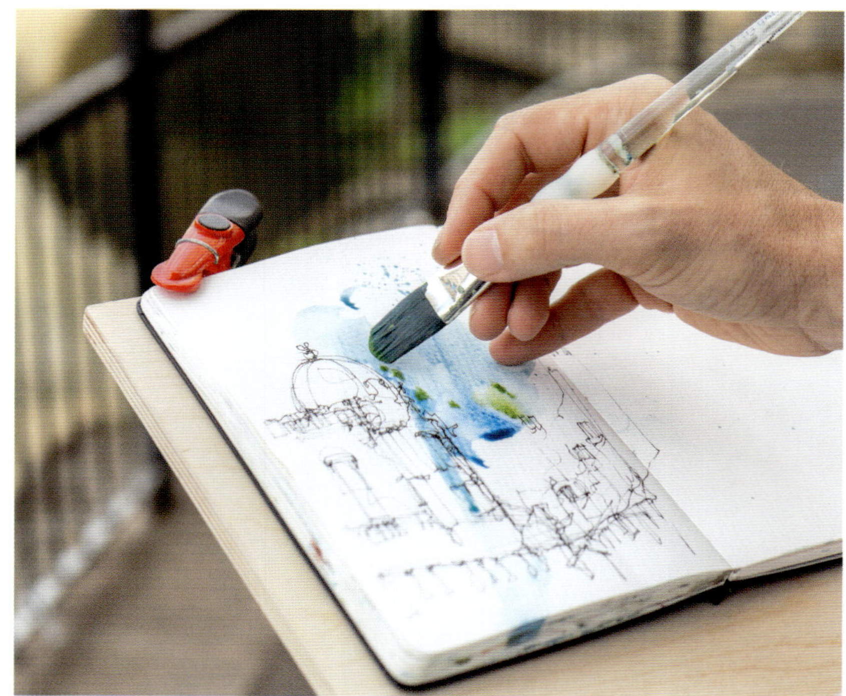

▶ I finish off the painting with a flick of the brush to add another layer of depth and movement – I don't want to start drawing birds in detail, for example, but I want to simply evoke the sense of movement in the sky.

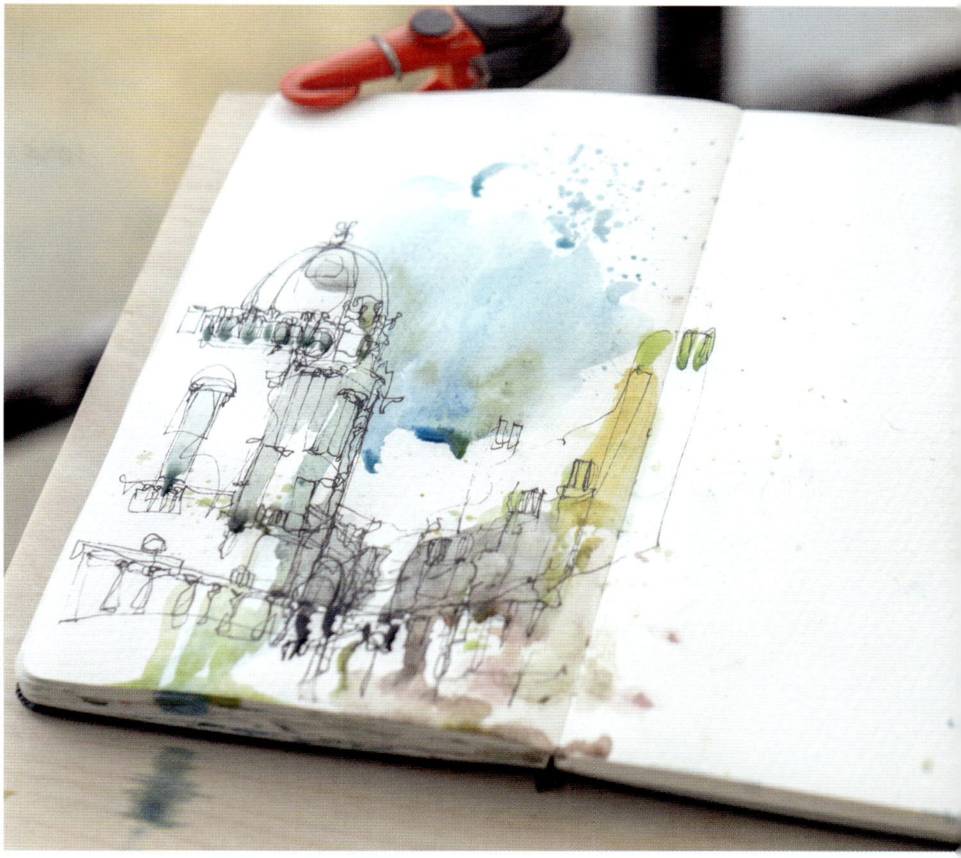

▼ Once the paper is almost dry, I jump back in with my pen. The slightly damp surface can unleash a beautifully dark black that will allow me to enhance the line weight on the dominant verticals, and show the details I want to present more prominently.

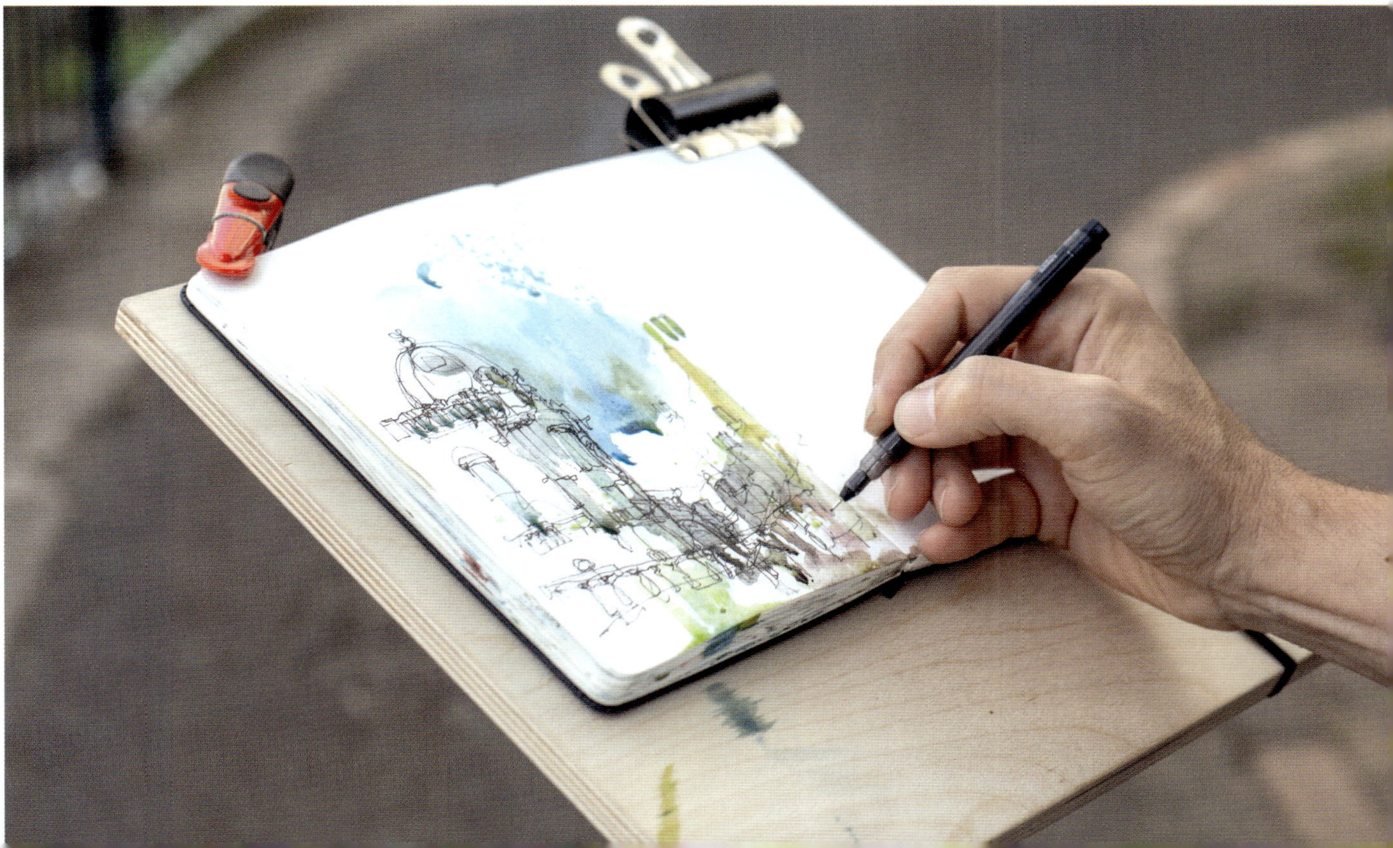

Simplifying the detail

The urban landscape can have a lot of intricate details. I love to simplify detail when sketching and, in fact, I will always favour a complex scene over something simple as I want my scene full of action, movement, noise, clashing rhythms and flow. These are all good ingredients.

We might not draw every window.
We might not draw every brick.
We might not draw everybody in the scene.

It's easier to remove elements from a scene than it is to add them in from your imagination. Often just shifting your gaze or position at a scene can completely change its character, perspective and complexity. I'm not advocating the removal of the most dominant focal point of a scene per se, just bear in mind that a different approach can deliver originality and a new context.

Don't be scared by the complex – we are about to break it down. Focus on the most important details that help define the building, such as windows, doors and distinctive features.

Focusing on specific details of an urban landscape sketch can help give it rhythm because it helps to create a sense of movement and flow in the composition. The details in an urban scene, such as the angles and curves of buildings, the placement of streetlamps, or the patterns in the pavement, can create a visual rhythm that leads the viewer's eye through the sketch.

People

People are a vital aspect of most urban scenes as the busy streets help to tell the story of the day. Capturing people can be a tricky task for the obvious reason – they move, and surprisingly quickly when you start to observe and capture! Again, the trap here is aiming for perfection and detail.

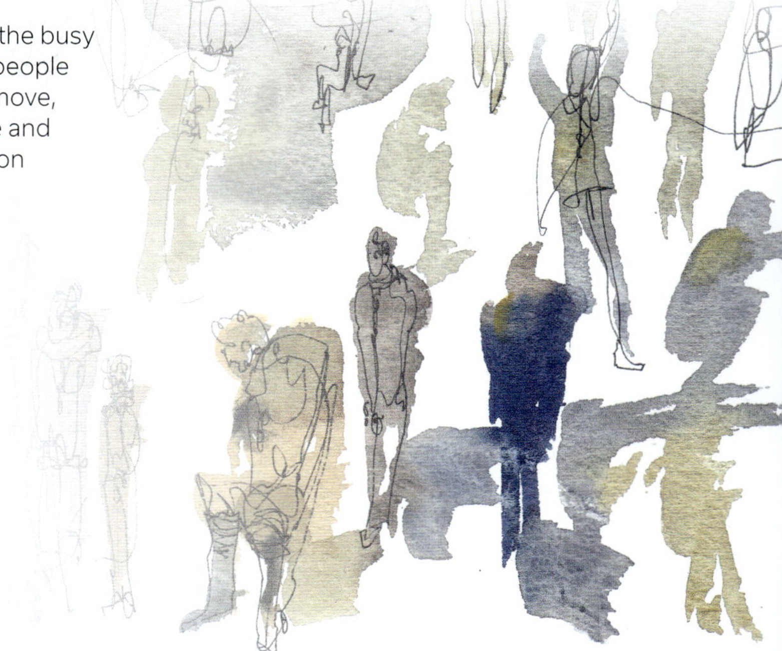

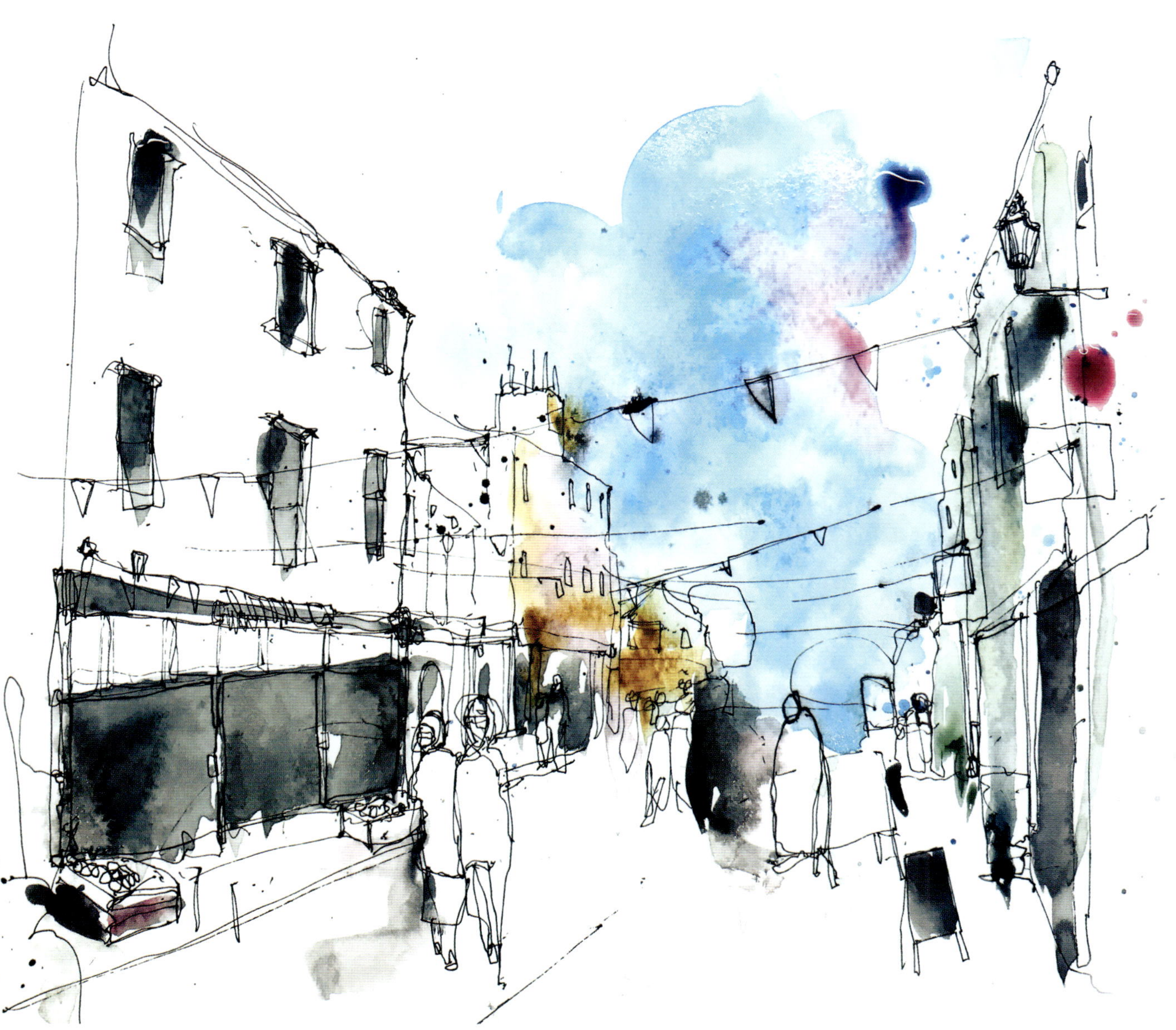

▲ The movement and mixture of colours here help to bring balance between the solid structures and the expressive sky. Focus on trying to capture the essence of the figures – try to convey their energy, personality, and mood through your sketching. Don't worry about mistakes – embrace the loose lines, the body shapes and varying heights. You'll see throughout my work that people are kept very simple. Often they resemble two small ovals: the body and the head. No feet, legs or even arms. Never fingers! Resist the temptation to draw what you know. As you practise more regularly, your tempo and confidence will develop quickly and you will become more comfortable sketching people in the street with freedom and expression.

Windows

The humble window. Windows have the power to offer so much frustration, but they can single-handedly knit a sketch together and make it fly. They are one of the single biggest challenges in all the sketching workshops I have done. The more you look, the more you'll see just how dominated we are by panes of glass in our towns and cities. Everyone interprets a window shape almost subconsciously.

Scale is critical for every sketch – if the windows are drawn too large, then the buildings can easily become unbelievable and dominant in the scene. Draw them too small and the building can potentially appear huge. The intricacy of window panes, frames and sills often catches people out as it throws up all sorts of complex perspective challenges.

Generally, as with every element of the page, backgrounds require less detail than the foreground and this is essential for windows. Try not to depict a window as you think it looks from memory. If you can't make out the individual frames from your viewpoint then don't try to recreate the detail you can't see. Keep them tall and majestic in line with the tall building. Use them as a guide to space out the scene. Generally, the further away, the smaller, as seen here.

My windows are barely windows, and as I work fast they tend to be just the impression of a window. I give more attention to the overall dimensions and relative height to make sure they effectively follow the line to a single vanishing point, helping give an overall and believable perspective.

If your calculation on how many windows there are goes wrong mid-sketch, simply let it be. Don't shoehorn in more to be graphically correct, stick to your flow and just put this down to experience. The vast majority of my fast-paced works have various inaccuracies such as this and would not satisfy an architect. Far more important than the right number of windows is the angle at which they are drawn. Windows and doorways need to follow along the vanishing point plane to avoid conflict. Pay attention to how the lines recede into the distance and use this knowledge to create a sense of depth and dimension in your sketch.

Master the power they have in suggesting scale and perspective, and the window can be your best friend! Don't fall into the trap of drawing every pane just because you know how a window looks. Concentrate on the relative size of foreground windows and background windows.

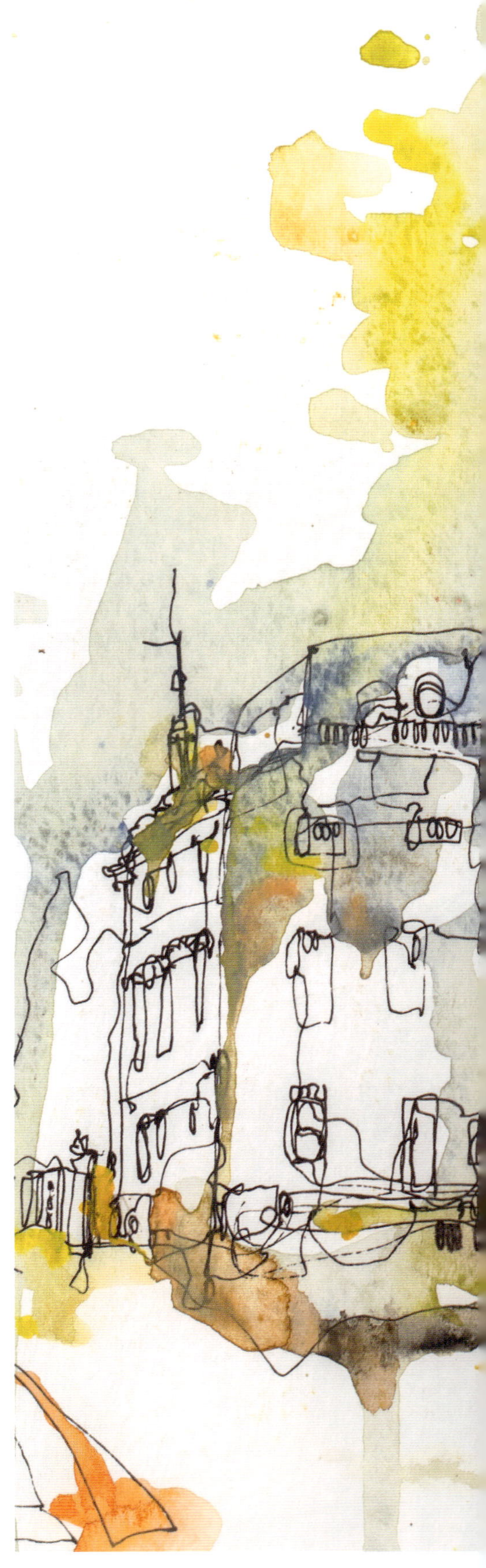

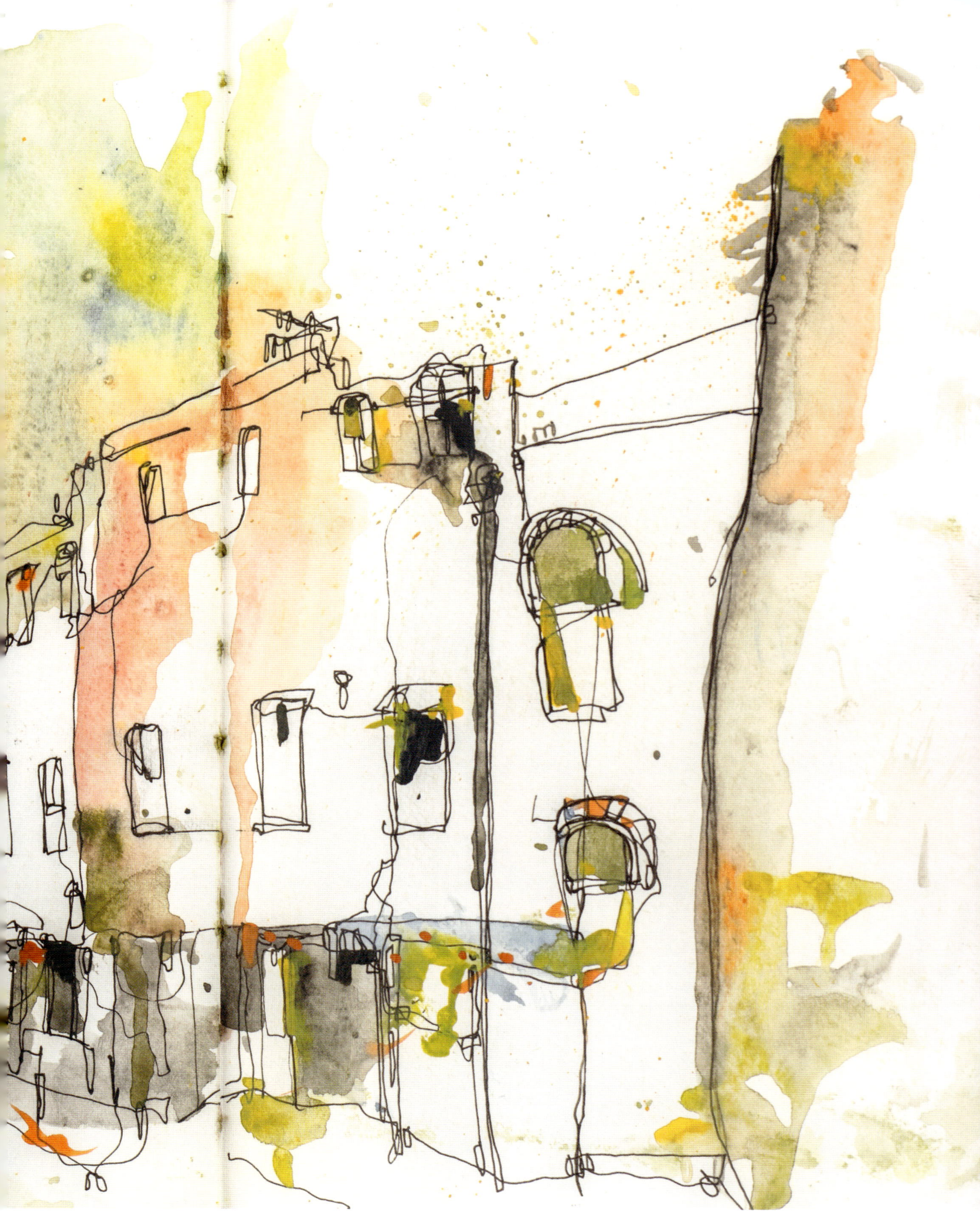

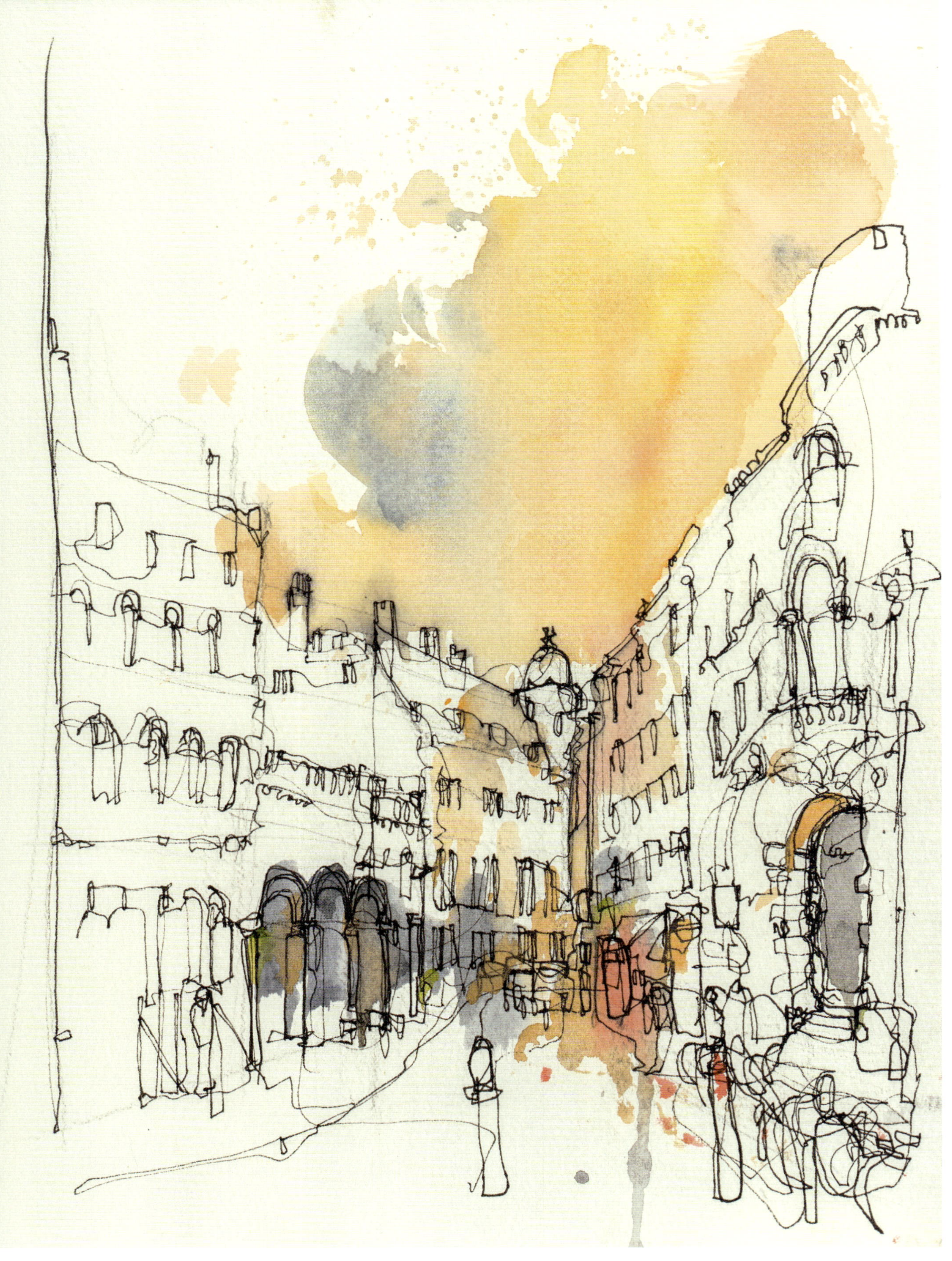

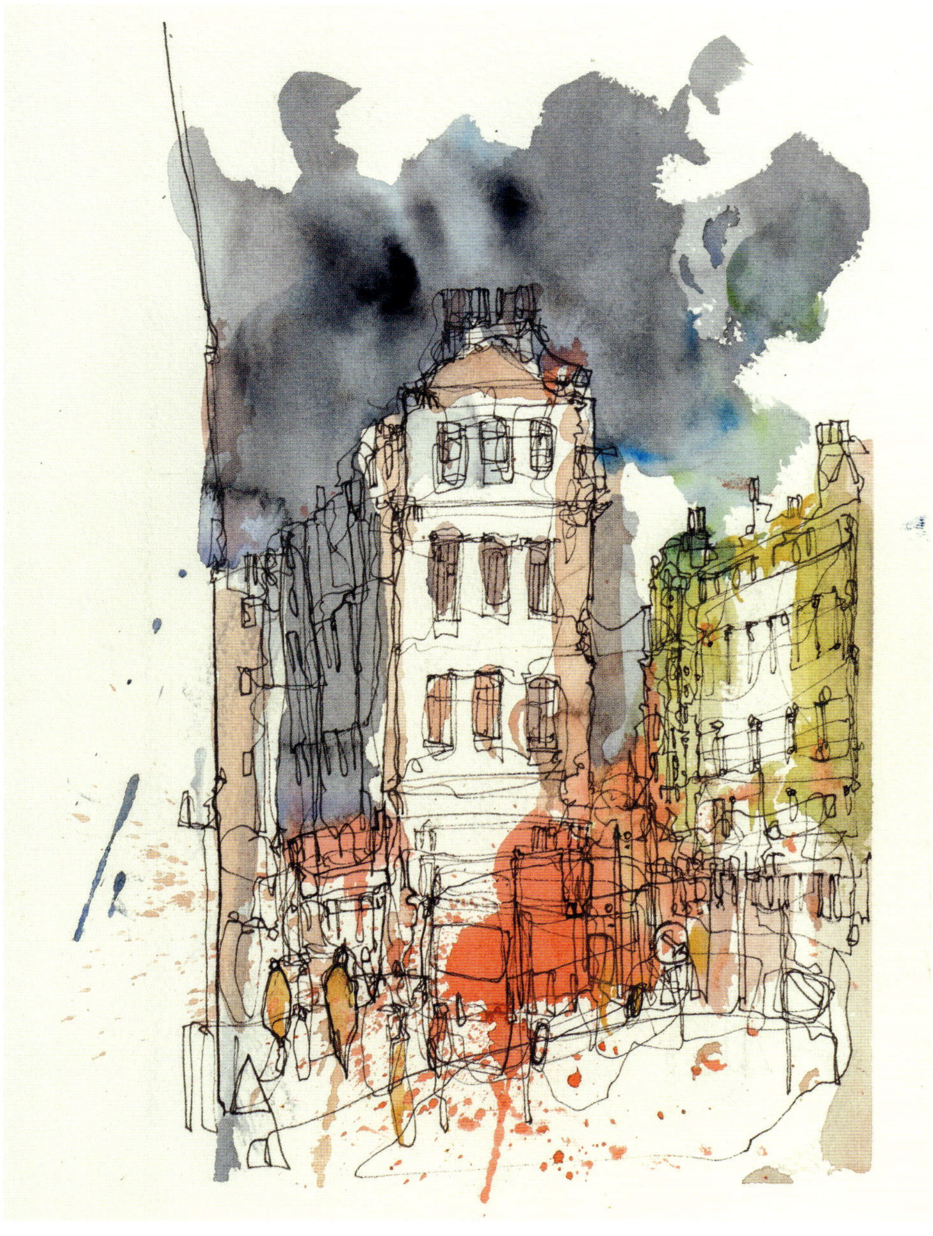

Notice how my sketches tend to massively simplify the window layout, and how the speed at which I work renders some of the shapes quite irregular.

Fill your sketch with shapes

To further simplify the complexity of a sketch and avoid drawing what we think we see, try to look for shapes. A chimney pot, the shape of archways, the dome of a church roof and so on. Throughout all my works I have actively found and simplified shapes. This complex sketch in central London (below) appealed to me immediately as it was full of conical domes, archways, triangular roofs, sweeping windows and globes. All great details to focus on and simplify. See more of this sketch in Out & About 6 on pages 118–125.

The second (opposite), also London, is massively simplified: I've taken the people out and reduced the complex foreground buildings to their basic structure. Left white and vacant, just the shell of the building remains. By contrast the right-hand side of the scene has more detail. It's this contrast that helps spark viewer interest and provides detailed areas to fill with colour.

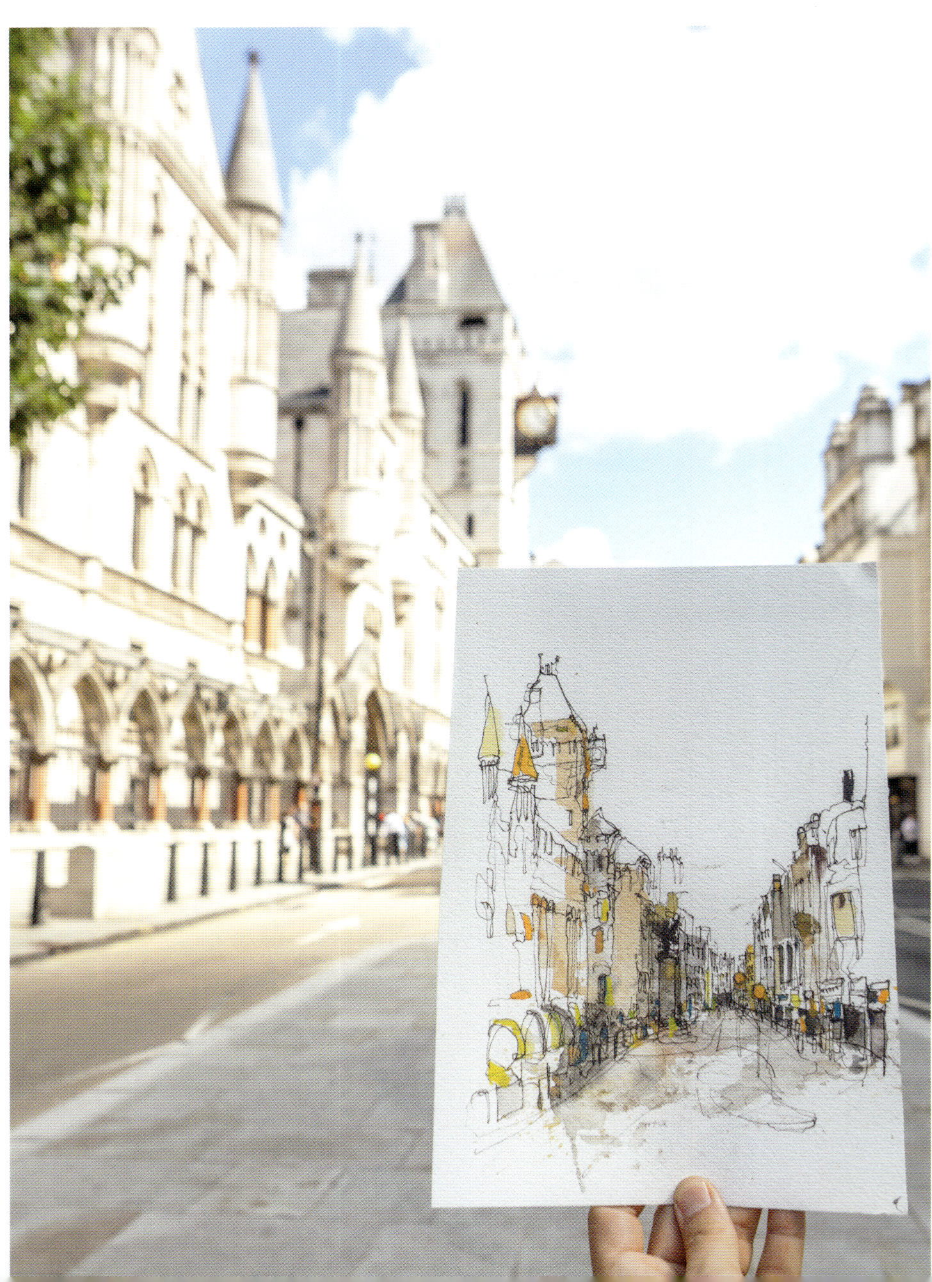

Specific details

A quick line can give the impression of a specific detail, drawn with the same fluidity as the main sketch. Try not to become too rigid when drawing a detailed area, but try to keep some familiarity in line tension. Small details such as lampposts, church spires, posts and the various junction boxes and oddities along the streets are good to include to further show scale.

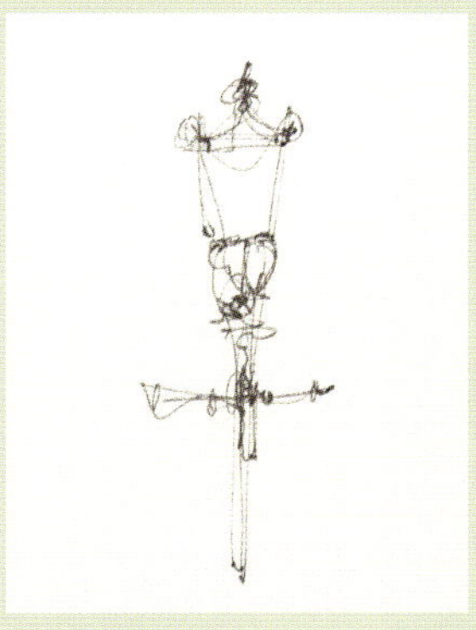 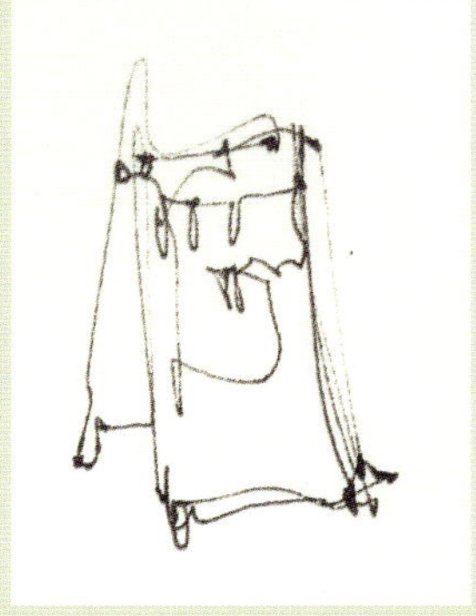 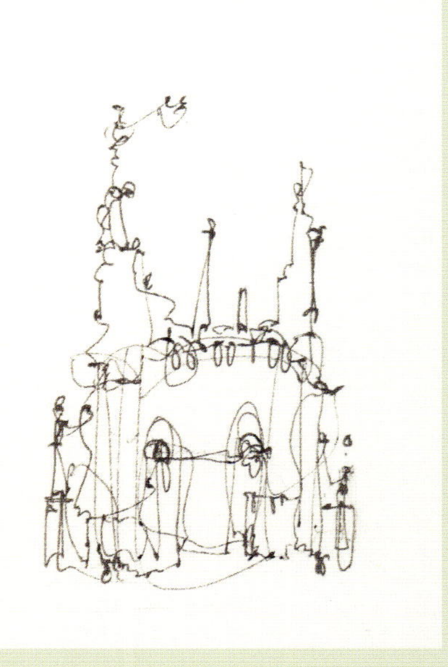

The church top on the far right here is deliberately loose and wobbly as it forms part of a background detail.

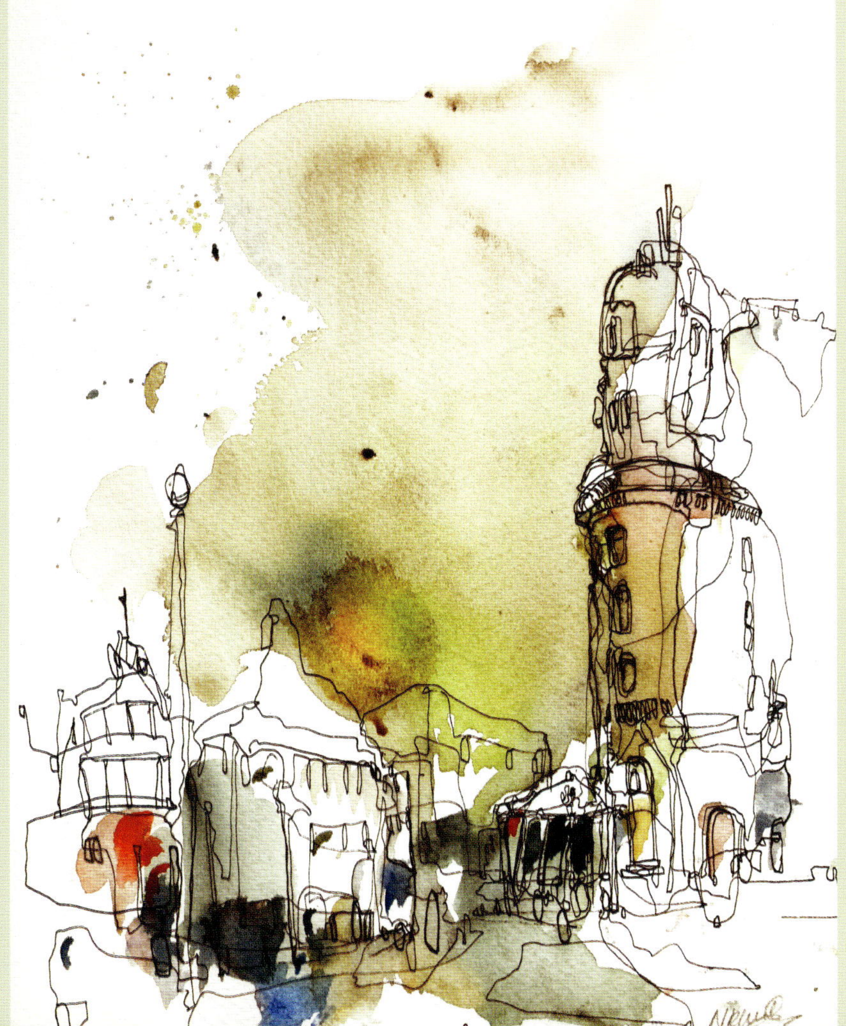

A collection of rectangles and loose lines.

Exercise

Continuous line sketch

Moving on from the pure contour drawing, I like to throw in another technique to free up the sketching arm and develop observation skills. A technique that I use a lot for both loosening up and for smaller sketchbook entries is continuous line sketching. This time we *can* look at the paper.

Just like the pure contour drawing, this doesn't have to be an urban landscape scene, it might be a chair, the view through the window, the dog asleep on the floor. You might want to sketch an architectural scene from a picture. Whatever you choose, try and pick something that interests you. Subjects with well-defined edges will make it easier to maintain the continuous line. That's why buildings lend themselves to this technique.

Set a stopwatch for 2 minutes
This will help you eliminate the unwanted detail and help you choose your scene.

Draw with a continuous line
Pay attention to the outlines and details within the subject. Follow the contours and shapes with your pen (or pencil), allowing the line to flow naturally. Don't worry about making mistakes or creating perfect lines; the goal is to capture the essence of the subject with a single, continuous line.

Let it flow – if you need to move across the paper, just let your pen press lightly; feel the varying use of line weight start to emerge.

Next steps
Try to combine your knowledge of pure contour and continuous line sketching to really free up your style. Practise regularly to improve fluidity, observation skills and line confidence. Like any skill, continuous line sketching improves with practice. With each sketch you'll gain confidence in your lines, improve your observation skills, and develop a deeper understanding of form and composition.

Tip

Start the line with the largest part of the scene so you don't run out of room on the page.

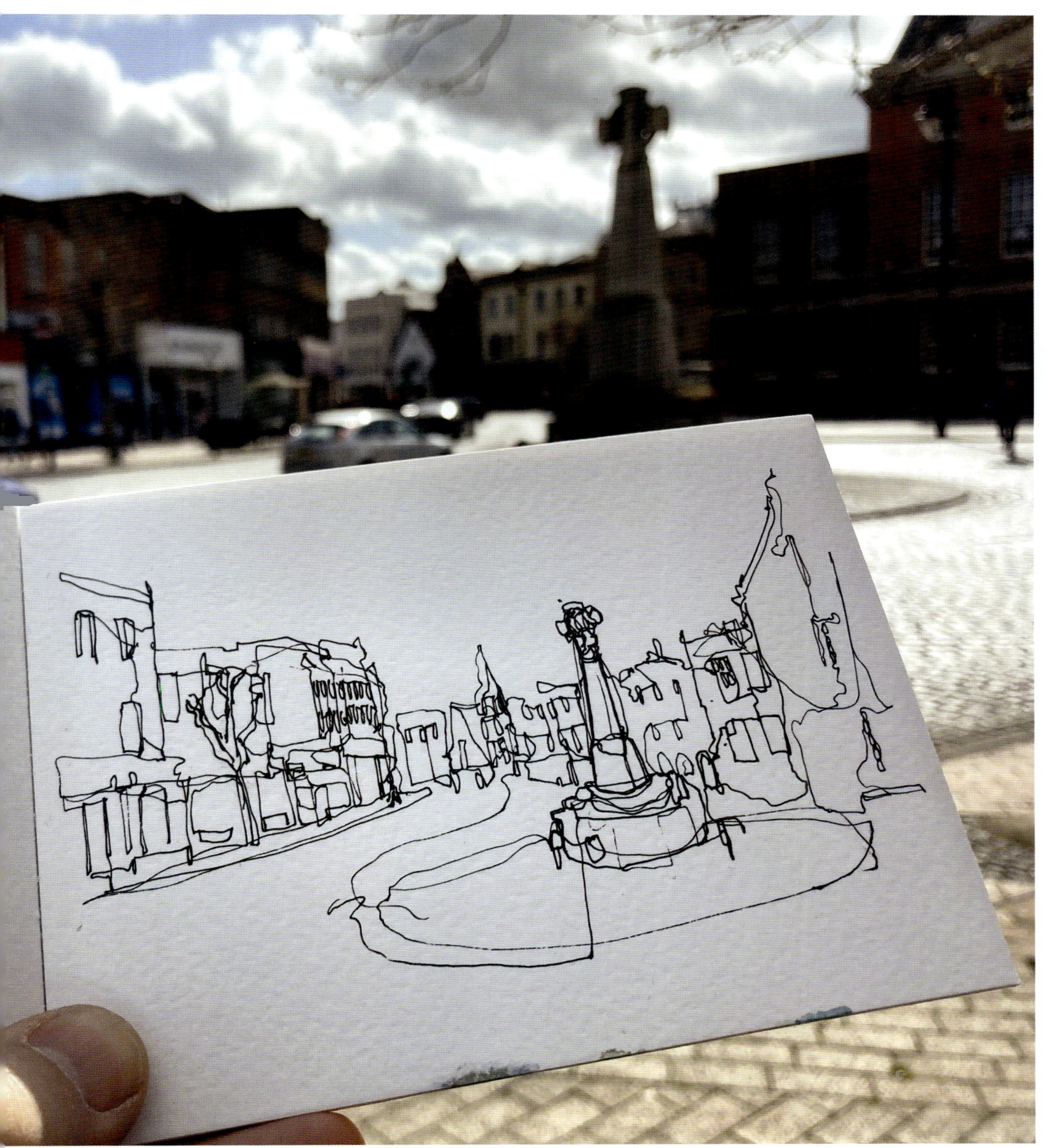

Watercolour postcard pads are a great way to start sketching. Here, the foreground monument is the focal point and sets the visible depth (see page 86).

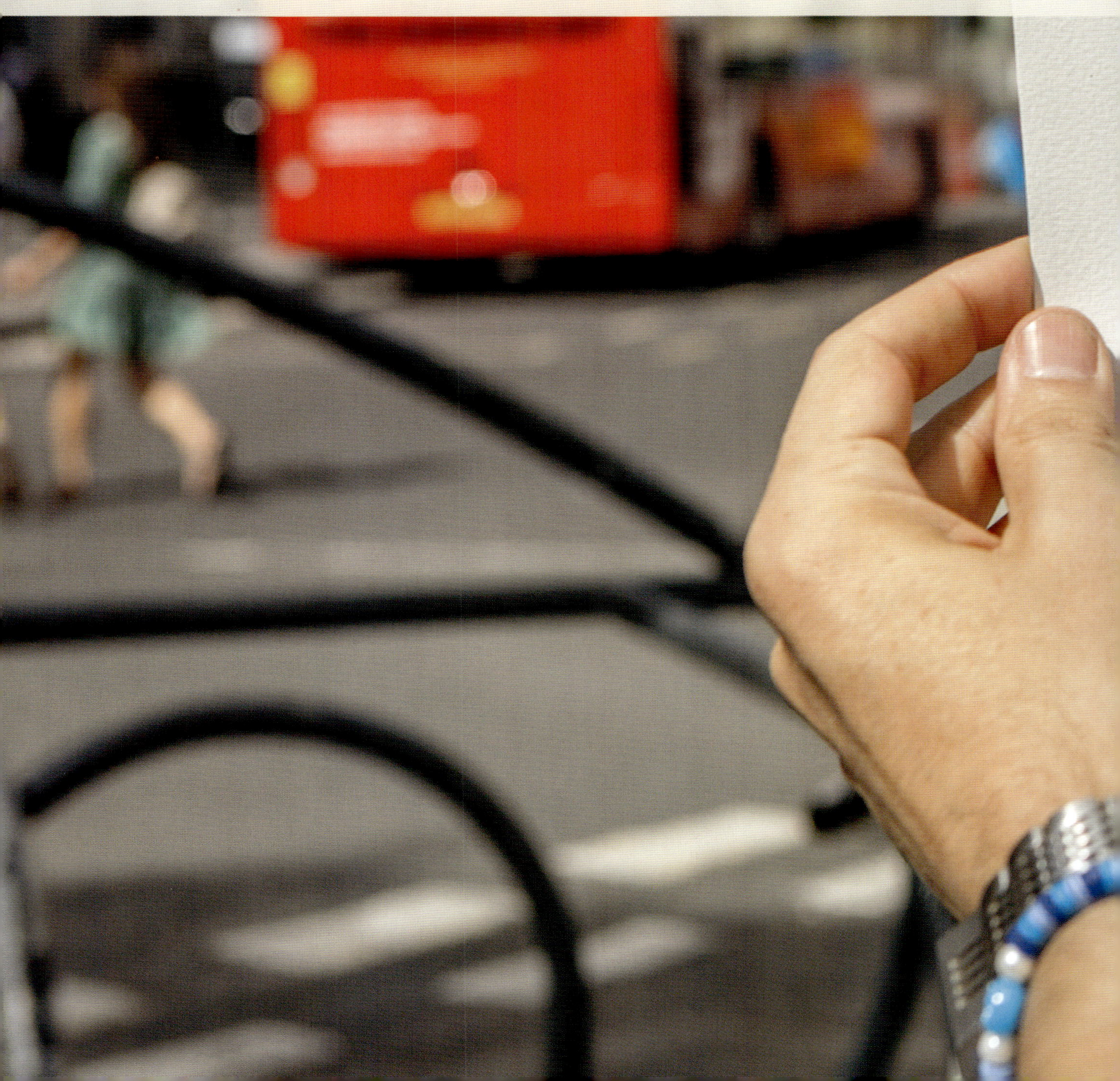

OUT & ABOUT 2
IN THE HEART OF THE CITY

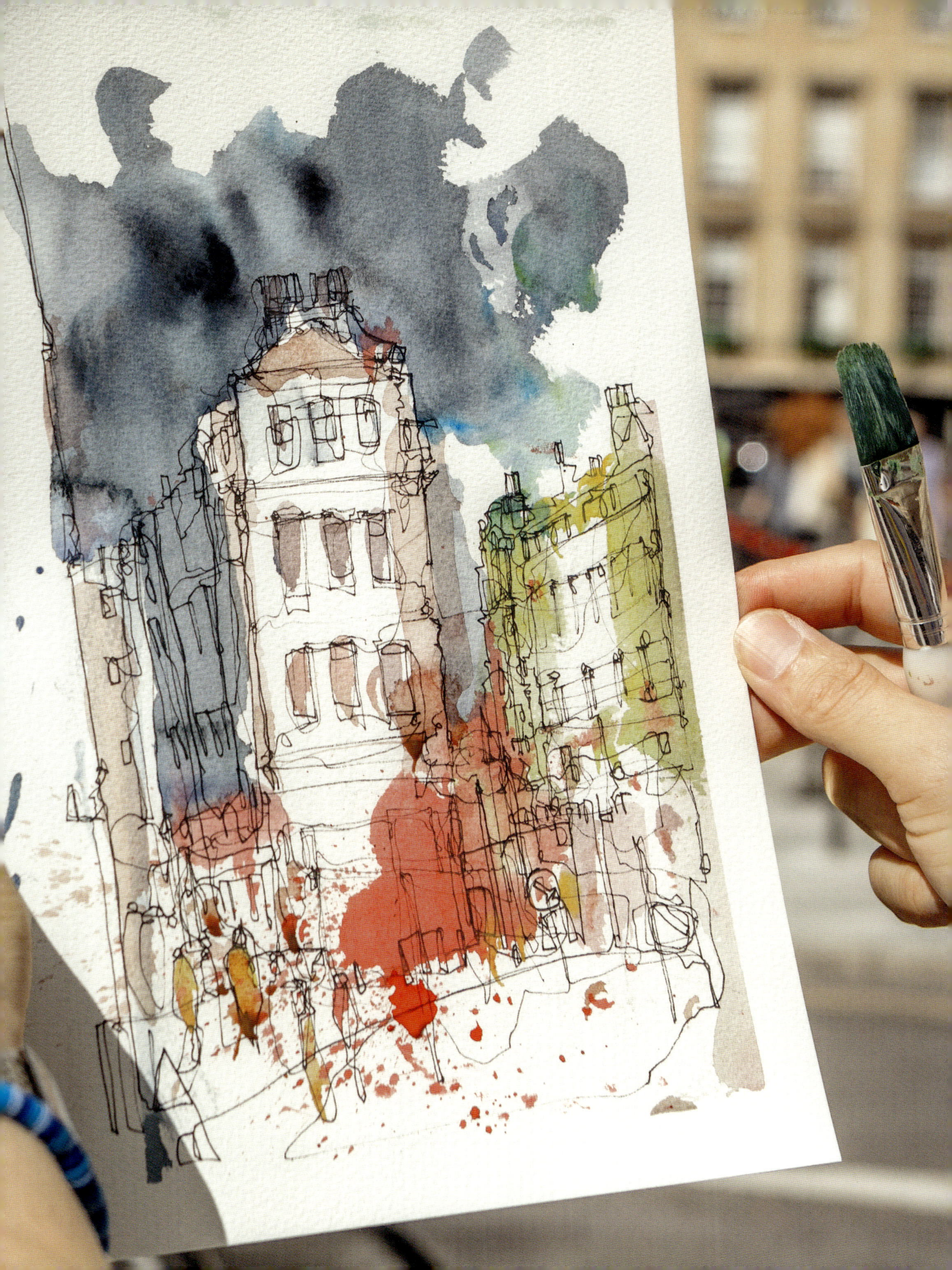

Capturing a bustling city scene

Seeking out the complex is always my first aim. Mix this with a cross-section of a strong skyline, foreground activity, a crisp horizon line, lots of movement, a good and obvious vanishing point (see one-point perspective on page 83) and the colours of the day, and you have the perfect recipe for urban landscape art.

I set up here early in the morning in a very open area and began attracting a few passers-by. This is always a interesting time! Seeing an urban sketcher getting ready does attract some attention – always good-natured; there's a real sense of intrigue from the general public. Fortunately sketching and painting on location is ever growing. I have learnt to love the social interaction and have met some amazing people who simply wander by and have a chat.

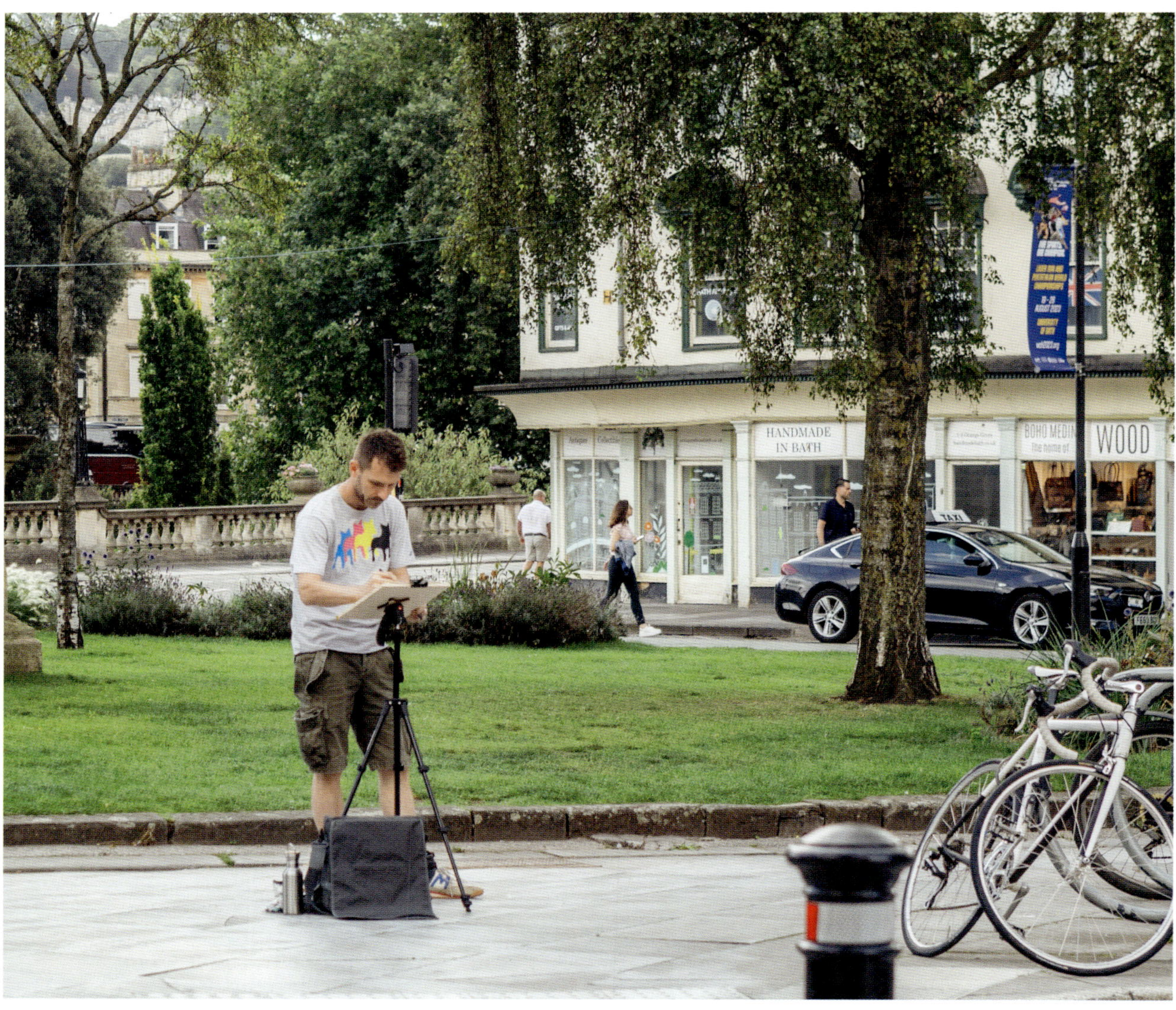

This scene below is super detailed – potentially overwhelming – and immediately lent itself to a visual crop. I used a makeshift cardboard frame (shown on the right) to bring some discipline to the scene and, like a target, I was immediately able to calm my senses and zero in on a potential scene. I didn't want to lose the busyness, but I wanted to capture more detail than my earlier loosener sketch on pages 40–47.

I decided to make my focal point a building nestled between the huge church structures. Again this was a conscious decision – when faced with a very dominant view, the majority of sketchers will all inevitably capture very similar scenes. I like to put my spin on the view and support the underdog, giving some welcome celebration of those less obvious parts of the scene.

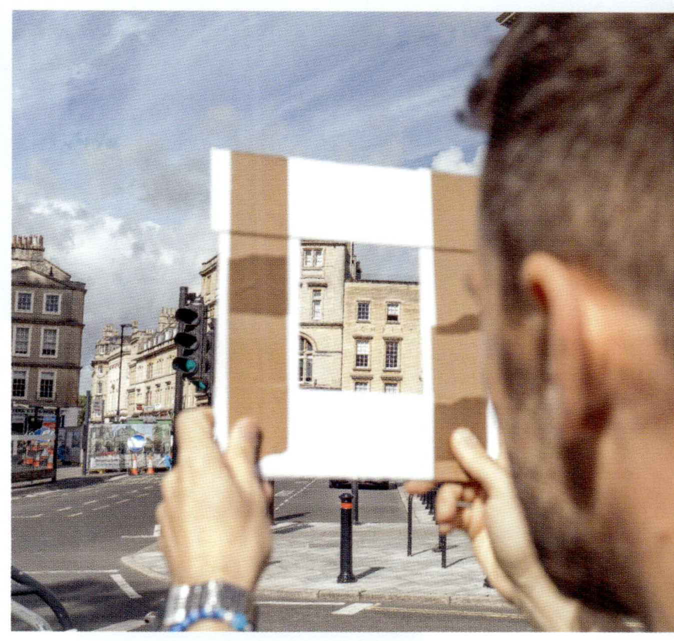

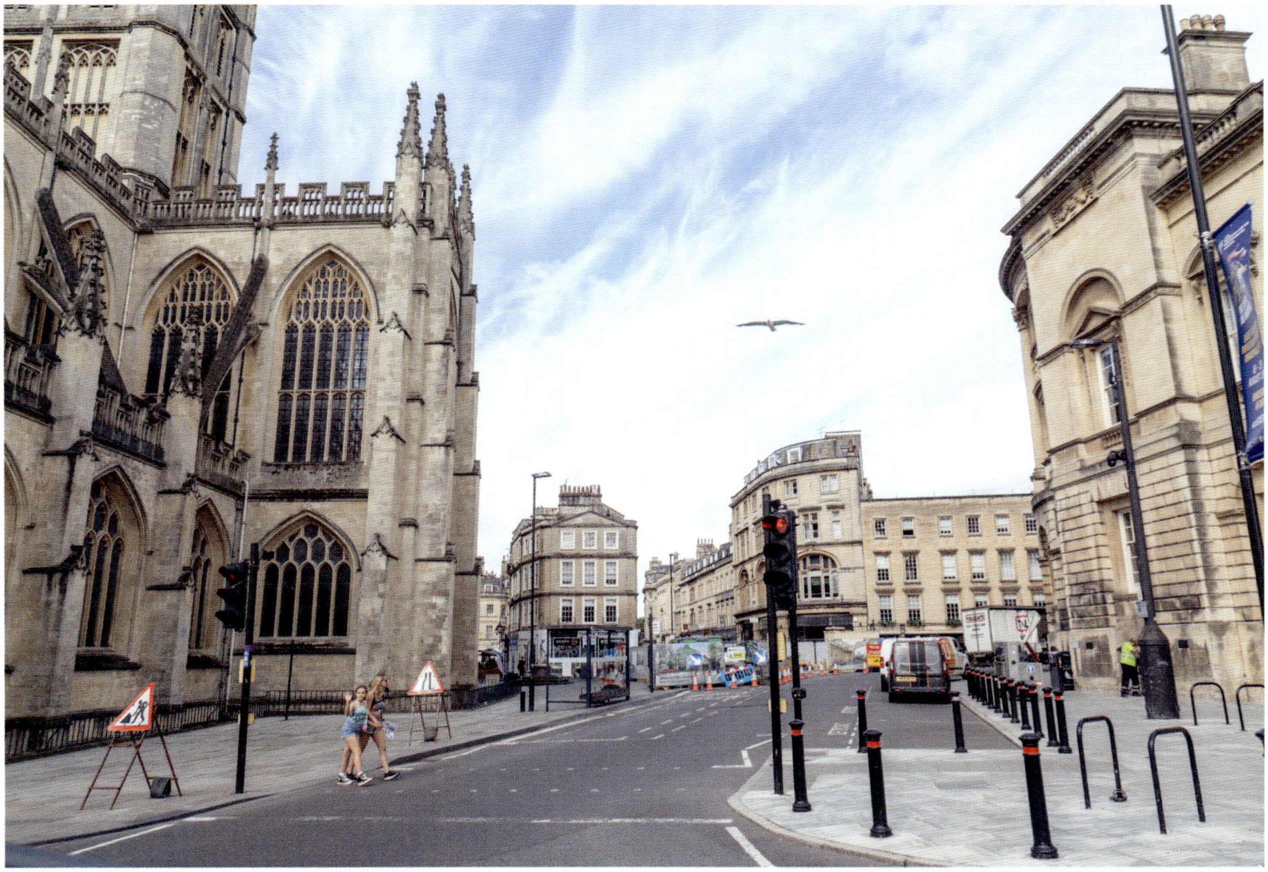

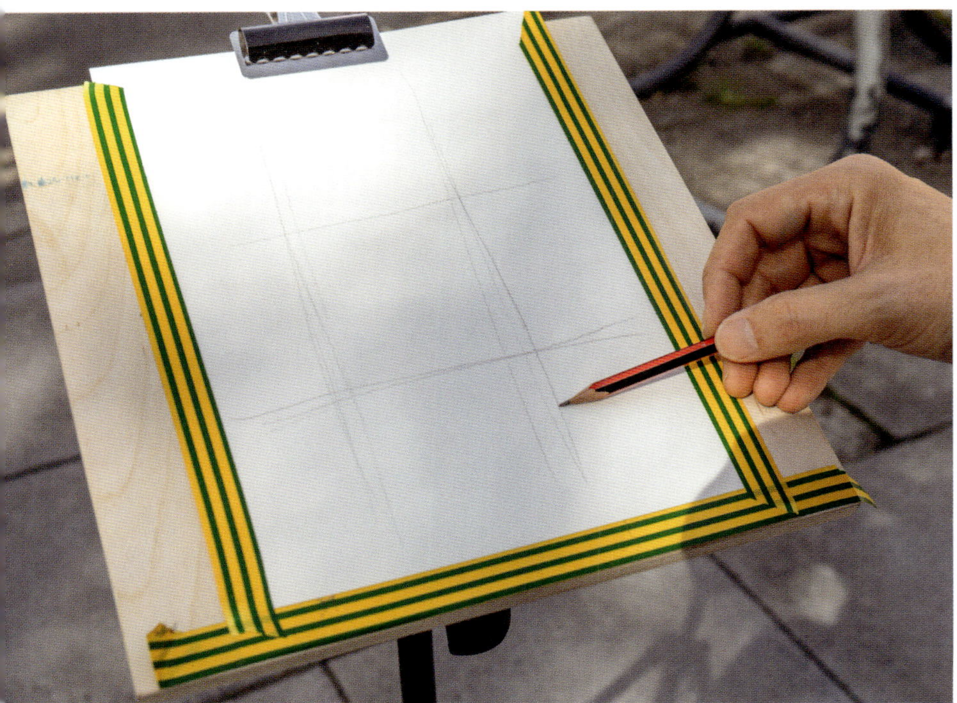

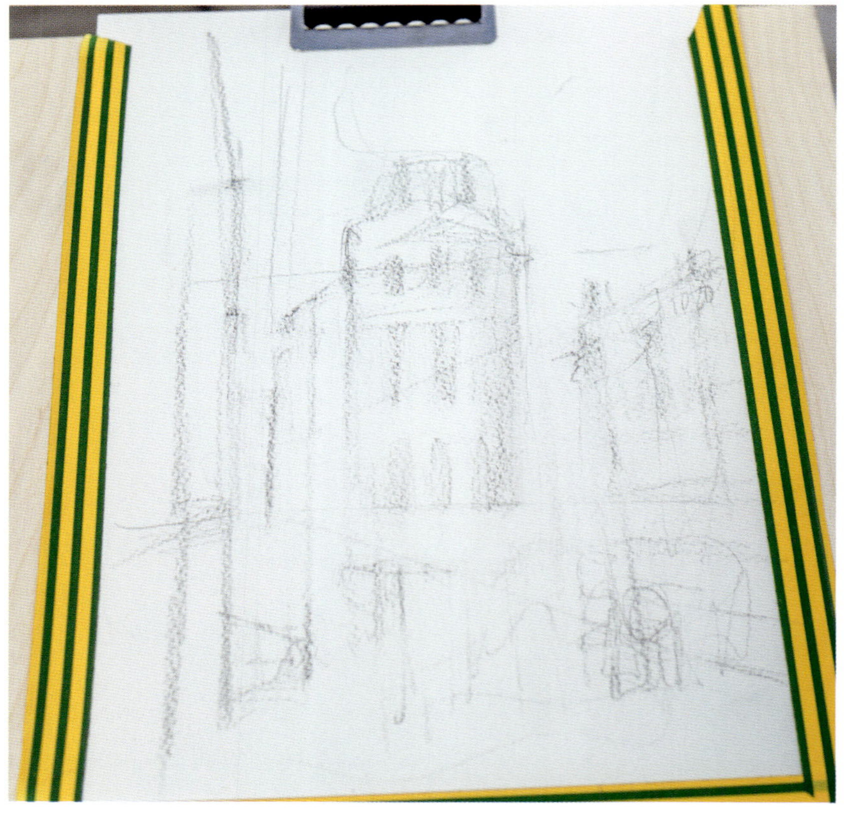

▲ I decided to work a little larger and on loose sheet paper. To help this, I taped down the paper with my trusty electrical tape and clipped the top firmly to my easel. It was quite a windy day, so keeping my base camp fixed and solid was essential! As before, I set out my kit so I had everything at my disposal.

When working larger I sometime like to plot the key intersections of the scene in pencil. This particular crop was going to involve two obvious skyline 'V' shapes, and I wanted to reserve the space for these (simultaneously this helped define the building outline).

▶ The vanishing point was not as prominent with my chosen angle, and was in fact off the page itself. This presented a different take, but the logic remains – the core rules of perspective were still in play.

▶ With the pencil sketch down, I don't waste time adding my ink – drawing with the same speed and flow as the continuous line style, stopping every now and then to breathe and view the scene. I tend to stop to look and consider what details I want to highlight – is there a particular archway, doorway or chimney that stands out? What can I see that makes it original and is interesting to focus on? Am I going to draw every window? Probably not. Will I simply hint at the complexity? Yes.

I made an early decision to capture the edge of the cathedral on the left but leave it untouched, by way of creating the natural frame.

This particular scene threw up one real challenge – the big red British bus. The scene became increasingly busy as I drew, so much so that the whole scene changed. My previously unobscured view was now in the epicentre of the sightseeing tours' parades. This happens on location and, even when working fast, cannot be avoided. Basically my earlier clear foreground view was now a haze of cars, taxis, buses, lorries and people. So that's what I decided to draw – but with the specific aim to capture the chaos. I took my pen for a walk and didn't look at the paper – a pure contour maze of lines and shapes, 100 per cent observation. To get any detail would have been untrue to the scene. I wanted to capture the rhythm in front of me. This is the kind of spontaneous uniqueness that working from still pictures can never recreate. What else could change?

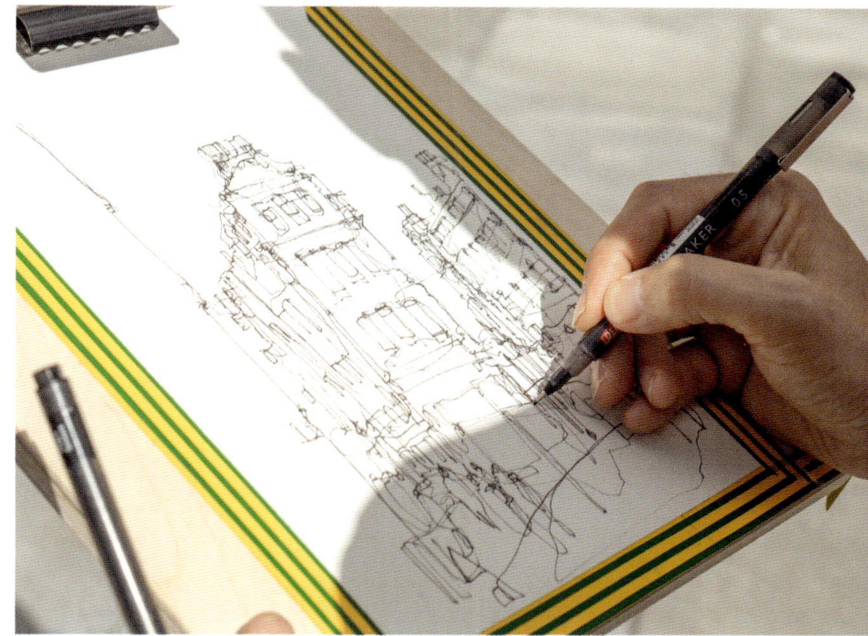

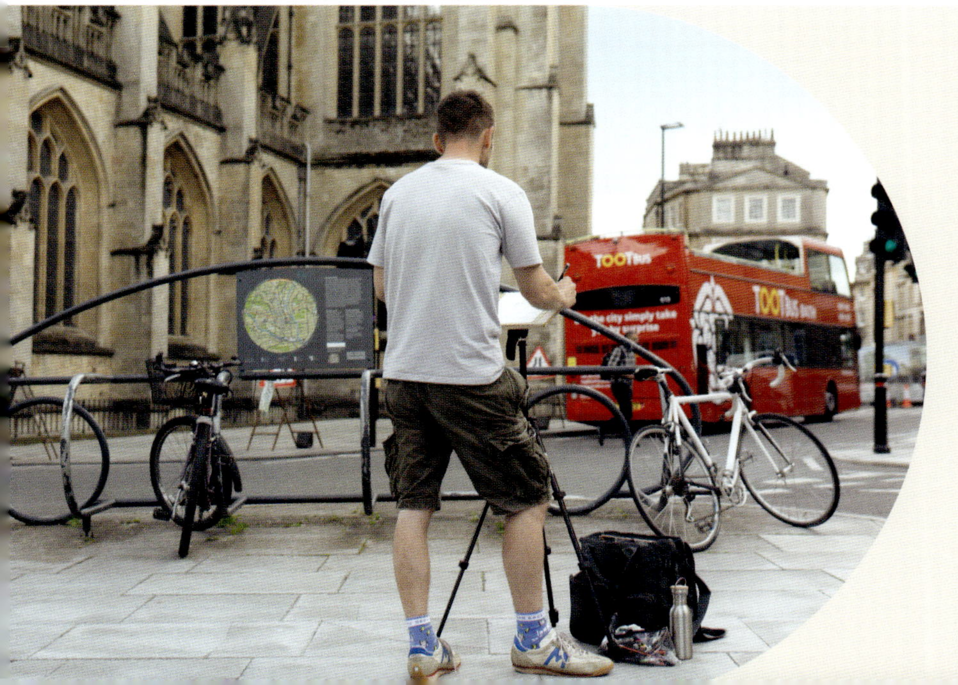

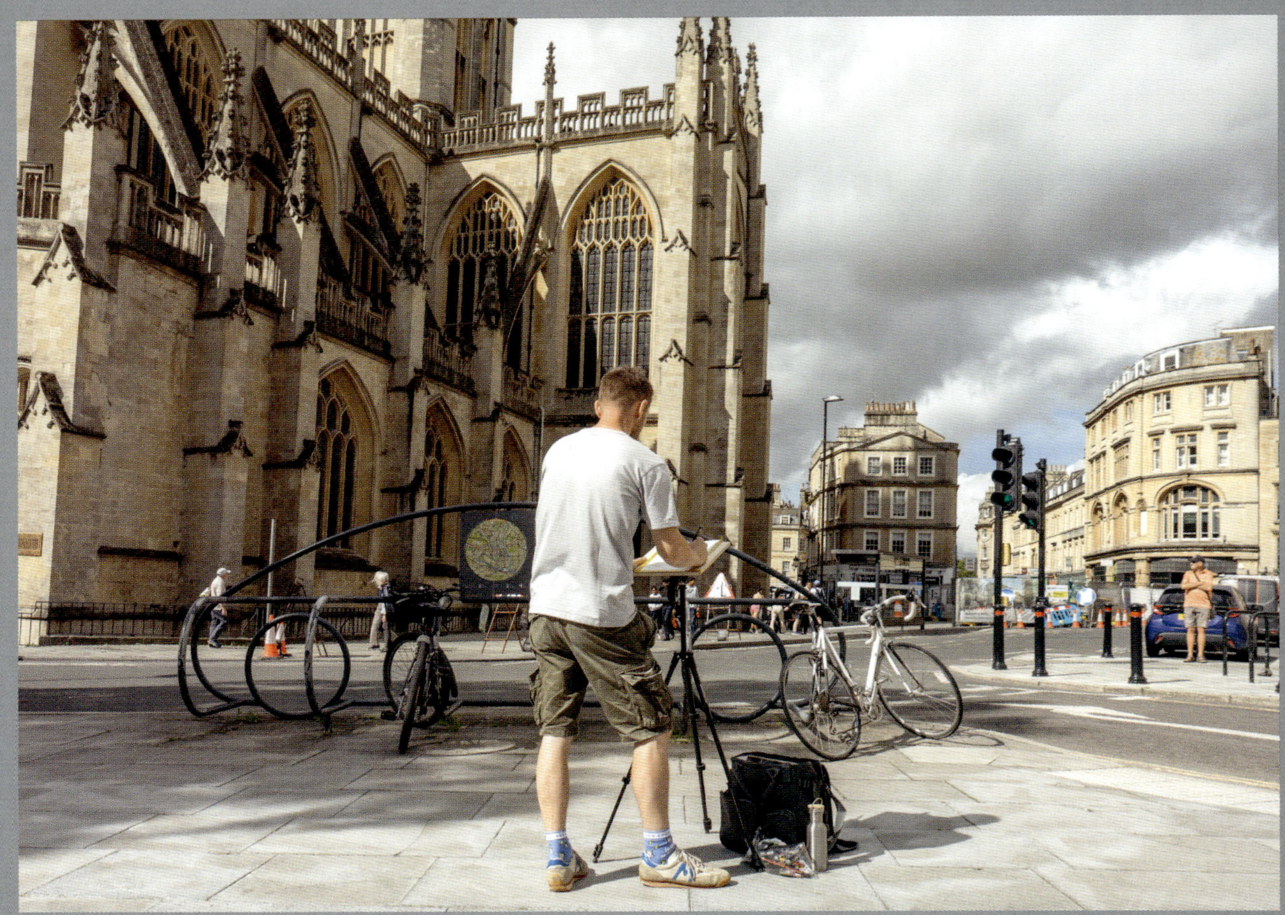

▲ How about some rain clouds? The scene drops another twist
as I decide to open my paint set. The red bus has moved again,
but the beautiful blue sky has turned a very definite angry grey.

The dark bruising sky prompted me to use a strong pigmented
tube of watercolour, and I didn't hold back. Tubes of watercolour
offer the ability to apply paint almost like thick acrylic paint.
I think I took some frustration out on the sky and some of the
paint settled with little water. Using Derwent Inktense cotton
paper here, the colour blends in really well. I fed the chunky
filbert brush into the paper and let the bristles fan out to create
natural coverage. At this point I had already decided to leave the
focal building almost untouched to deliver maxiumum impact to
the dark sky. I did, however, decide to bring the grey down to the
horizon line to help show the dark shadow of the focus building.

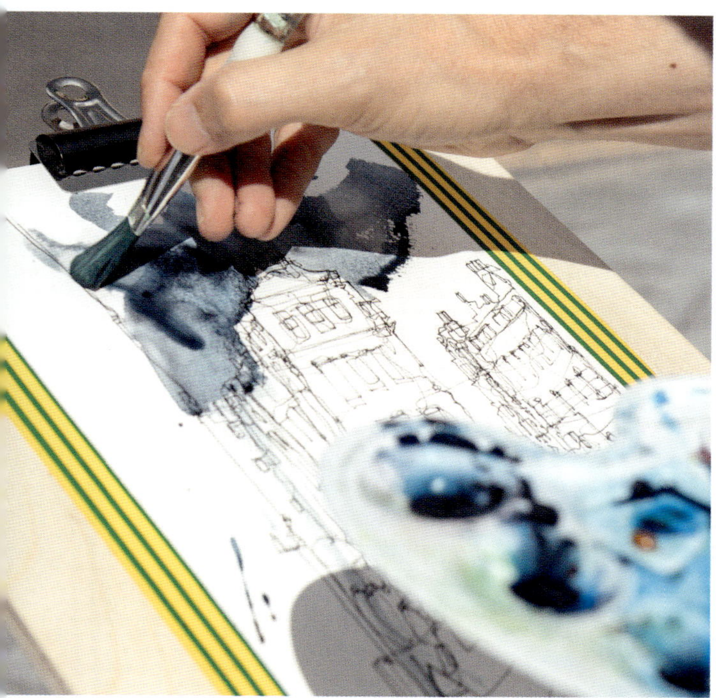

▲ The dramatic sky takes shape with a generous amount of dark tones and water.

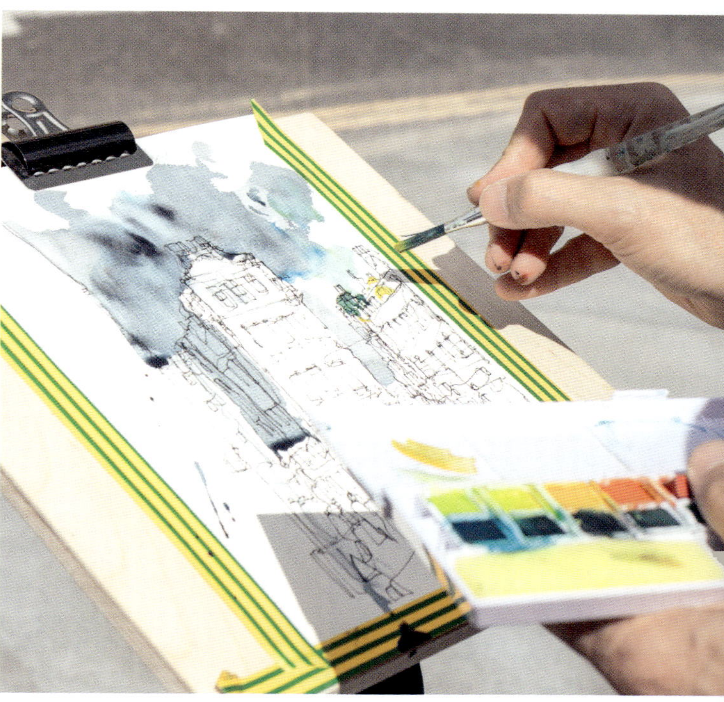

▲ I then offered up a more neutral colour to the building on the right. I simply let a warm yellow mix run along the contours of where the sunlight was reflecting – no detail here. The foreground of the sketch is where it's all happening, so a calmer area to the side helps deliver more visual contrast.

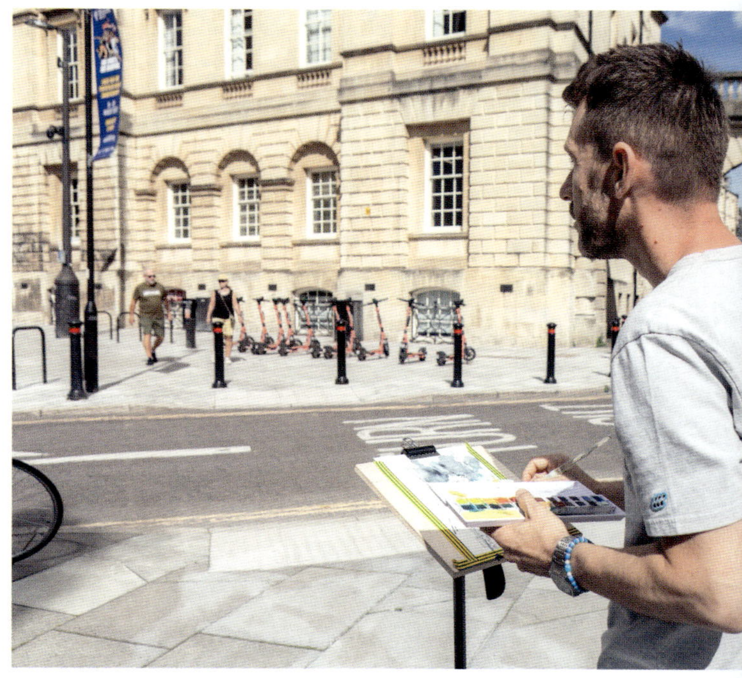

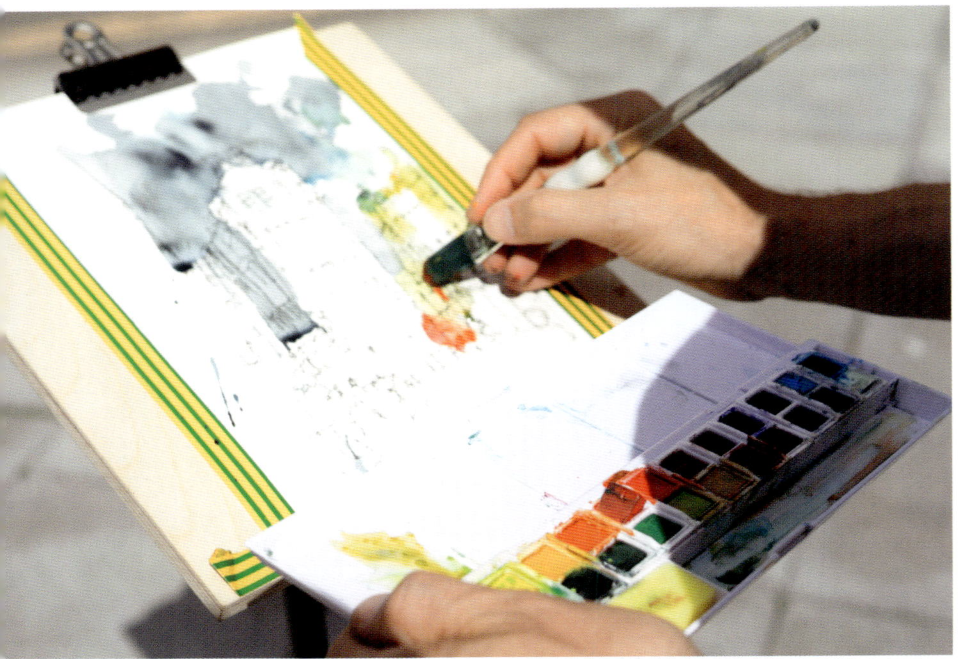

◀ The foreground was a merry-go-round of movement, colour and confusion. By now the rain clouds had passed and it was a hot, sunny day again. Almost like a time-lapse video, I had a complex trail of lines, the movement of people and all the various shapes of wheels, buses, posts and pavements.

▼ I splashed the red where the most promiment outline of the bus had been, and set to work adding splatters and speckles to add the excitement of the scene. Some of the pure contour drawing lines had naturally created a closed shape, and I intentionally added paint to these to create some solid objects inside the line frenzy.

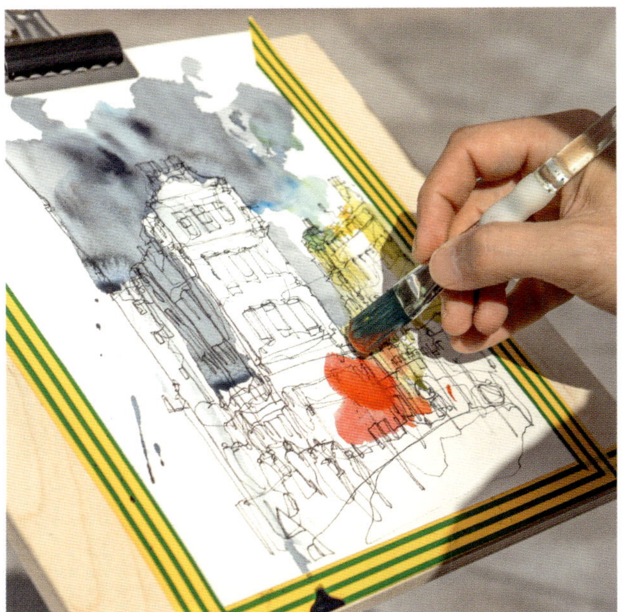

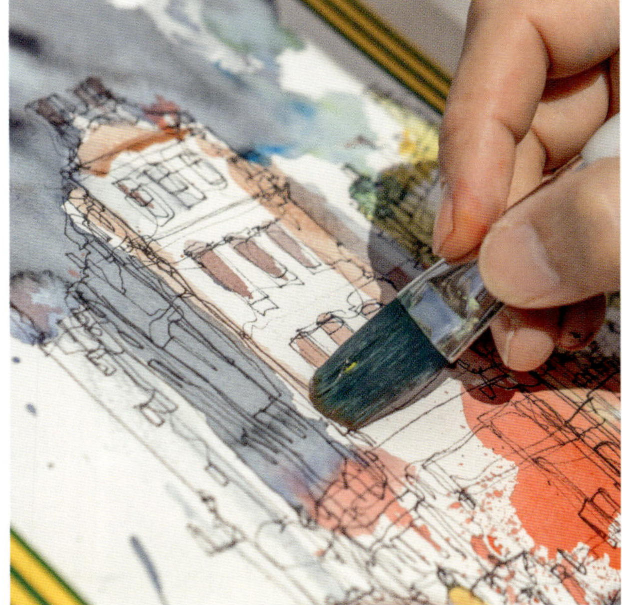

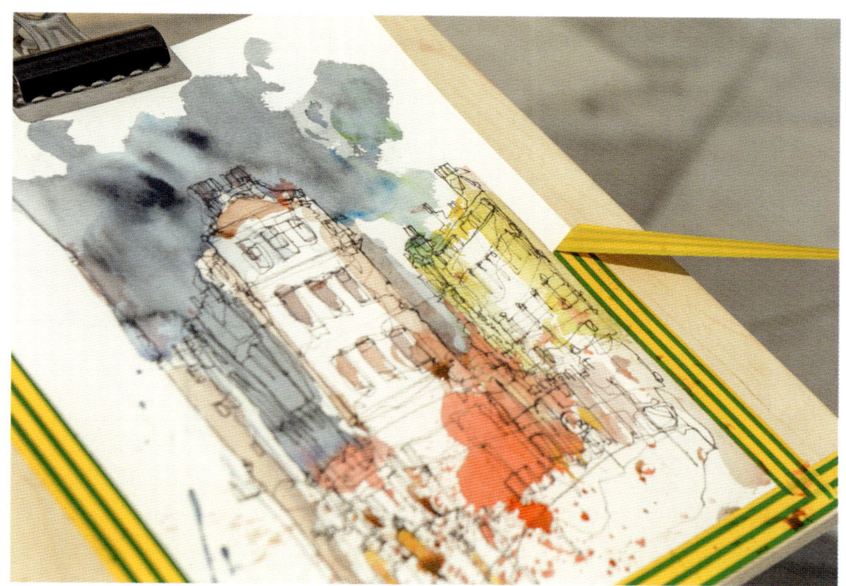

The final piece, completed in around 30 minutes,
featured the strong white building edge on the
left-hand side, a bold sky and a foreground melee
that could never have been imagined.

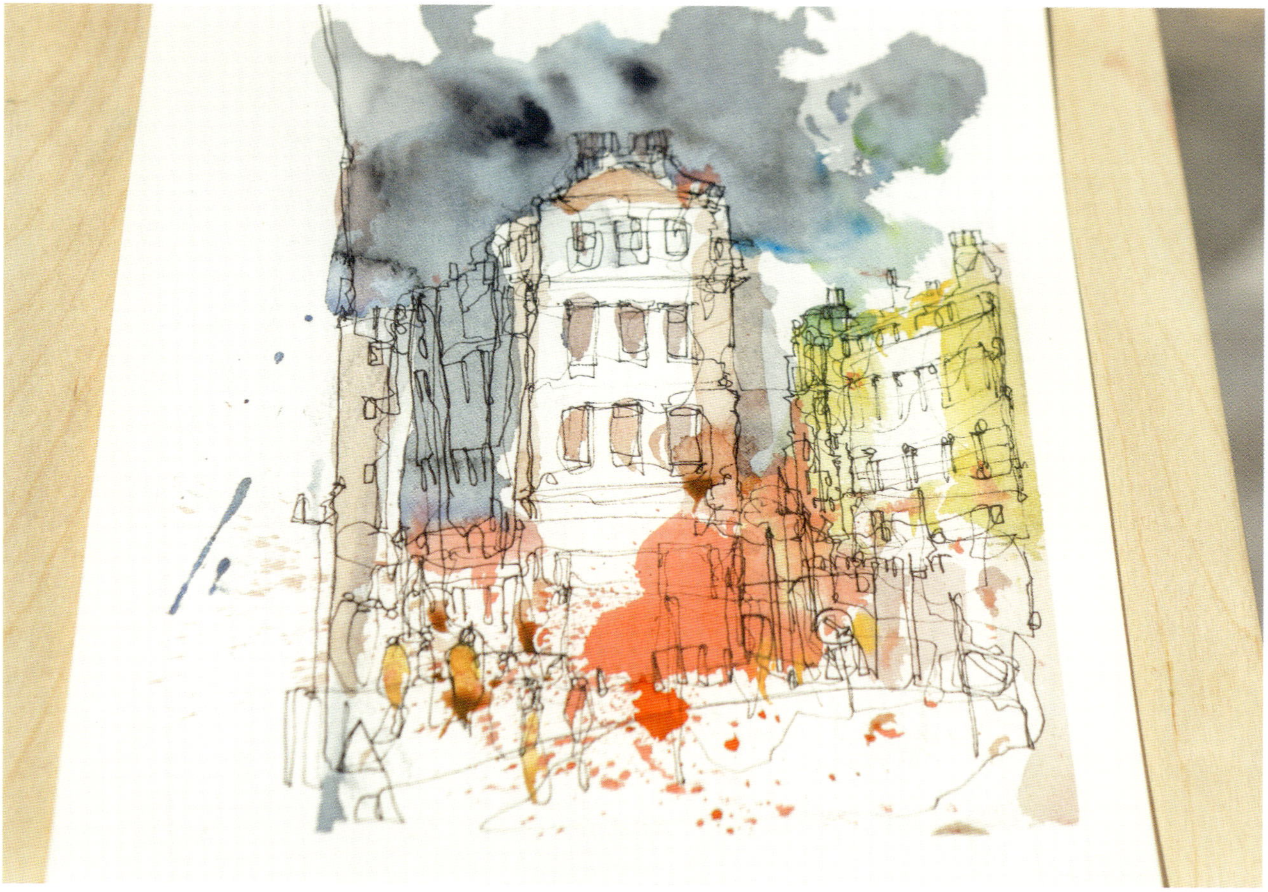

Measurement and scale

Accurately depicting the relative height and width of the urban scene is crucial to make the sketch appear life-like and correct. There are a few techniques that can help you get to grips with this key skill and ultimately lead you to having a more natural way of assessing the scene visually. It's important not to get too obsessed with rigid accuracy as you might find such tight scrutiny stunts your creative line-making process. The overall goal is to keep the proportions correct in relation to one another, so as to not make a sketch unbalanced.

Like all the lessons in this book, experience and repetition will bring results. Once you are comfortable you'll find that measuring the scene starts to become second nature.

Pen measurement

Using your pen to measure a sketch is a very common technique used by all kinds of artists to gauge the size and proportions of their subject. It simply involves holding up your pen (or pencil) and using it as a relative reference point to compare the size of objects in the drawing. To use this technique, first identify a key object in the sketch (ideally the largest object, so that you can gauge the likely overall dimensions and available space on the page), hold up your pen and then refer to this relative size when comparing to other objects in the scene.

You can mark basic pointers on your sketchbook to depict the base, the width and the roof of a structure. These pointers can be simple dot with the pen or with a pencil. Measuring in this way will help give a consistent way of estimating distances to help kick-start the sketch.

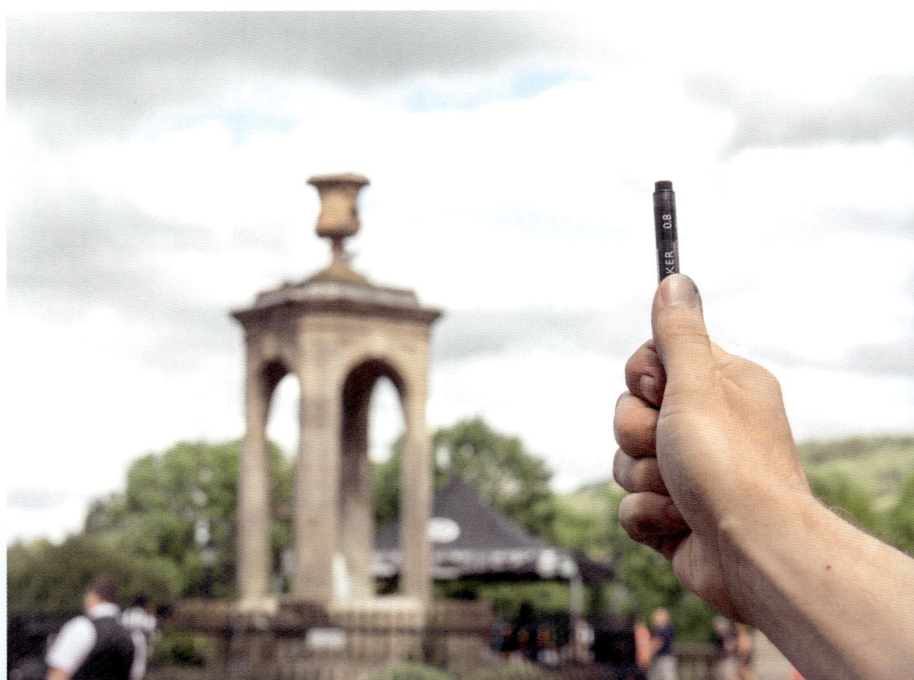

Angles

Perspective can fool the mind, and the simple act of holding a pen or a finger at the same angle as the subject helps clear away the confusion of many merging lines and angles. I use this technique all the time to keep me on the right track. Typically I will hold the pen at one end and tilt it until it mimics the angle in view. Then it's just a case of identifying this angle against what we know as horizontal. Lines of perspective that are very close to the horizontal (or vertical) are incredibly easy to misread but are crucial to the sketch. If I'm working on a larger scale I will use my arm to measure the angle.

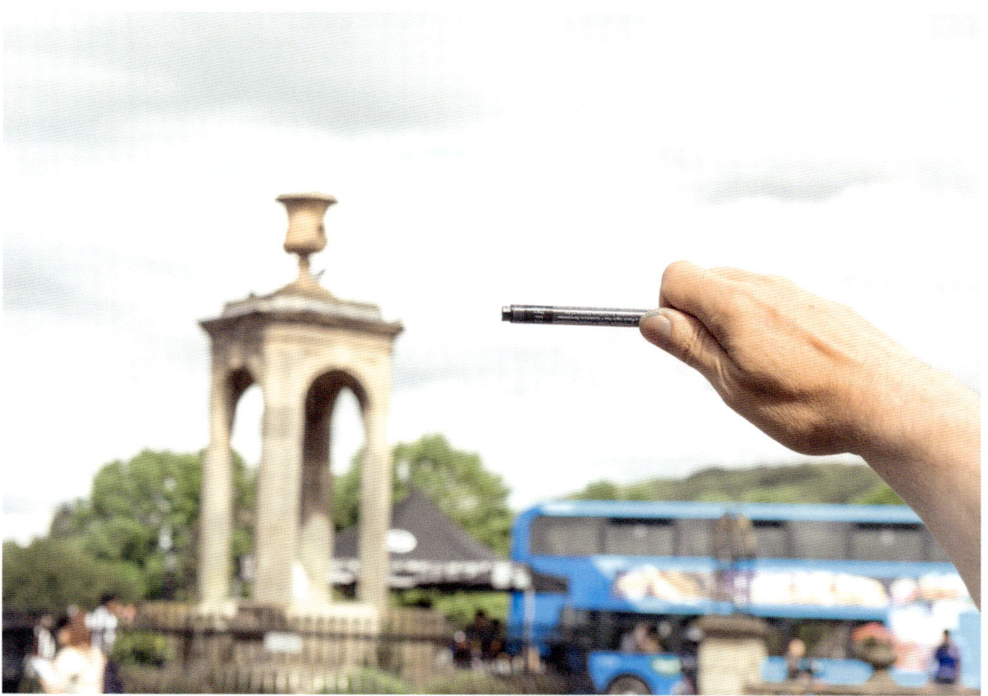

Exercise

Measure the scene

The key to measuring a scene is making sure that the relative sizes of the scene align as much as possible. It's okay to have some slight variance as this can add character, but too much can make the scene's proportions incorrect.

Select a focal point
Choose a specific object or point in your scene to focus on. I usually pick the most prominent building visible, but for this exercise it's good to start with a basic scene to measure, perhaps the inside of a room or a window view.

Use your kit
Hold your pencil at arm's length and use it to measure the height or width of the focal point, and then use your thumb to mark off the height or width on the pencil.

Other parts of the scene
Next, use your pencil to measure other objects in the scene relative to your initial measurement. For example, if the height of an object is approximately twice the height of your focal point, use that ratio to estimate the height of other nearby objects.

Keep checking
It's a good idea to regularly check and adjust your measurements to ensure that the proportions of objects in your sketch accurately reflect those in the scene. Pay attention to relationships between different elements, such as the spacing between buildings or the size of windows relative to doors.

In time, this process will start to become second nature. Practice makes better!

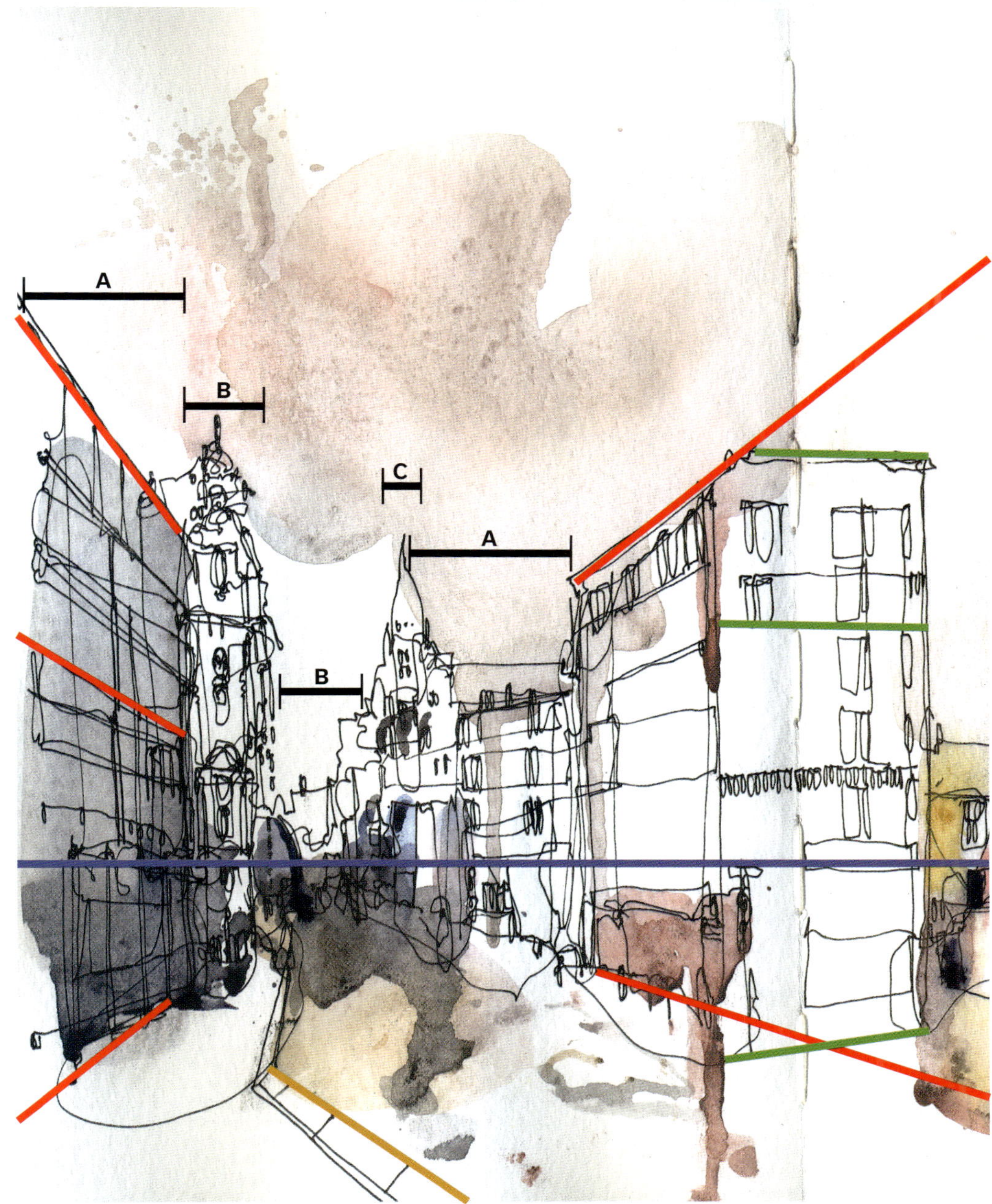

The following three base widths really help simplify the relationship of the whole scene:

A = I used this as my standard width measurement.

B = half the size of A. The large grey structure on the left appears much wider due to the strong perspective lines, but this can be deceptive.

C = half the size of B.

The red lines lead towards the vanishing point and vary in angles – hold up your pen and physically trace the angle in the sky.

The angle of the yellow pavement line is quite extreme but it really helps illustrate the depth.

The blue is the horizon line, grounded at the lower third of the page.

As the sketch panned right, a secondary vanishing point was starting to appear and these green lines just start to capture it.

OUT & ABOUT 3

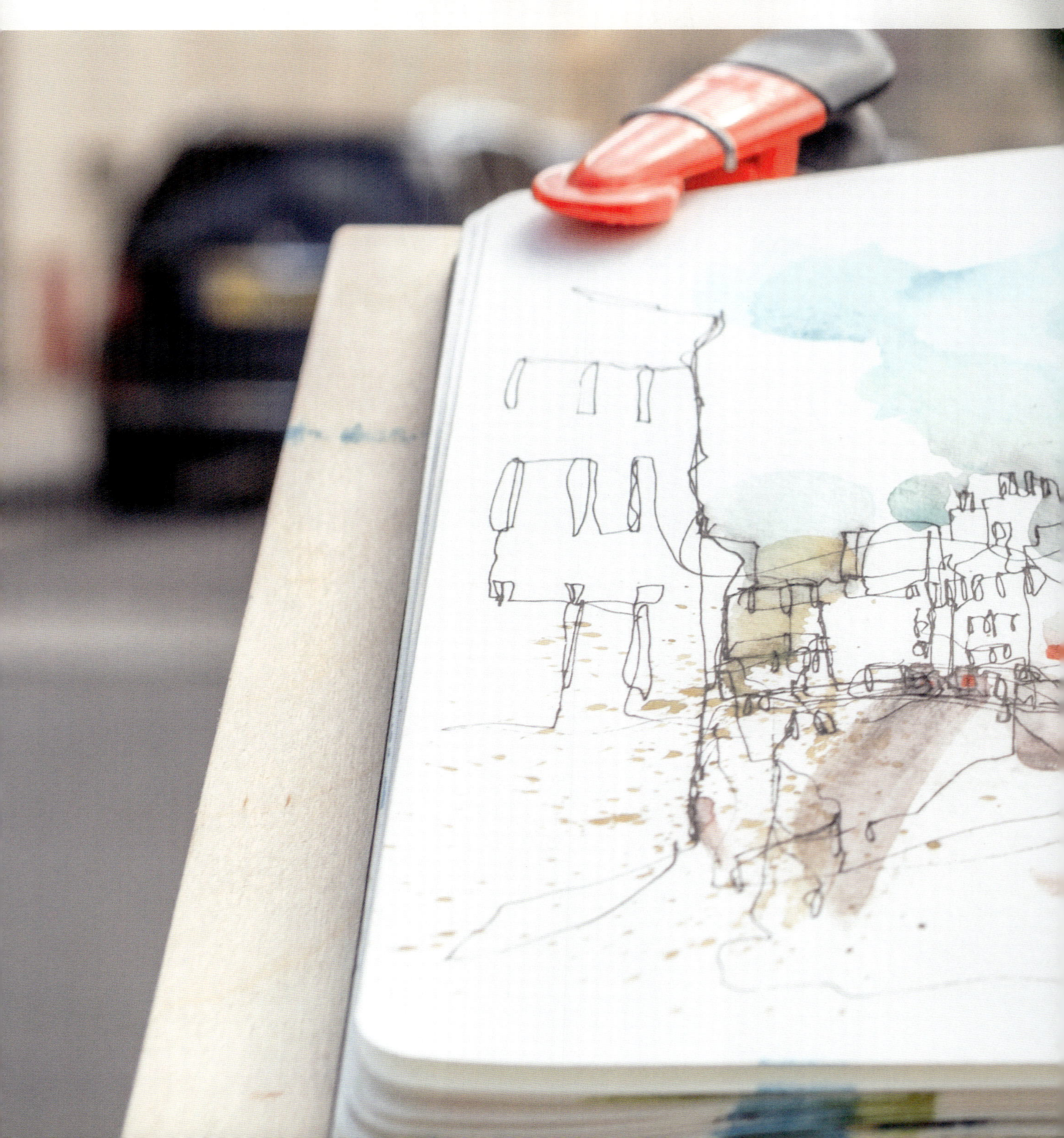

MEASUREMENT IN PRACTICE

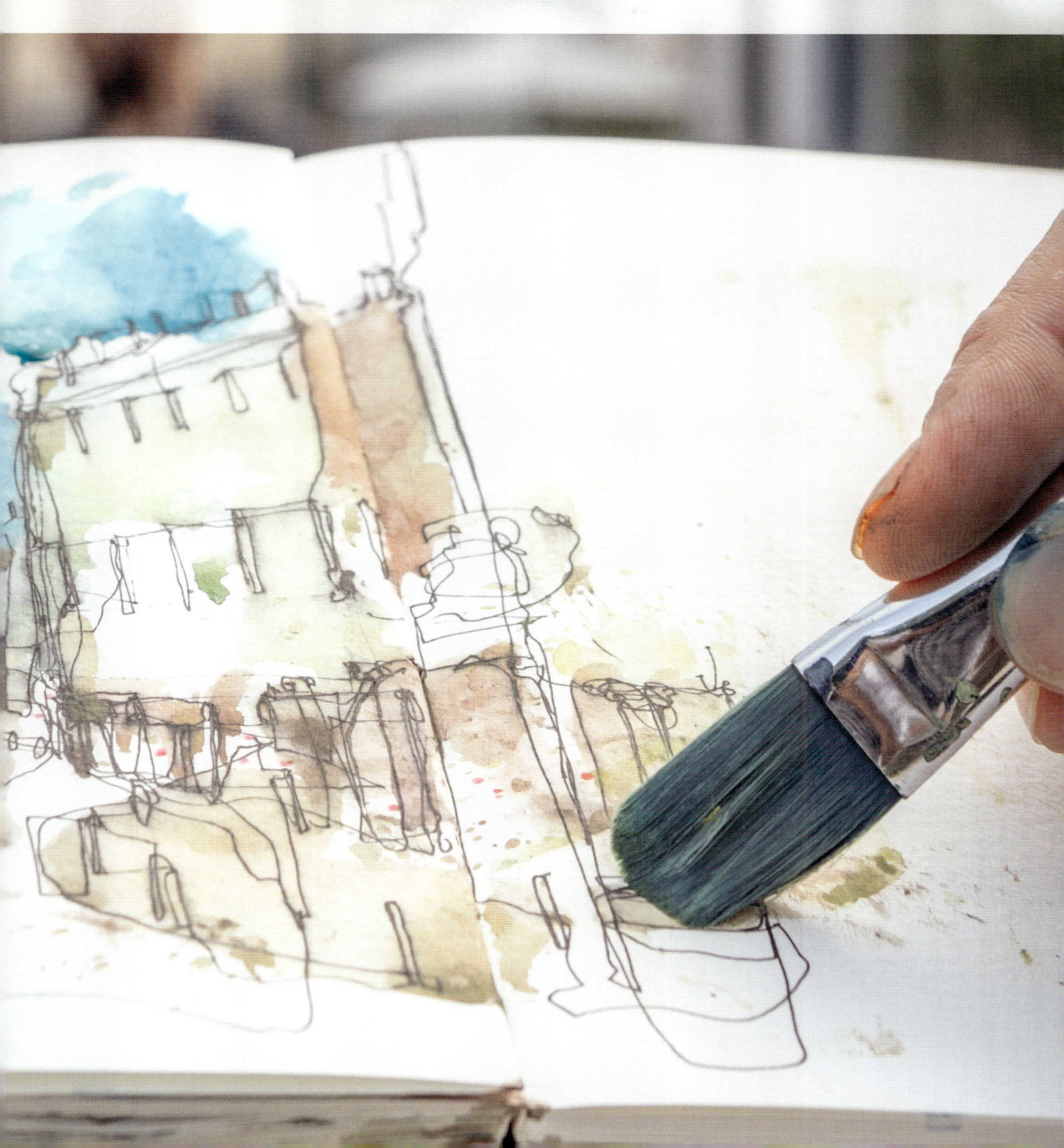

Measuring the scene on location

Not drawing the most obvious part of the scene is one of my quirks and this is where originality can come alive. Shifting the focus to a less easily scrutinized or dominant structure can encourage a little more freedom. Faced with the scene below, I was first naturally drawn to the striking building front with the greenery – the doorway and the windows make it the obvious choice – but my focus shifted to look for the perspective angles in the road to the left with a dense collection of smaller windows and street detail.

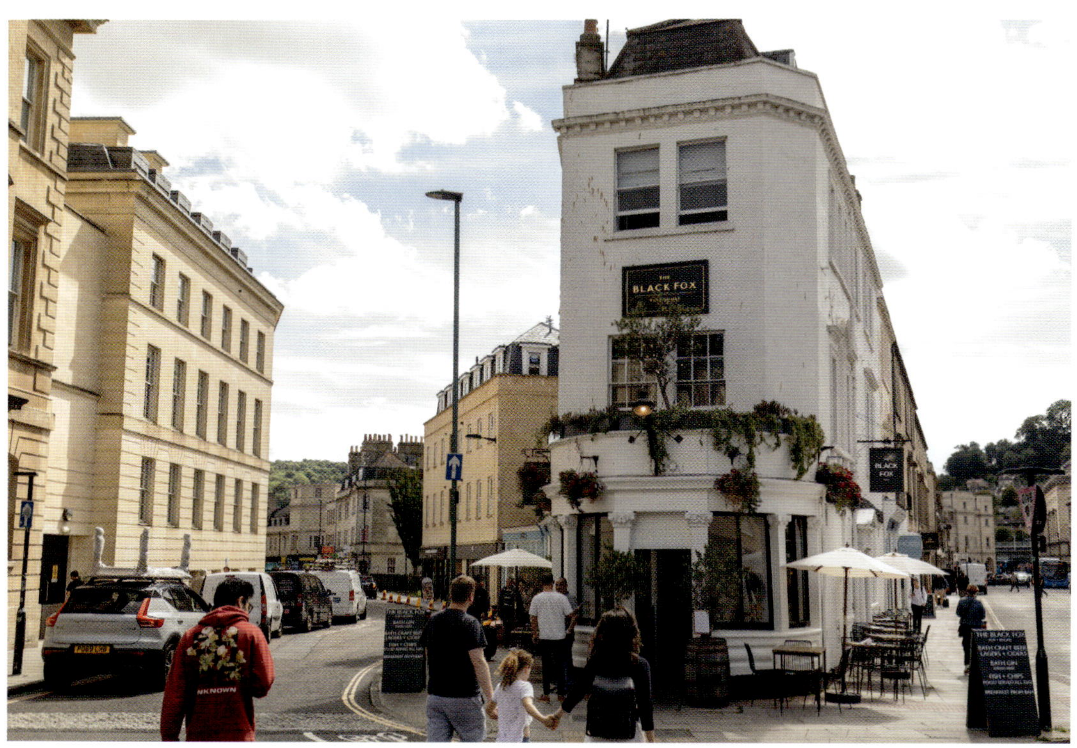

▶ The bold face of the building on the left was my start point for measuring the scale of each shape. As detailed earlier in 'Measurement and scale' (see pages 68–71), I used the width and height of this building as a guide to each space. I was able to see that the main shapes were similar sizes. This simplified the entire process and I was able to add a couple of pen marks as guides and then go head-first into the sketch, starting on the left.

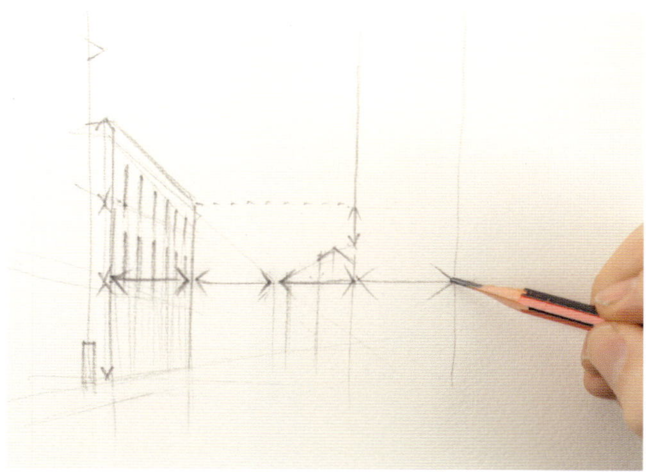

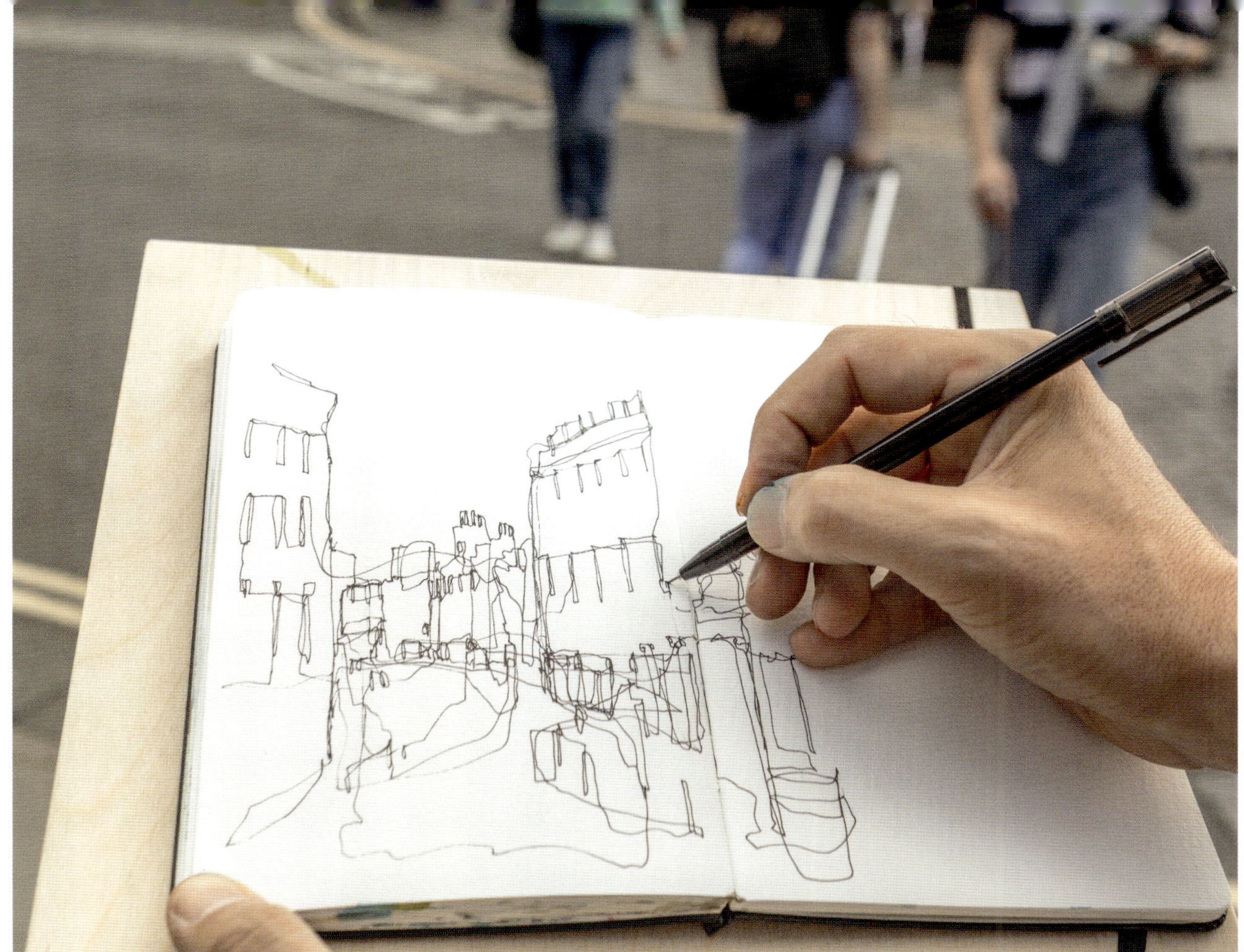

▲ Using the measurement process both horizontally and vertically soon helped to outline the negative space of the sky. The shapes began to form across the main elements and, with a horizon line a little higher than usual, I was conscious to include some of the shapes in the foreground to really start to lay down some scale. To further balance out the horizon line, I chose to continue parts of the foreground onto the next page in my sketchbook. This is a technique that can really help balance the sketch and makes for a nice twist in the sketchbook. Perhaps this subconsciously compensated for the exclusion of the main building.

The windows, becoming thinner as they recede, are mere outlines but I made sure that the heights of all were relative, i.e. the height of those in the background is much smaller than in the foreground – a simple point but easy to overlook. The marks for the chimneys and other background details are light and just enough to indicate the shapes in view, with minimal detail.

My pen strokes are definite and consistent (I resisted the temptation to use cross hatching or to rework the line and make it too jagged). More prominent are the shop fronts and doorways in the foreground. I made sure to use a stronger line weight here in expectation that the watercolour process would probably mix well and drive the lines a little darker.

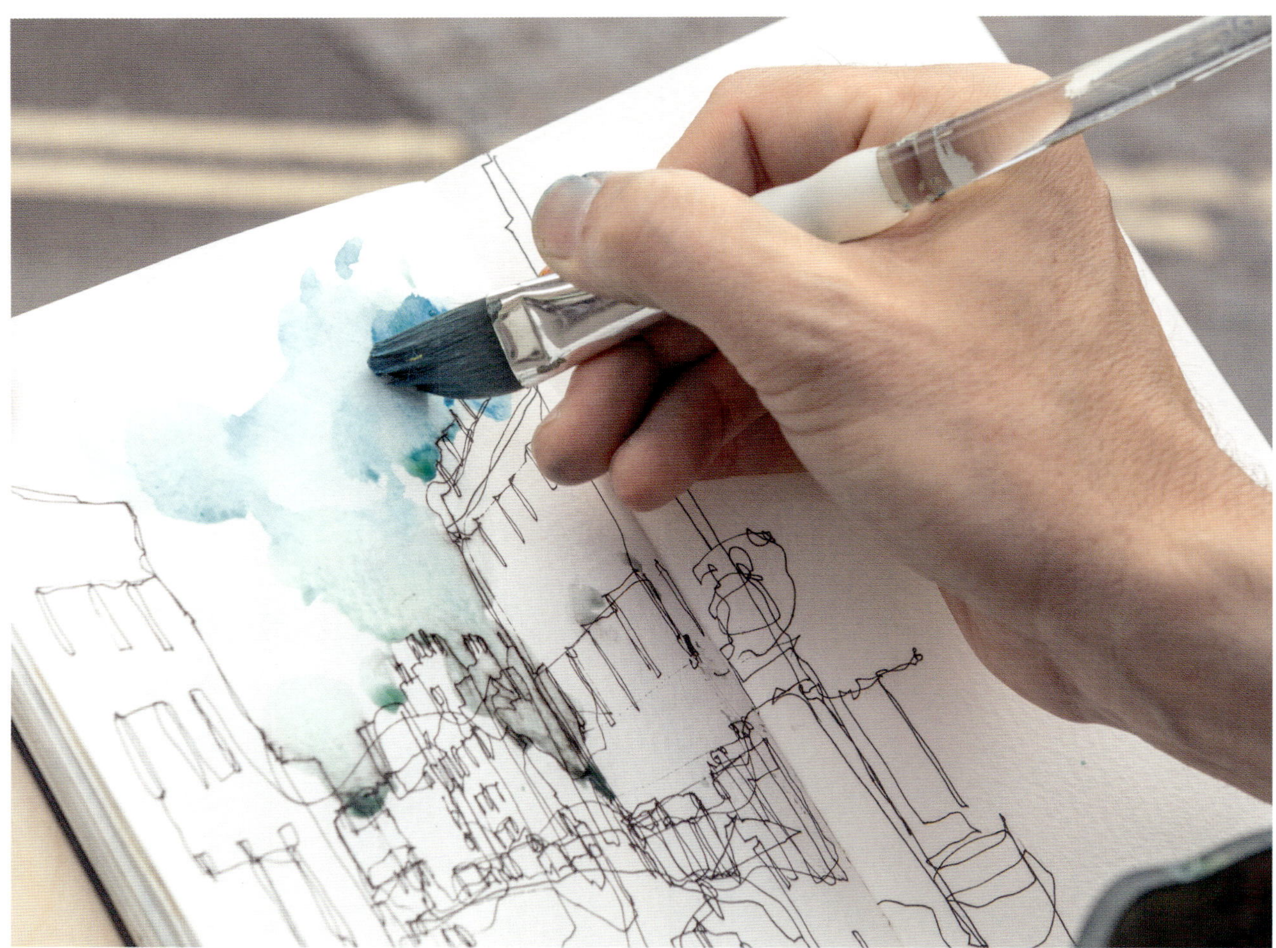

▲ With the line work done and passers-by looking over my shoulder, it was time to throw down the watercolour wash. I added a mix of phthalo blue and some bright yellow to bring out a slightly greener shade of sky. Feeding my usual thick brush into the page, I deliberately made sure the darker pigment was aligned to the roof to add drama, depth and contrast. I extended this to the left with a few strokes of the watered-down mix to give the impression of a distant blue sky. Drawing this down over my pen work created a pleasing shade of grey, which naturally further defined the contrast between the foreground structure and that behind.

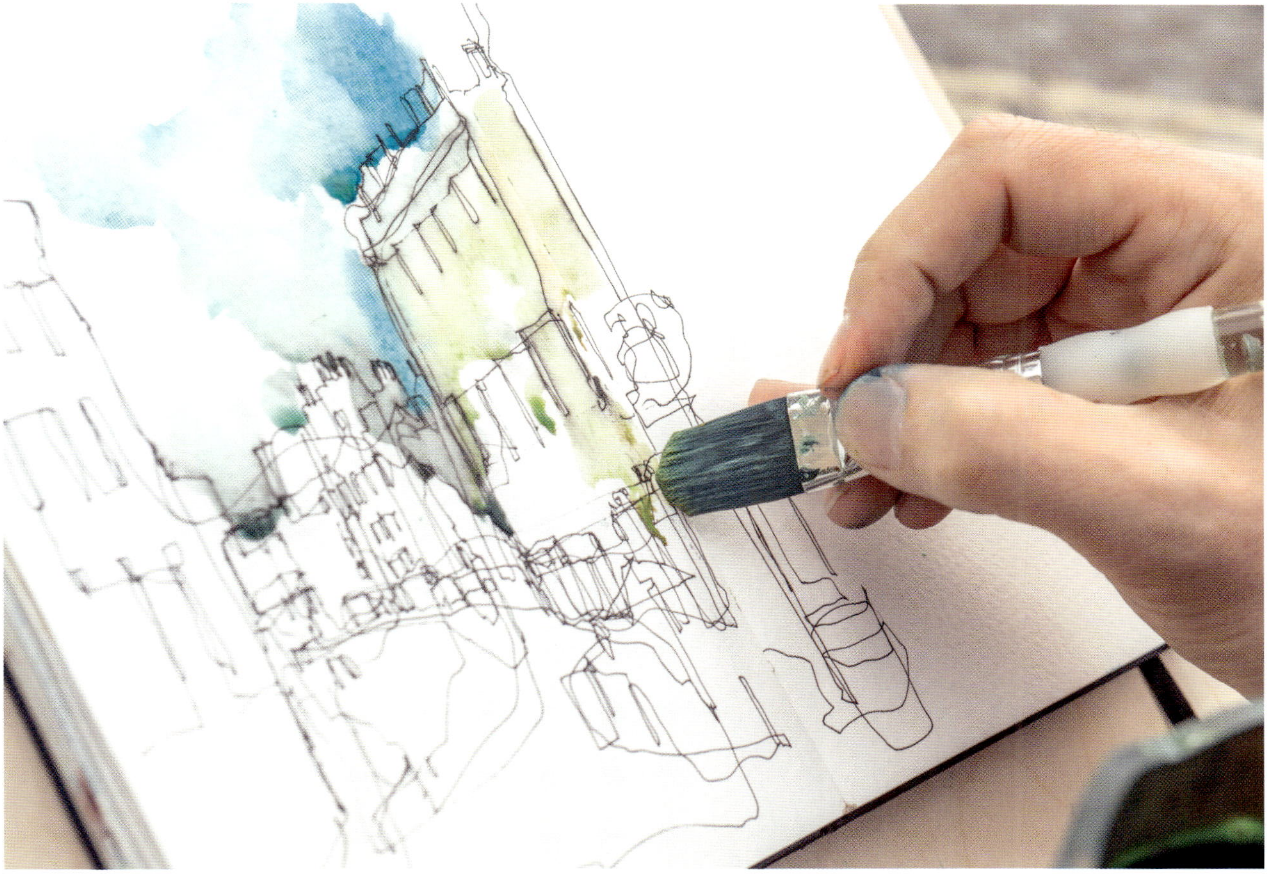

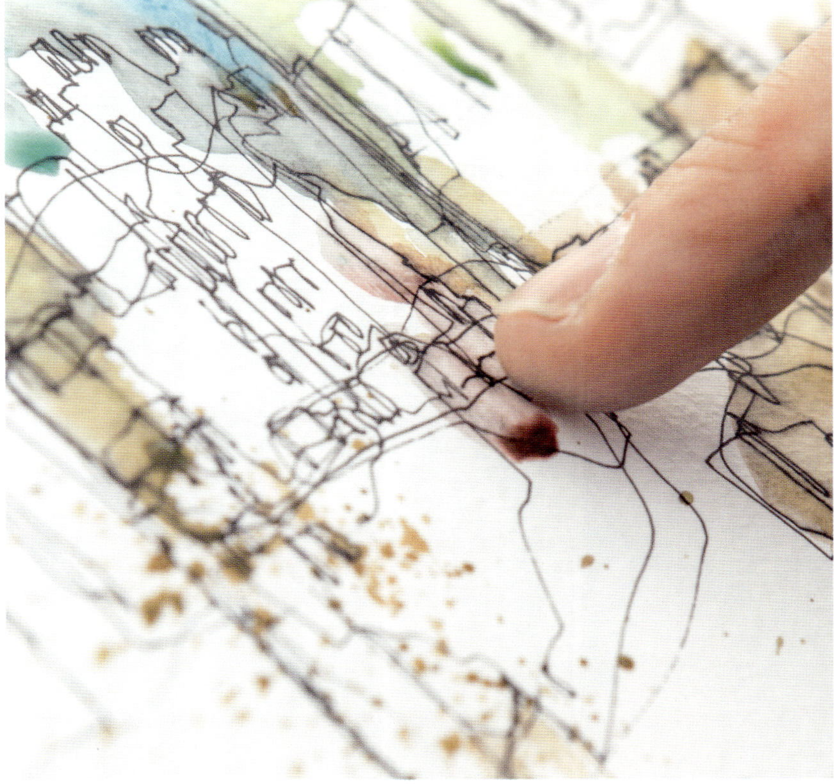

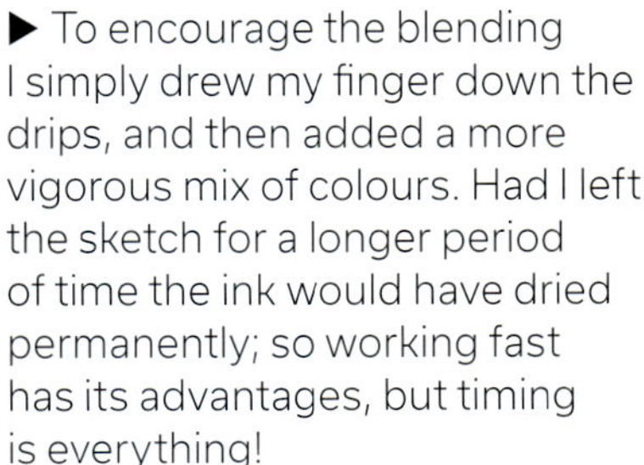

▲ I then picked up some of these dark drips and offered them to the ground-floor windows and doors that had been drawn with a thicker line.

▶ To encourage the blending I simply drew my finger down the drips, and then added a more vigorous mix of colours. Had I left the sketch for a longer period of time the ink would have dried permanently; so working fast has its advantages, but timing is everything!

These dark sections will be further darkened with a second layer of ink.

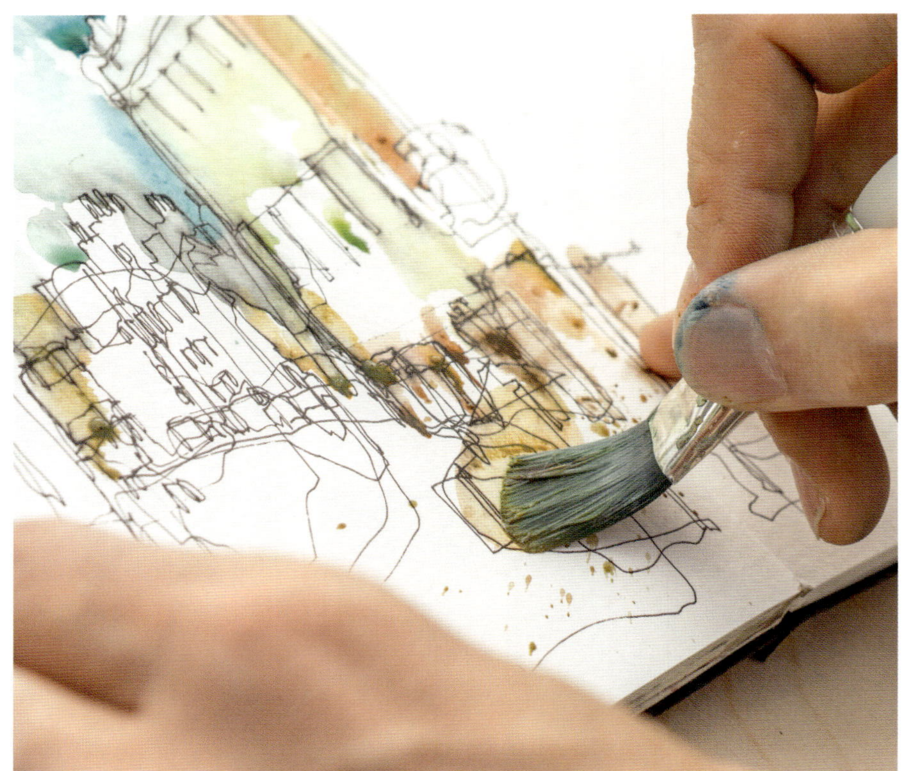

◄ I chose to introduce only one more colour, an orange tint that illustrated the sunlight on the buildings and the heat of the day. This mixed gently with the sky to wash over parts of the right-hand building and was my colour of choice to add some speckles of movement.

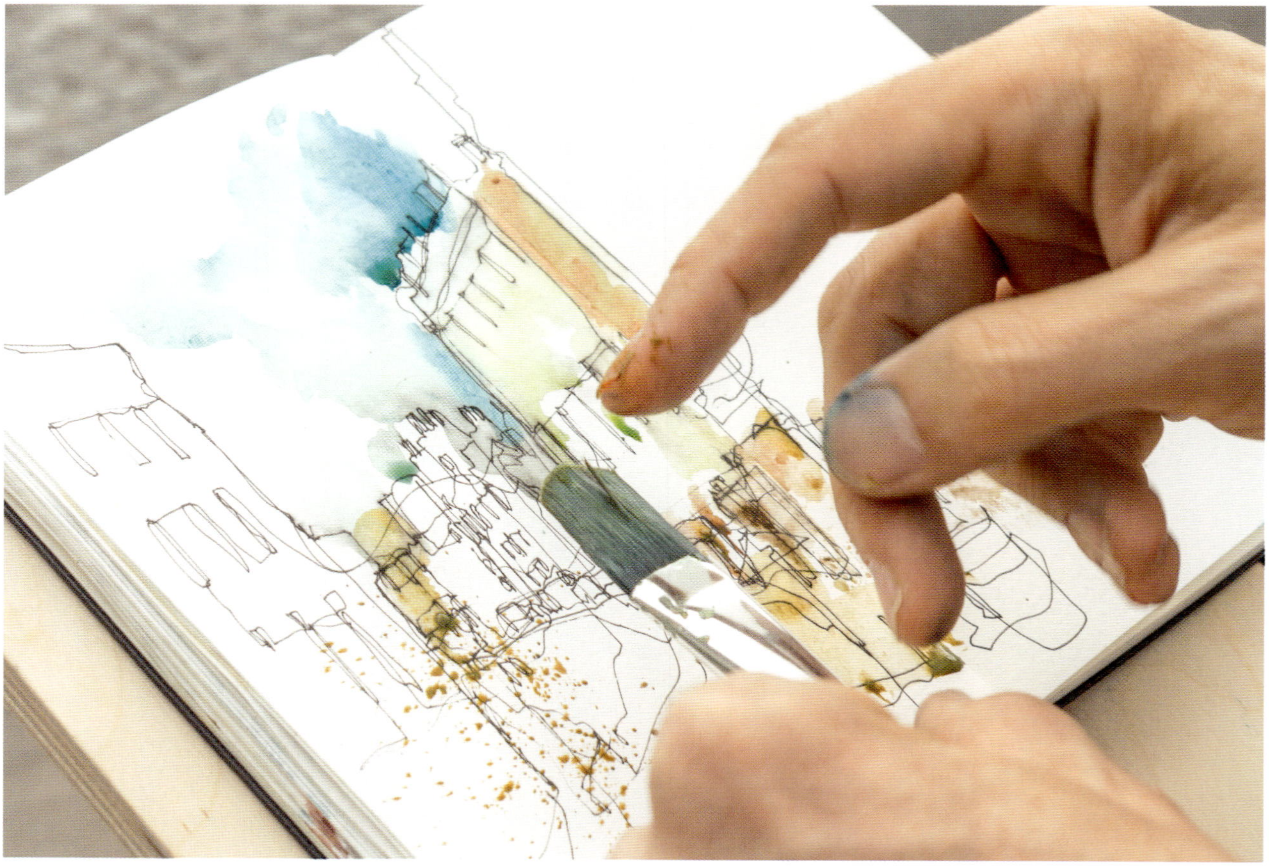

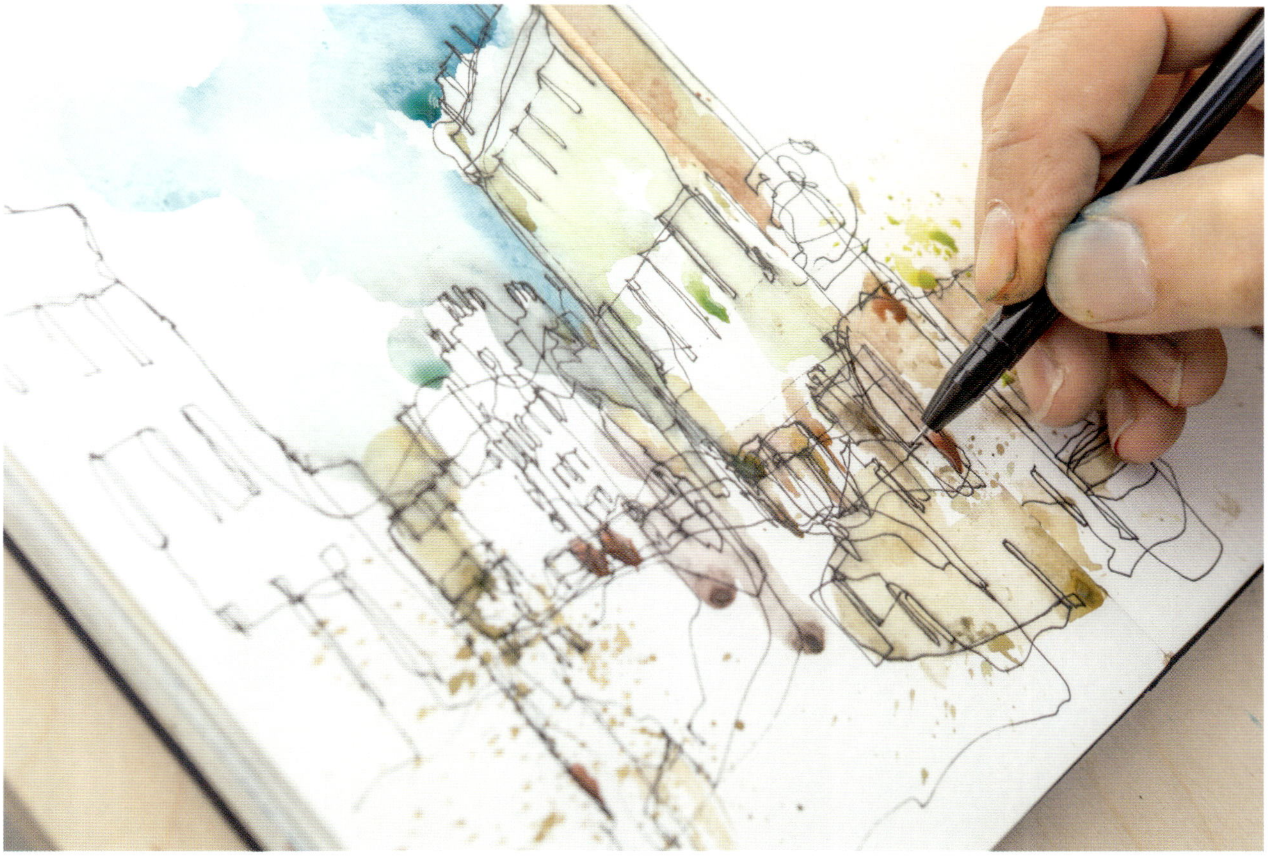

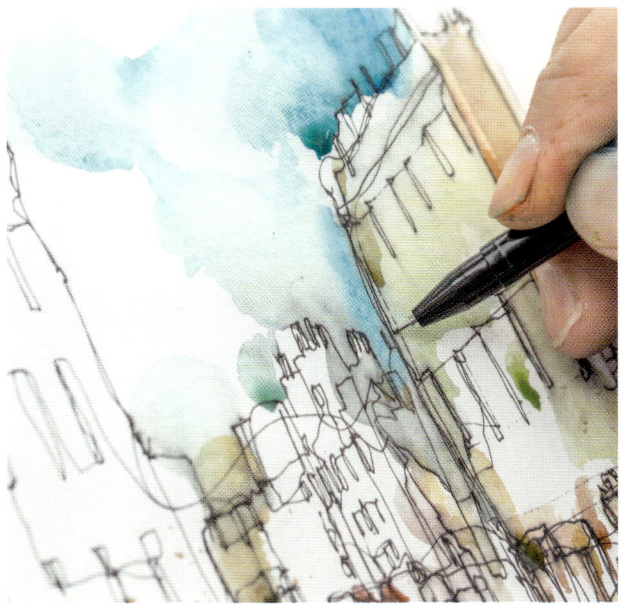

▲ The second dose of line work was next, with damp paper and drips flowing. I picked out a range of lines in the foreground to darken the ink and to make them thicker. Depending on the pen you have, it is possible to drag both the line and the water residue together and start a capillary action, but the results are massively unpredictable. I have been known to use a standard ballpoint pen at this stage as they are less expensive than fineliners and cartridge pens.

TIP

Drawing on wet paper can be unpredictable and can clog up your pen so use with caution.

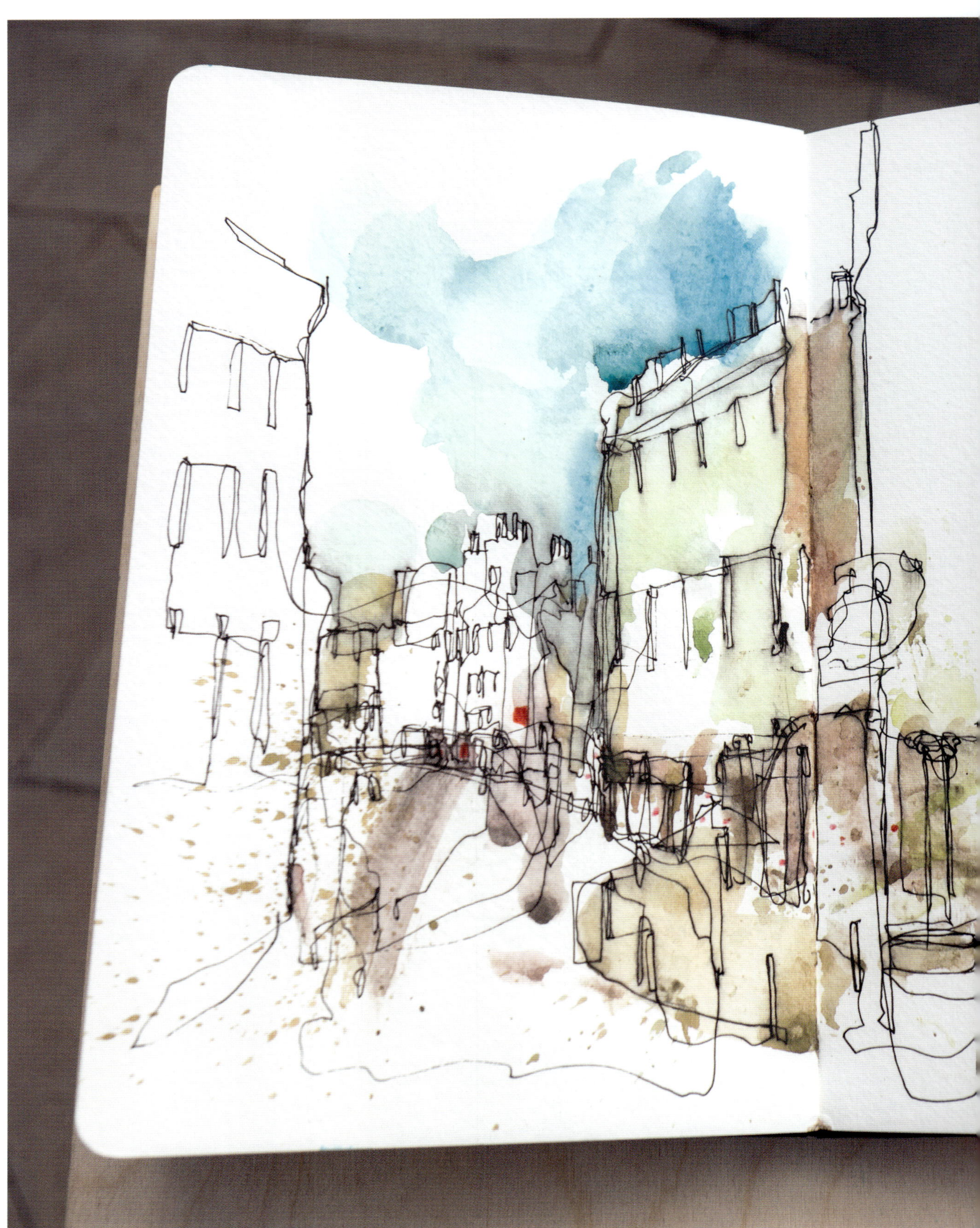

◀ The finished sketch offers a sense of depth as the road snakes away to the left, bringing emphasis to the buildings and foreground shapes, hinting at activity in the street. This piece uses minimal colour but reflects the atmosphere of the day, and creeps into the right-hand page to effectively shift the viewpoint. The left-hand side is left untouched, guiding the viewer down the street.

This was sketched and painted in 30 minutes – it has lots of detail missing and not every window is accounted for, but it's an original take on a pleasing scene.

Composition

One of the fundamental steps to creating an interesting sketch is finding the best composition. Over time, this can become a natural thought process and a way of seeing that can be trained like any habit.

Let's talk through the key areas of scene selection. I thrive on simplifying complex scenes so I would encourage you to keep this in mind as we explore the various techniques around composition and scene selection.

The rule of thirds

Fundamental in photography and the reason why camera viewfinders and mobile phones come equipped with a viewing grid is the ability to slice up the scene into nine squares, or three vertical and horizontal sections. I adopt the same method when sketching and painting. Placing the key areas of interest at the intersections creates visual depth and a way to encourage the eye to wander and explore the scene. However, this is only a guide, and we don't want to overload the scene with four bold focal points. Just try to keep attention on placing a key element on one of these four intersections. Typically, the horizon line can occupy the lower third of the page and the sky the top third. This leaves four key points that can be a major focal point.

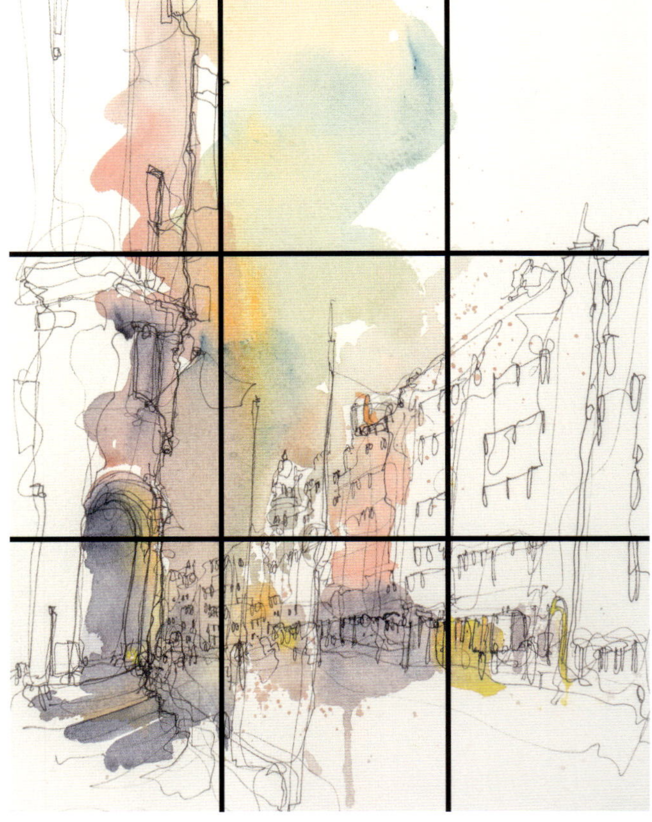

The rule of thirds.

Perspective

With this skill and way of seeing the viewing grid in your mind, it's time to add perspective into the equation. Perspective needn't be a scary thing, it's our friend – it creates depth, interest and realism. It can come in many forms and ranges from one-, two-, three- and four-point perspective.

A fundamental skill to architects, perspective in most of my urban landscape artworks has just one or two points. I recommend sticking to the basic rules but with some allowance for artistic licence. If perspective in the sketch is wildly out then, yes, the sketch will struggle for harmony, but that doesn't mean you should approach it with laser-like precision – there is plenty of wriggle room to balance technical accuracy and artistic endeavour. Most of my work presents perspective errors – this is why I have so many lines on offer to the viewer. Think of them as 'lifelines' for the sketch.

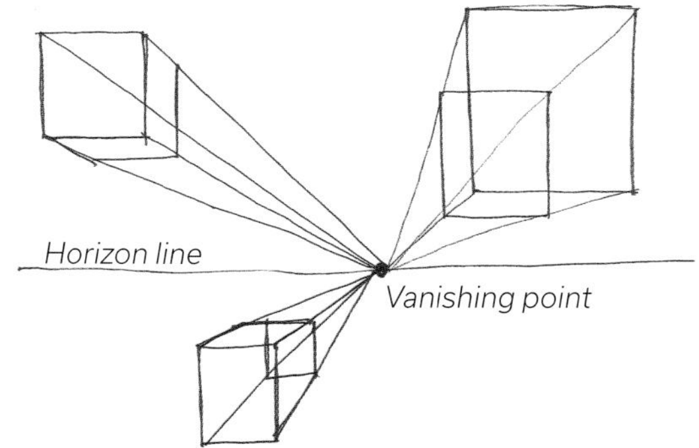

One-point perspective: all lines appear to converge at a single focal point (often set at a rule of thirds intersection for dynamism).

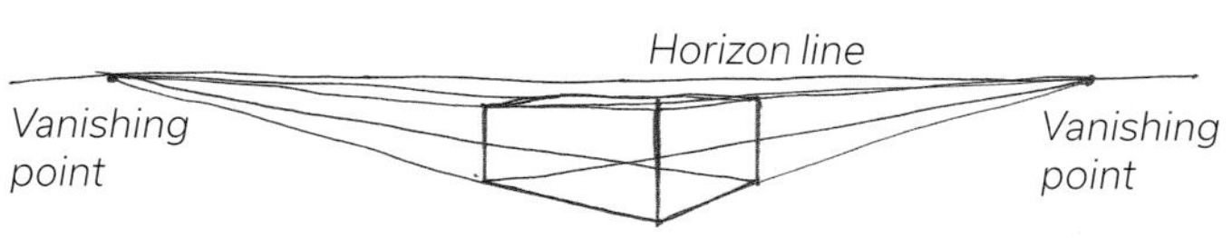

Two-point perspective: the building lines disappear off to both sides (often a building edge or front fascia is the core focus).

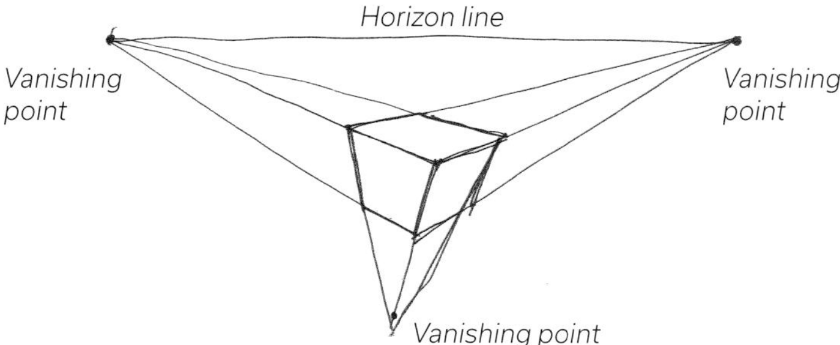

Three- and four-point perspectives: this is associated with more extreme views such as at ground level or from a great height.

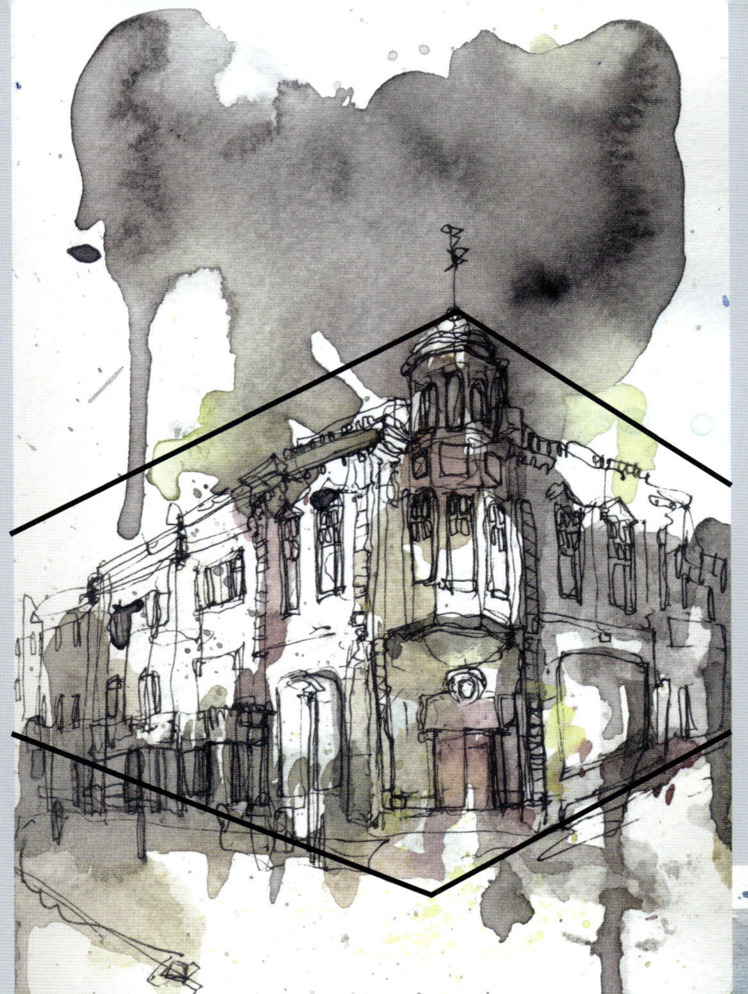

The examples on this page demonstrate the range of perspective views on a street scene. Notice how the working lines track back to the same location or 'vanishing point'. Practise these as much as you can so they become second nature.

The vast majority of my works are done in one-point perspective. The rectangular planes of the buildings, including the windows and doors, appear to converge towards a single vanishing point on the horizon line. In two-point perspective, the rectangular planes appear to converge towards two vanishing points located on the horizon line. And in three-point perspective, the rectangular planes appear to converge towards three vanishing points, with one point located above the horizon line.

Above: two-point perspective.
Right: one-point perspective.

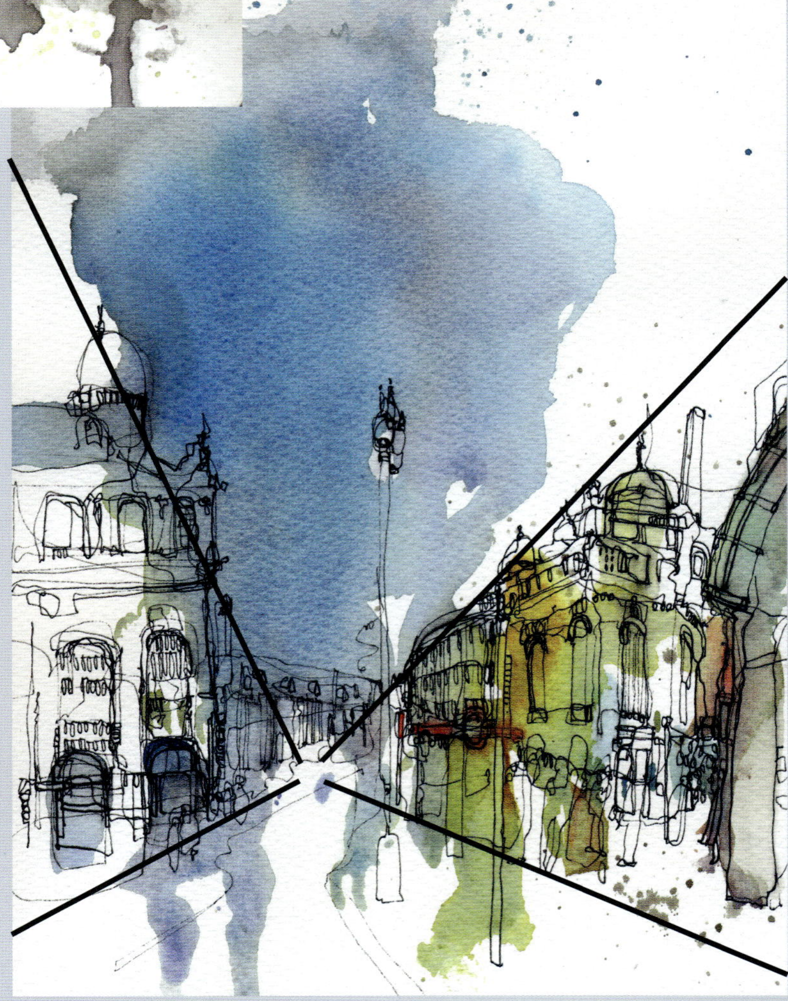

▶ The vanishing point is where all parallel lines meet. A very identifiable aspect of my work is how I place the vanishing point in the sight lines of my rule of thirds. This is a very conscious decision and provides a natural journey for the eye to travel, pause and explore.

▼ The following four scenes show my thinking process: rule of thirds, perspective shift and vanishing point positions.

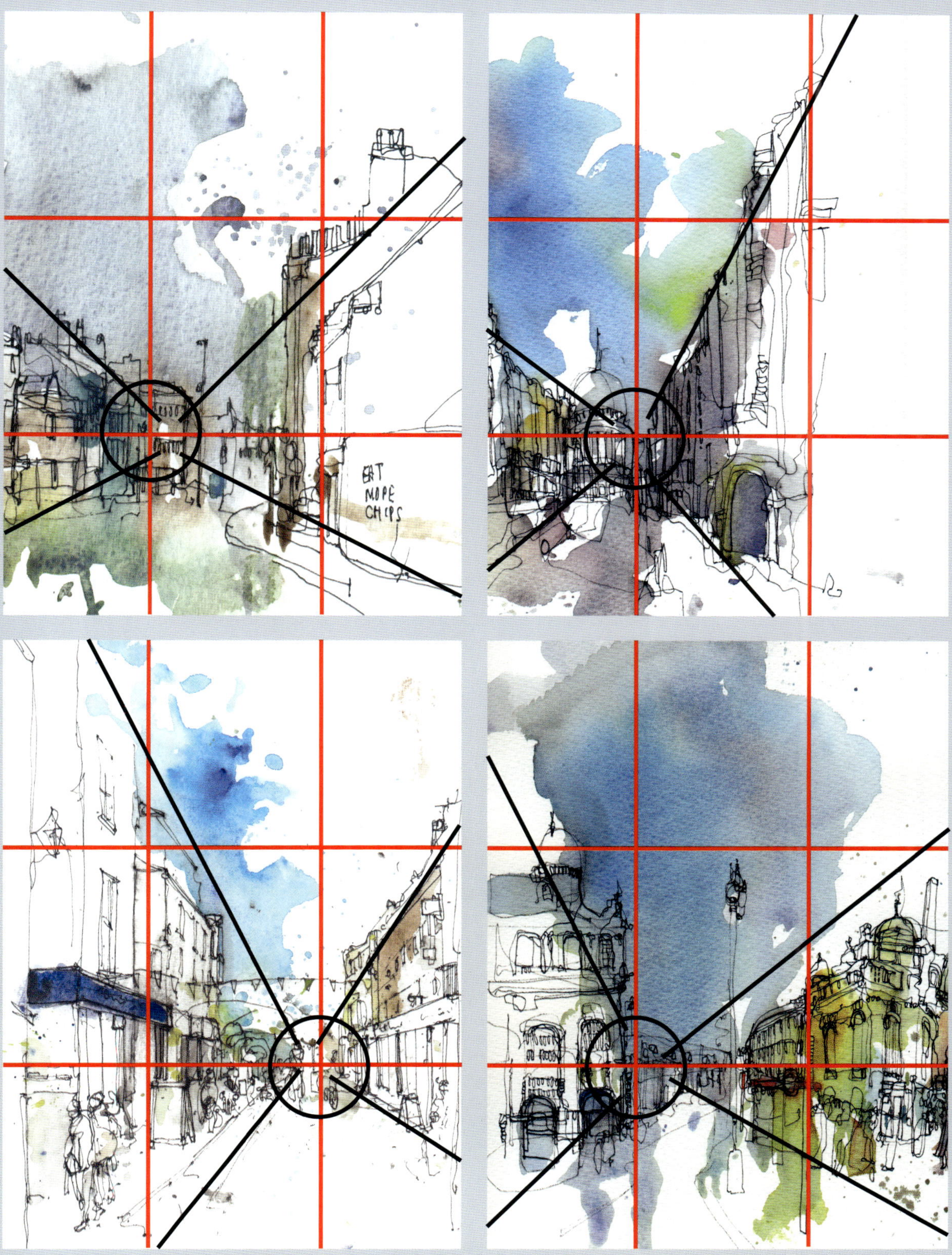

Visible depth

Another key component is visible depth – if the perspective and offset vanishing point are in place, then the depth should follow naturally. As mentioned earlier, my horizon line often sits on the line of thirds, this time horizontally. This helps the artwork breathe and presents the opportunity to add some detail. Naturally, whatever is closest in a scene will offer more visible detail.

Typically in my work, I will pick out the pavement in the foreground, a street sign or a kerb. You can add some detail to the foreground aspects, but be wary of too much detail in the background and not enough in the foreground, as this can create an imbalance and a conflict of visual scale.

Explore drawing perspective in different positions but keep your lines nice and loose, don't grip the pen or pencil too hard as it will create unnecessary tension. We're training the brain and the hand to identify and capture scenes that are believable and interesting. I treat buildings as blocks just like this but often just the front face of the building is visible.

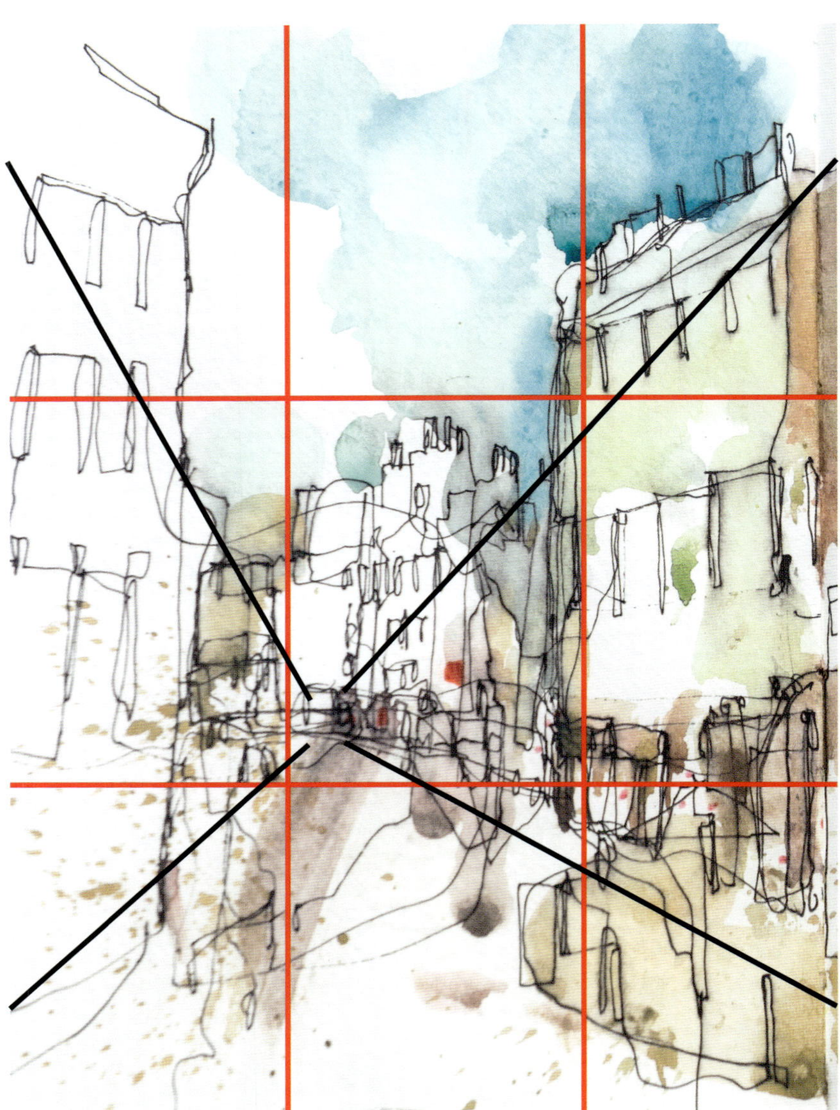

The road snakes away in the area of the lower left intersection.

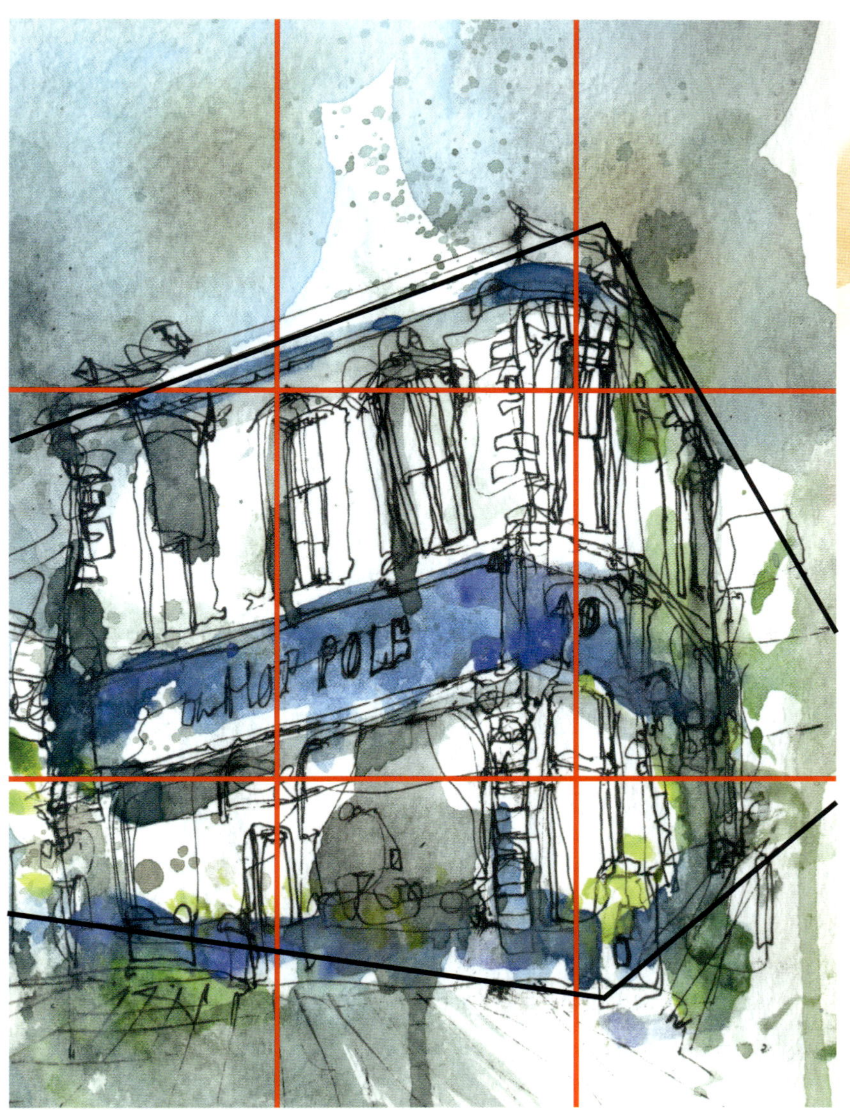

The edge of the building sits on the right-hand red line, giving it a strong composition.

Tip

Use loose lines to guide the eye towards the right perspective. Use natural guides such as windows – think of them as track lines heading towards the vanishing point.

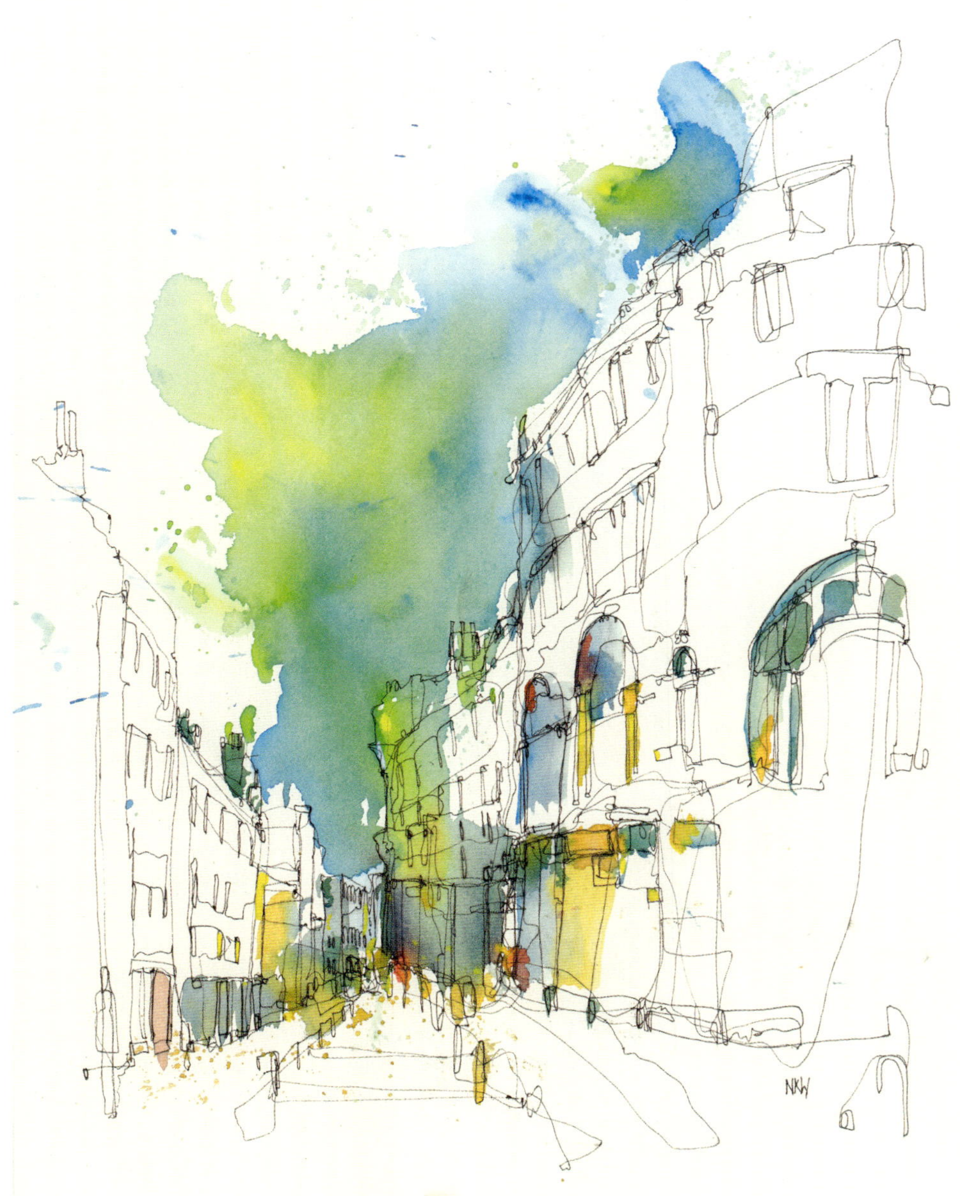

▲ Notice how most of my work is in portrait layout – there's no coincidence here. The page echoes the scene. I would encourage you to draw tall rather than wide. Occasionally I exaggerate the height to bring more presence to key landmarks. Simplifying the scene and the urban landscape into simple shapes is a habit that will develop over time as you practise and begin to banish the fear of the blank white page.

Framing the scene

Frame your scene to eliminate unwanted distractions. Nothing expensive is needed – I use a cardboard mount from an old picture frame or look through the camera on my mobile phone.

It can be overwhelming when sitting down in front of a complex scene, and defining where your boundaries are is a great help. This is what I call 'the first crop' – if working large enough you might add a further crop to pinpoint the parts of the artwork you want to frame.

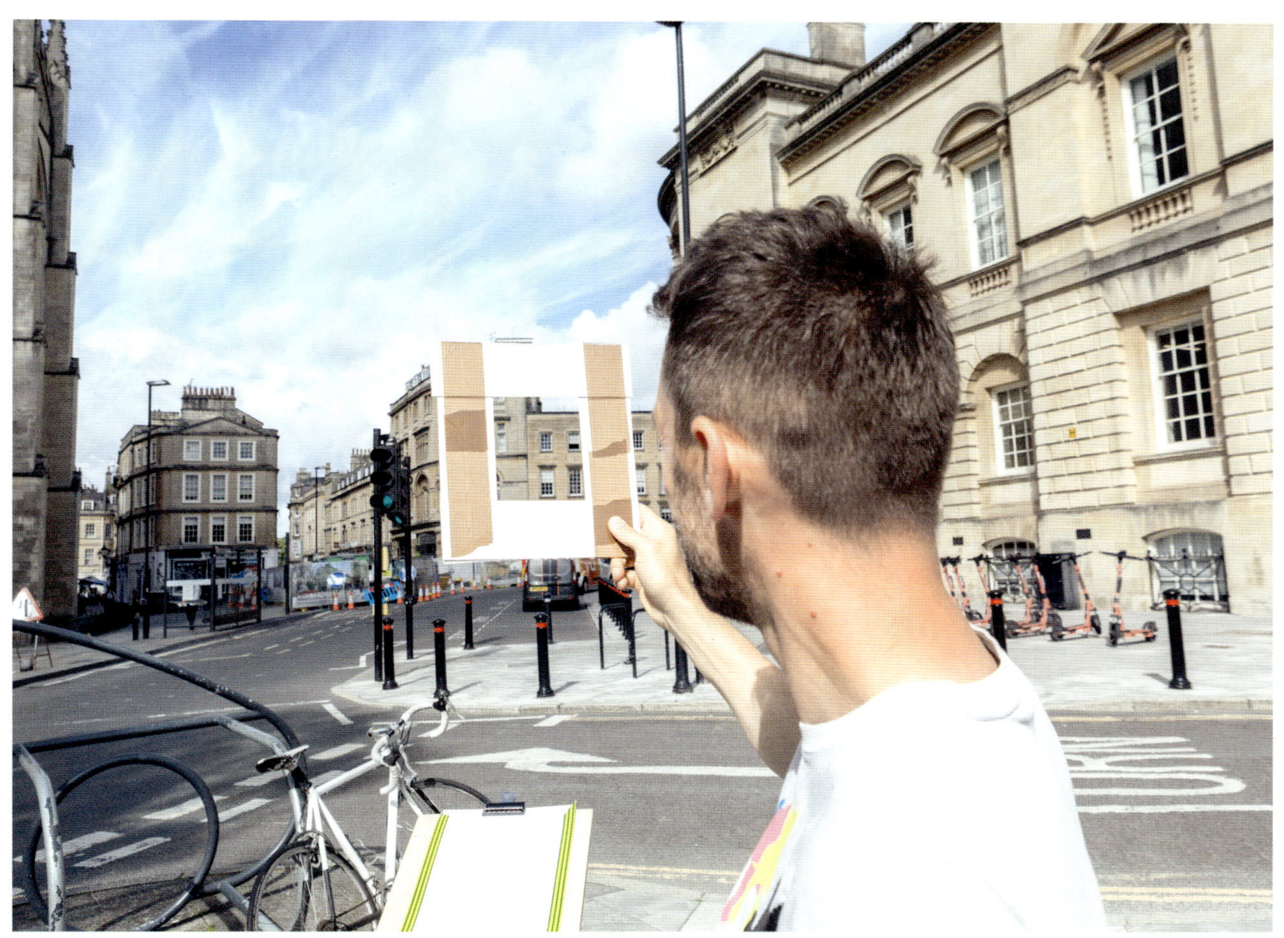

Exercise

Composing your scene

The fundamental rules of perpective can be picked up with some patience and observation. A popular part of my workshops is to find the vanishing point and change the view. Practise this using some simple steps.

Take some pictures or browse the internet and play around with the rule of thirds. Think about the following:

1 **Where is the vanishing point?**
Not every scene is so simplistic but generally there is a line of perspective to be found – this will depend on how close you are to the subject.

2 **Does cropping the scene make for a more dynamic view?**

3 **How do we make a scene more interesting?**
Not every detail is needed.

4 **Where is the horizon line?**
If it's in the top third of the page you'll have a good deal of foreground to work with, if it's low down then the sky might need to come into play to balance the work.

5 **How can you work with the horizon line?**
With a horizon line central to the page you'll have some symmetry in the scene.

6 **Which aspect deserves more attention?**
Whatever the situation (and there is no right answer), consider what the composition presents to you.

Opposite: The horizon line is high – I've sacrificed a big bold sky to focus on the foreground. It's still one-point perspective but I've made sure to balance out the dominant light with some bright colours.

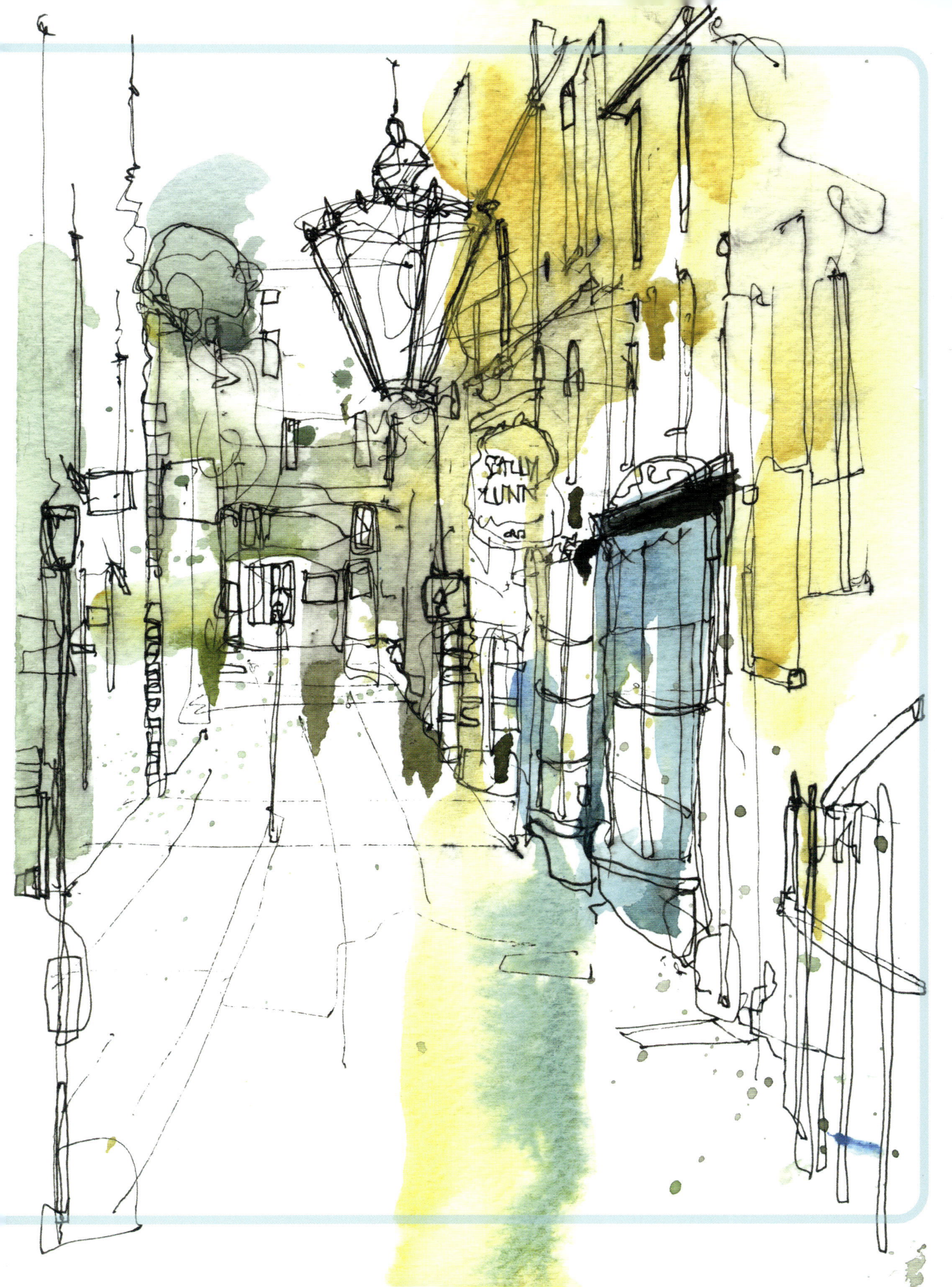

SALLY
LUNN

EXTENDING THE TECHNIQUE

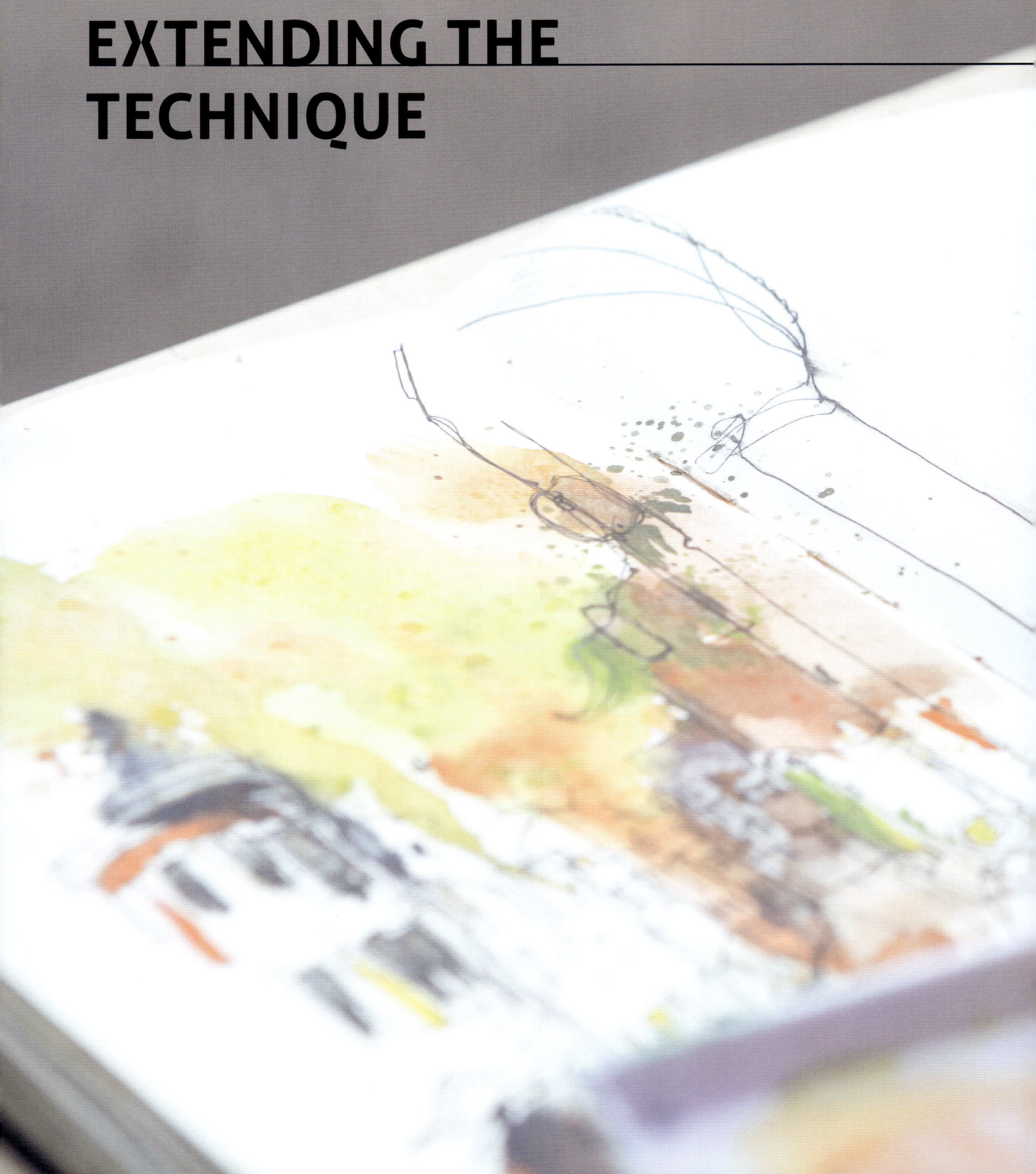

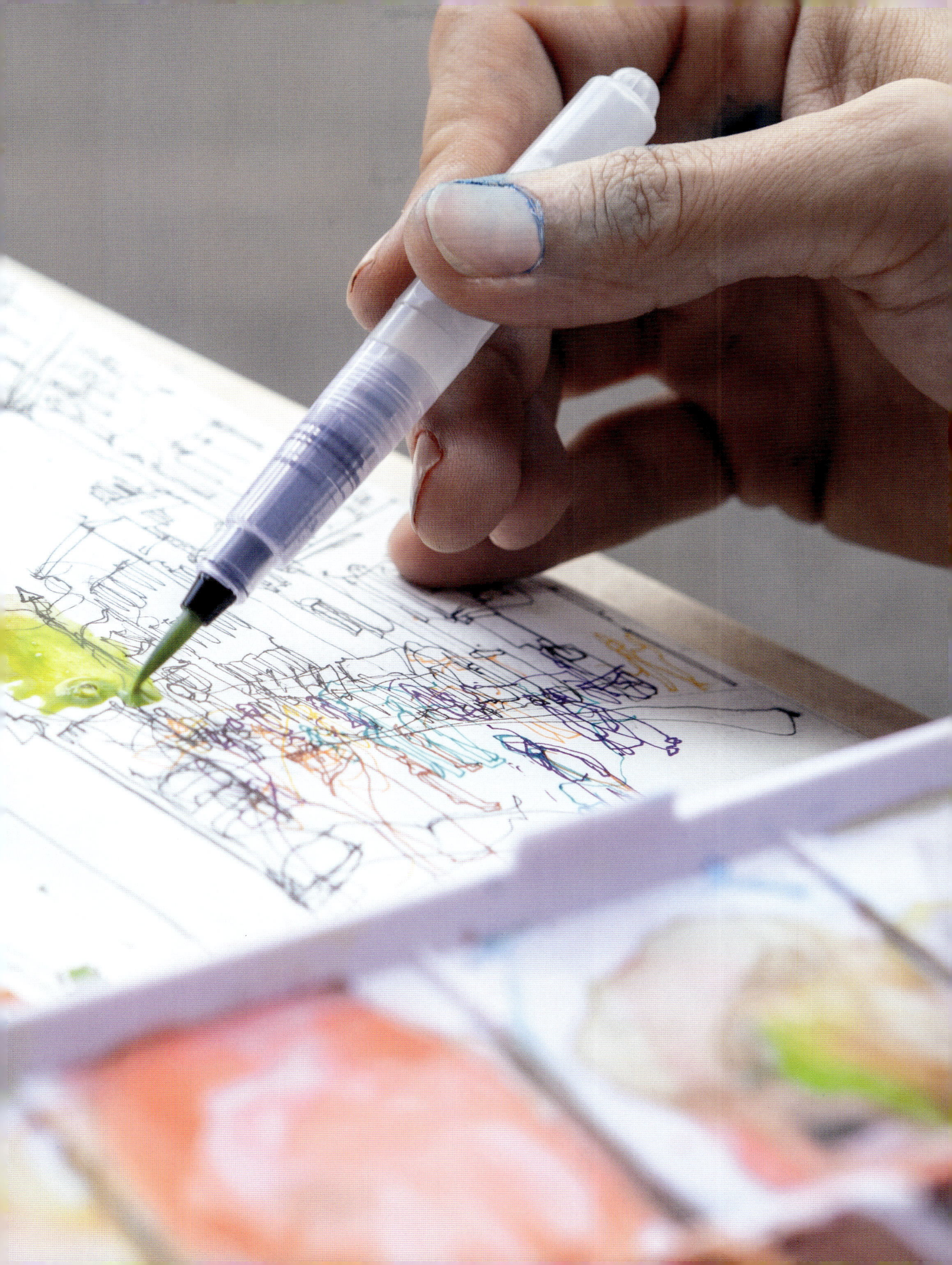

Experimenting with colour

Vibrant colour is present throughout most of my work: I love to use colour to make my work come alive and to bridge the gap between observation and imagination. I will usually reach for my trusty watercolours once the sketch is done, either on location or later in the studio, but an alternative is to use coloured pens. I carry a good range of fineliners in a range of colours – much easier to transport than a watercolour set and they don't require water (which I have a habit of forgetting – indeed, I've been known to substitute coffee for water, which can give interesting results!).

Using a reduced amount of kit, I set about capturing the scene shown below. This scene had much of what I look out for – one-point perspective, bold and clear 'V'-shaped skyline, plenty of windows to guide me towards the vanishing point, people moving around, not too many cars, a good mix of colour (strong green tree and bright yellow road markings) and a lovely sweeping foreground curve.

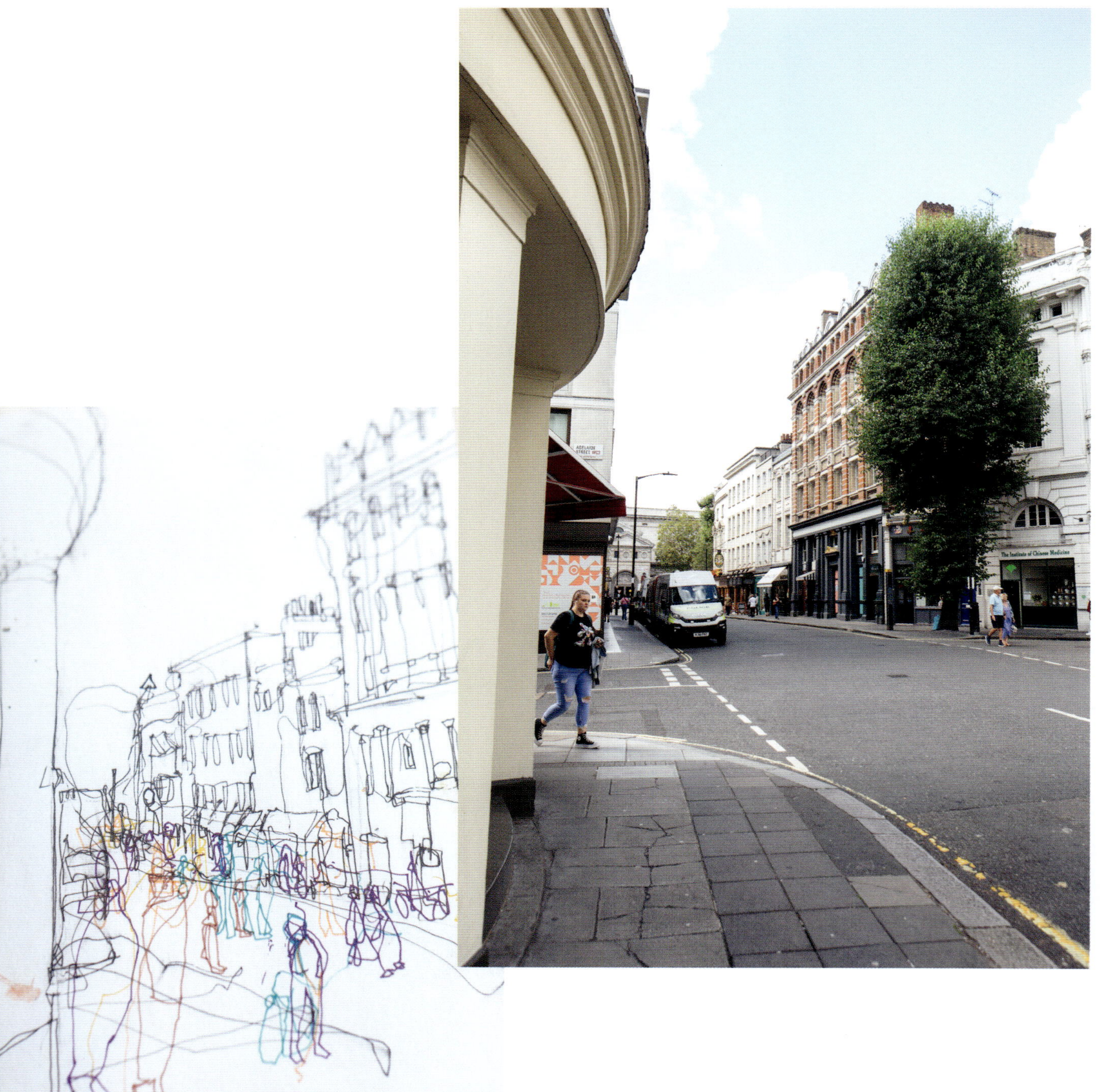

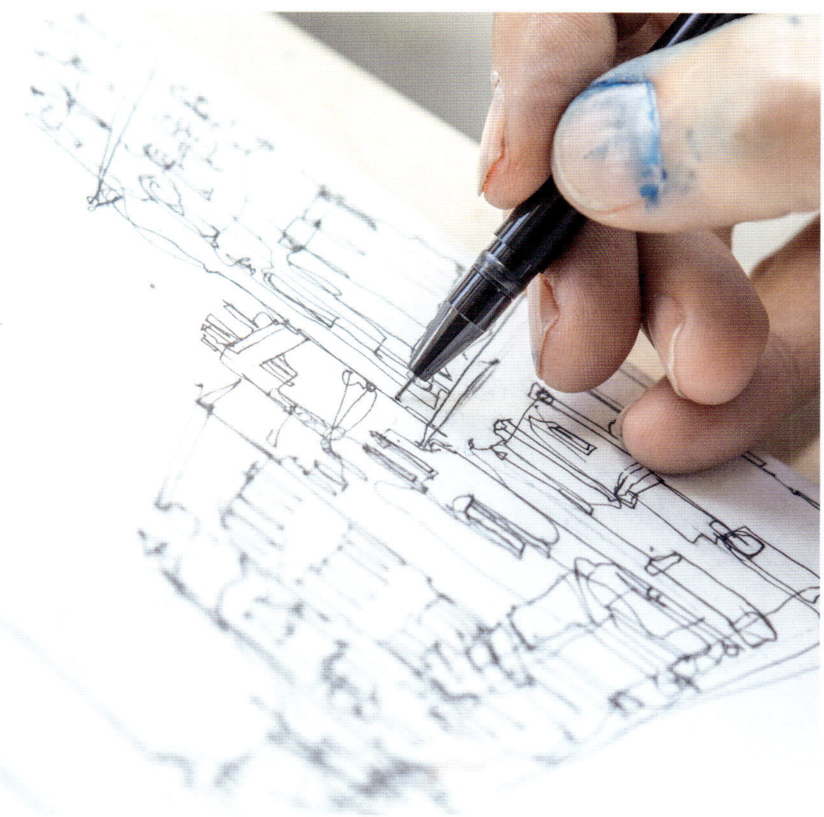

◄ The sketch takes shape fast, as usual. The speed leads to inaccuracies but it delivers rhythm and flow. I'm not an architect. Not every window is there, not every chimney, not every architrave but the essence of the scene is on paper.

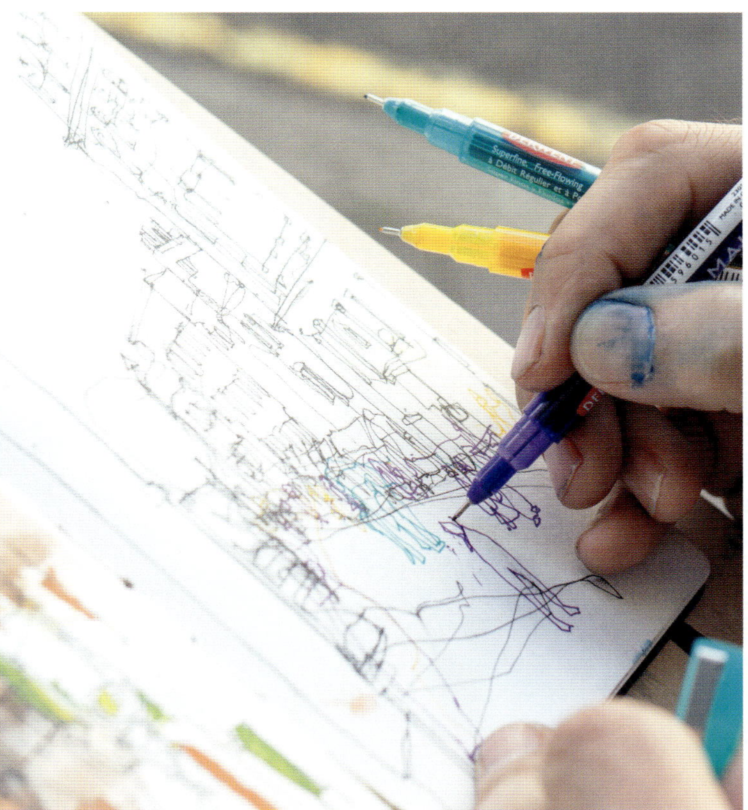

◄ The street became busier and I decided to make this sketch work almost like a time-lapse piece, overlaying the movement of people in a 30-minute period. With no paints to use, I decided to change pen colour every few minutes and add outlines of the passers-by onto my scene – it became almost like a repeating pattern.

I made a much more conscious decision to capture the shapes of people rather than draw people – so I sketched the outlines, the legs, even feet (but only if very nearby so as not to throw the visible depth perception).

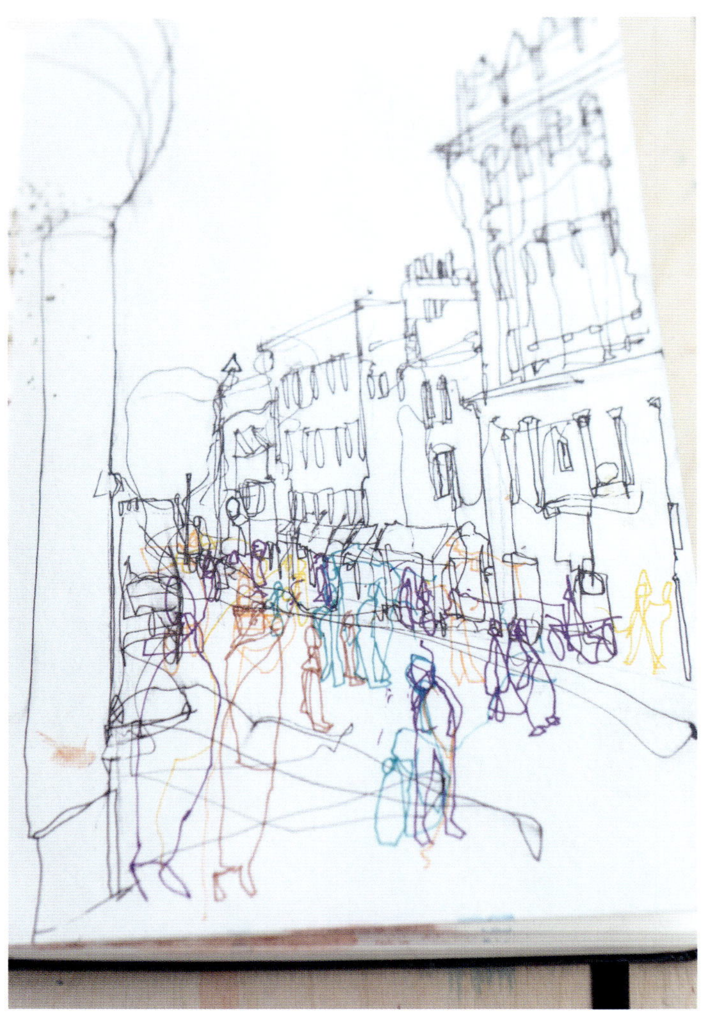

◀ This technique is quite removed from my standard style, but as is the nature for anyone sketching and painting, I would always encourage you to try new things. Do things that are challenging or that stretch your comfort zone, and one day you can look back at your sketchbook and see how you've developed, experimented and tried new things.

At this stage (when I thought the peice was finished), it was certainly different from my usual style. I introduced some felt-tip pens into my work (I borrowed my daughter's!). Some of the red and yellow speckles and splatters are just the simplest of pen marks.

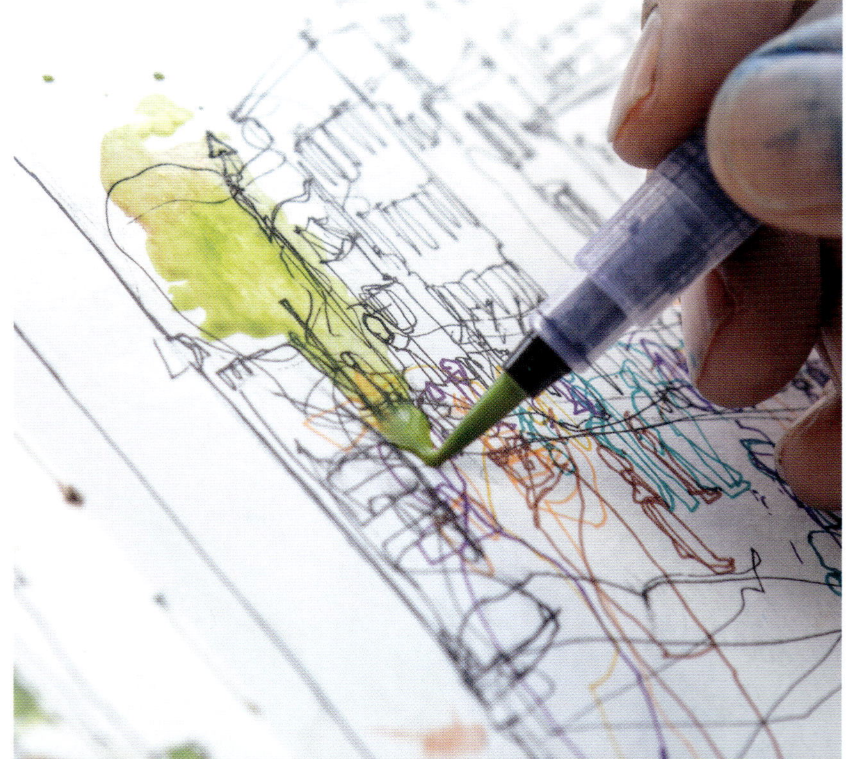

◀ Later at home I felt like something was missing, and had the compulsion to include the green of the tree which was cropped out of the original sketch. I added this with my brush pen – a super handy brush with an inbuilt water reservoir. I resisted the temptation to add any more – once you start looking, it's time to stop!

Opposite: the finished sketch.

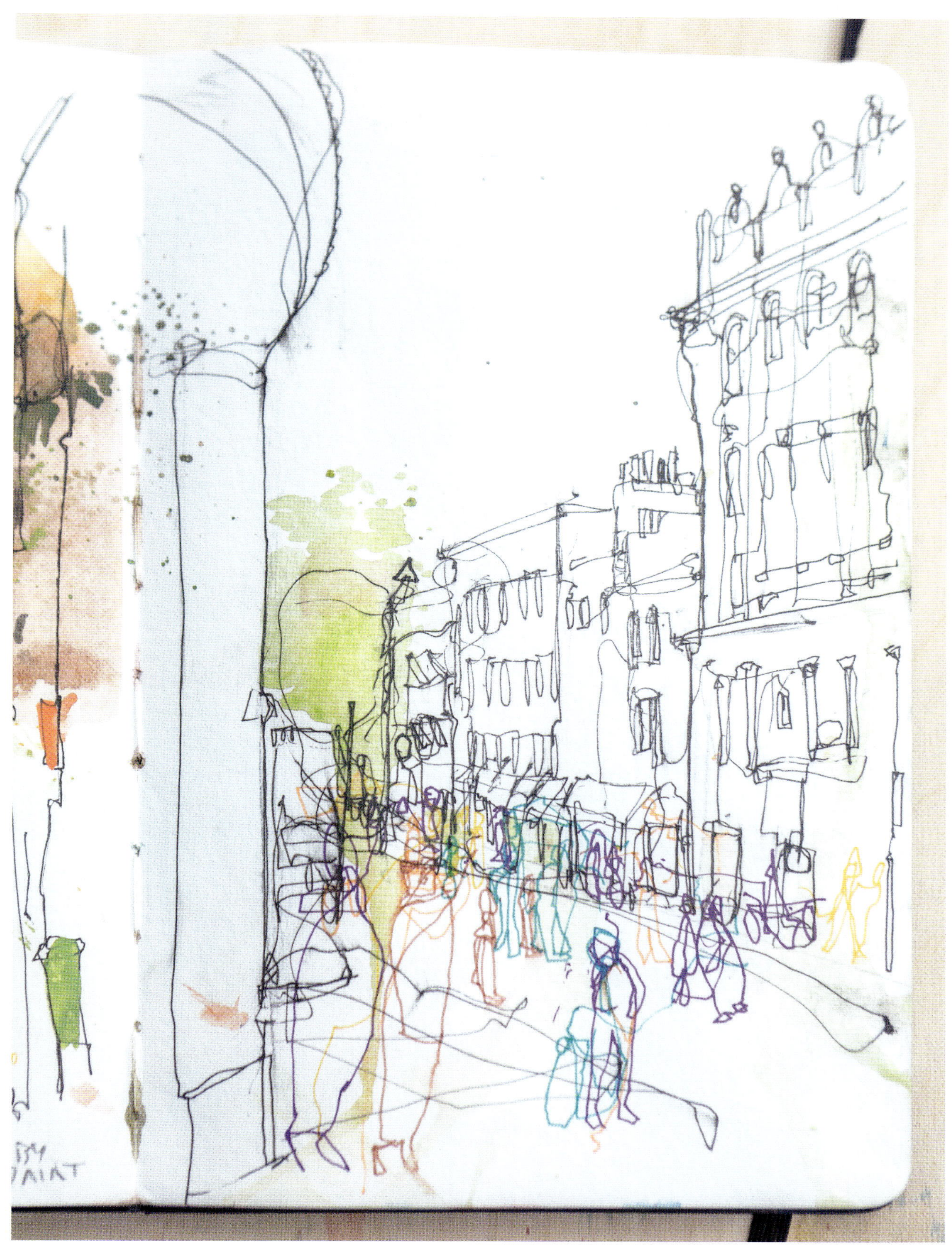

Negative space

There's no denying it, a good element of my work is left untouched on purpose. This white or negative space can be your friend and often it is good to plan for some white space as this protects you from the dangers of overworking. Watercolour can sometimes be unforgiving, so leaving an element 'unfinished' is in fact a perfect way to finish.

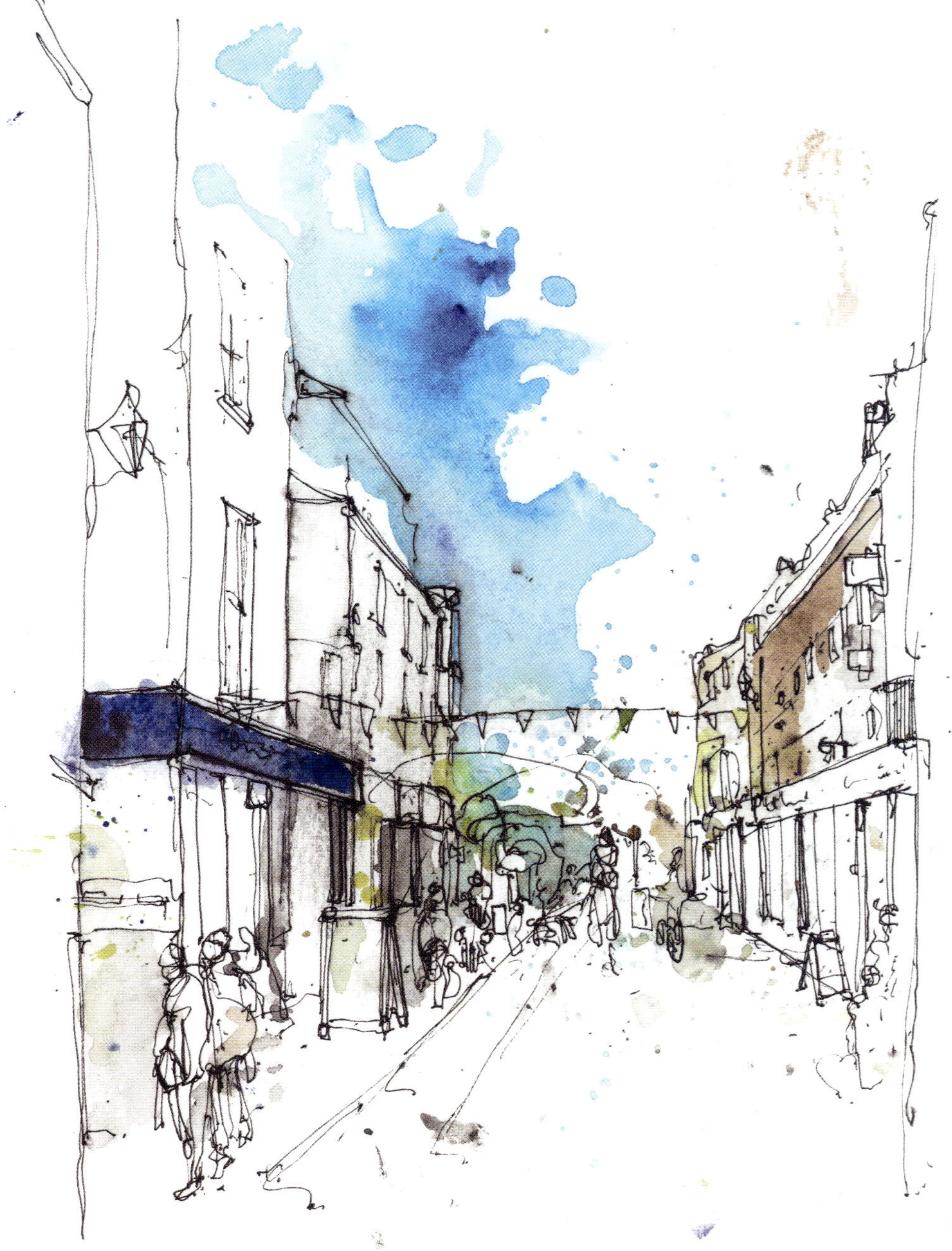

The building on the left remains white and serves up a nice sky contrast, as well and helping the grey window shadow to appear much darker.

White space is your friend

Traditional watercolour artists are masters of light and tone, and are adept at layering shadows and varying levels of opacity – a technique that can be tricky to deliver when urban sketching. This is mostly due to time constraints (I love to work fast, as you know) and a desire to keep a piece vibrant and boldly expressive. So the main question I hear you ask is, 'Which parts should I leave white?'

White space can deliver stunning contrasts between key parts of the artwork. I will usually offer up a vibrant sky in most of my works and deliberately leave an element of foreground in pure white to really make the scene pop! At other times I use white space to add a playful element to my works to help highlight a feature, structure or space. These 'white islands' work well as places to rest your eyes, almost subconsciously, and they can help knit together the scene and avoid a crowded sketch.

Be careful, however, to not be too rigid – the washes and negative spaces don't usually adhere to the lines of the sketch. Embrace a little creative freedom as the paint moves around the page.

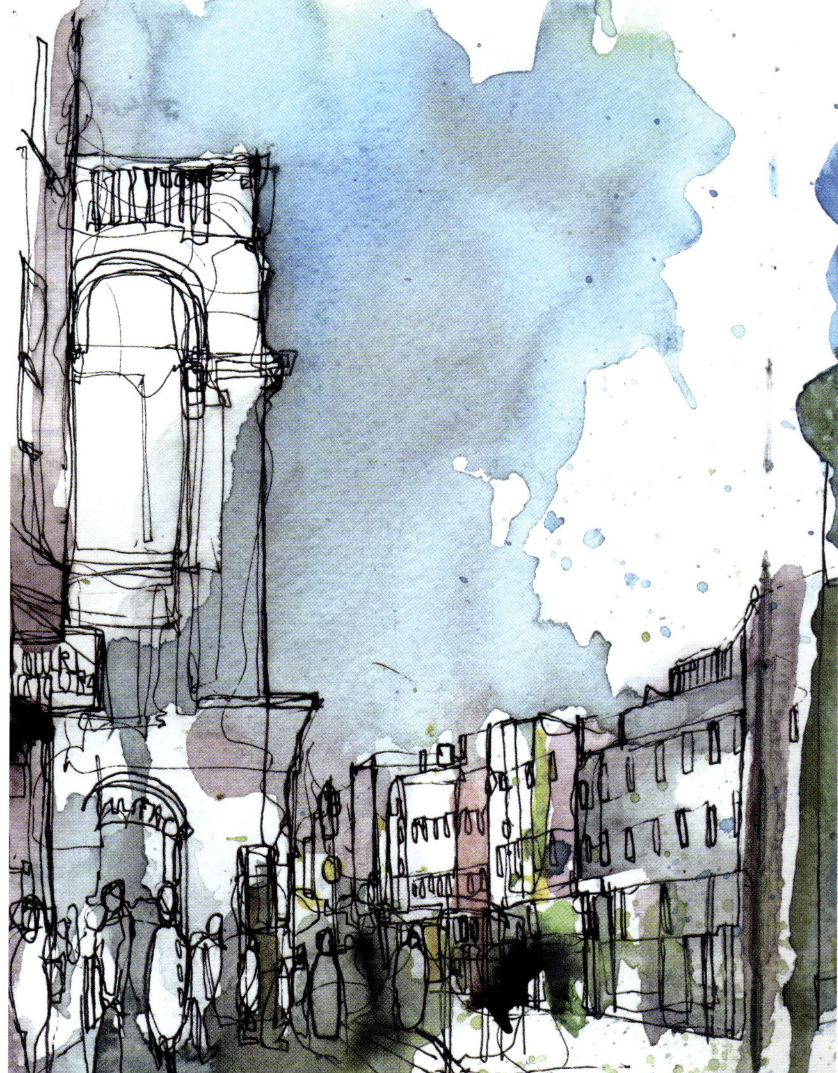

The white space left in the window delivers the strong contrast against the sky and also helps the sky appear more vertical.

Draw the shape not the thing

Try not to focus on drawing the buildings but draw the space in between. Once you have measured up your page and you're comfortable going into the sketch try this – choose a scene with a good defined sky and, rather than drawing the buildings, simply focus on drawing the shape of the sky. This helps to shift the focus and make sure your buildings appear nice and tall and in scale.

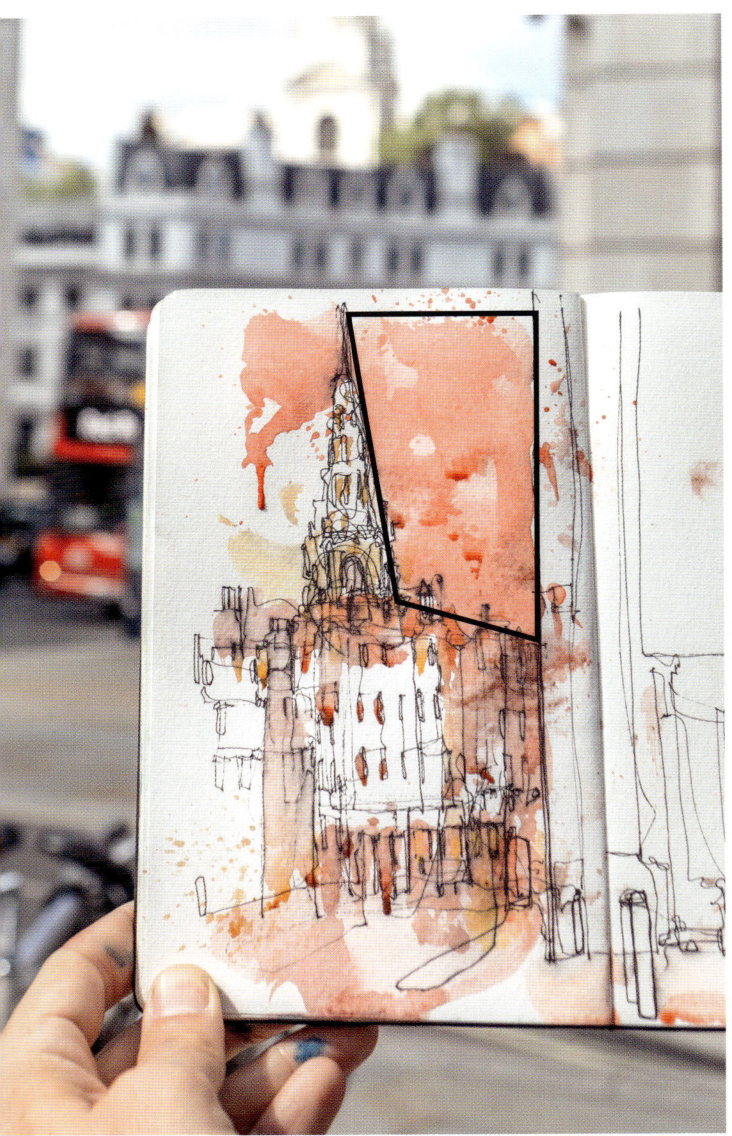

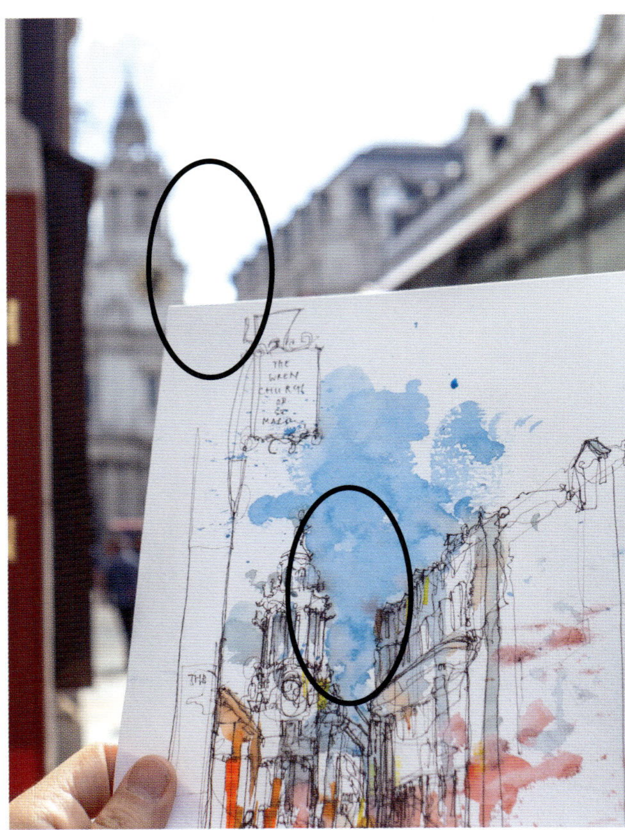

Observe the space between the structures. These simple shapes are a good aid to look for when choosing a scene. The more you look for these visual clues, the more you'll find.

White space can also act as a natural way to frame a sketch and increase the implied depth. Do this by deliberately placing a strong chunk of white space to one side of your painting.

The example sketches below immediately feel narrower by making use of foreground white space, which further helps to give the sketch more height.

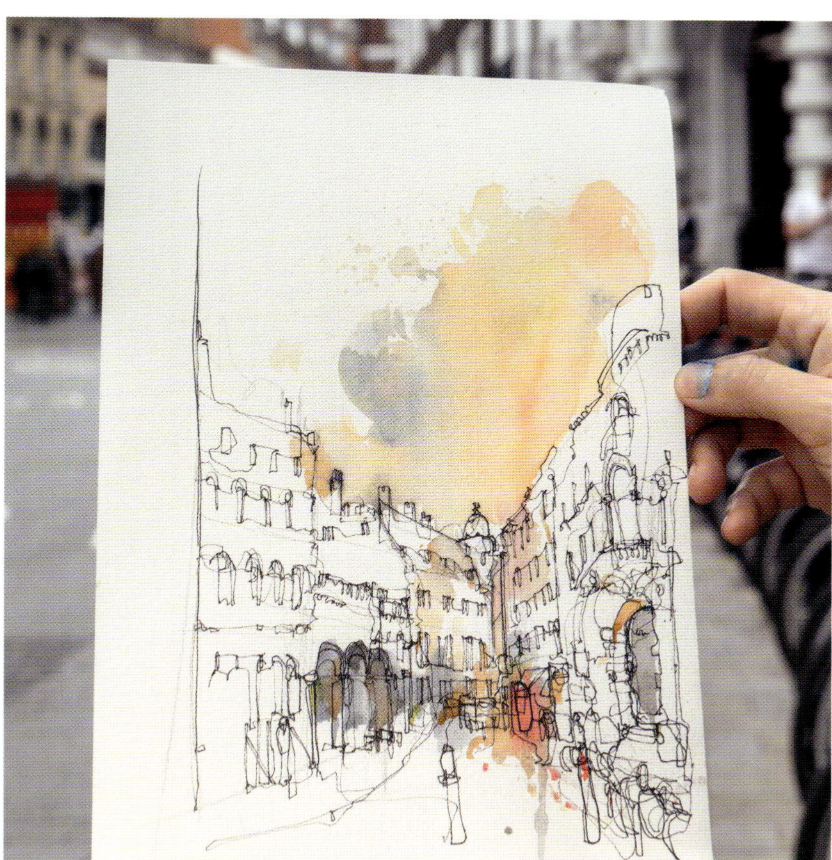

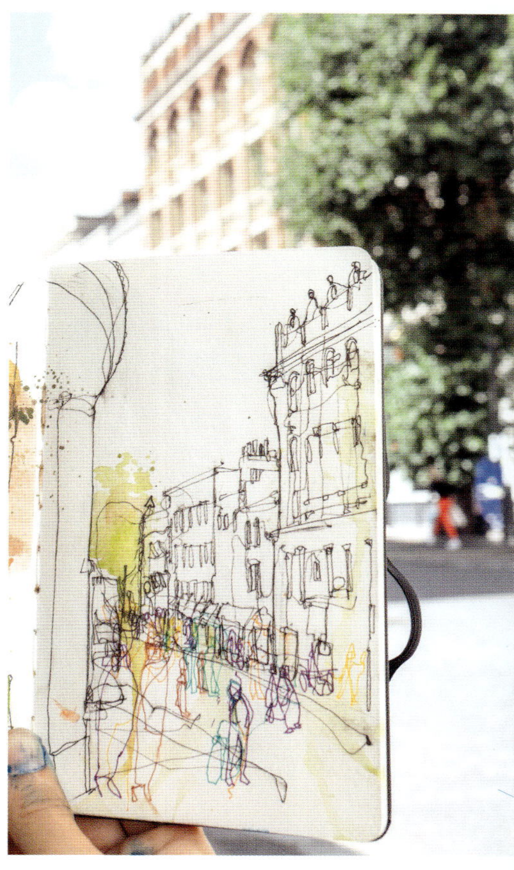

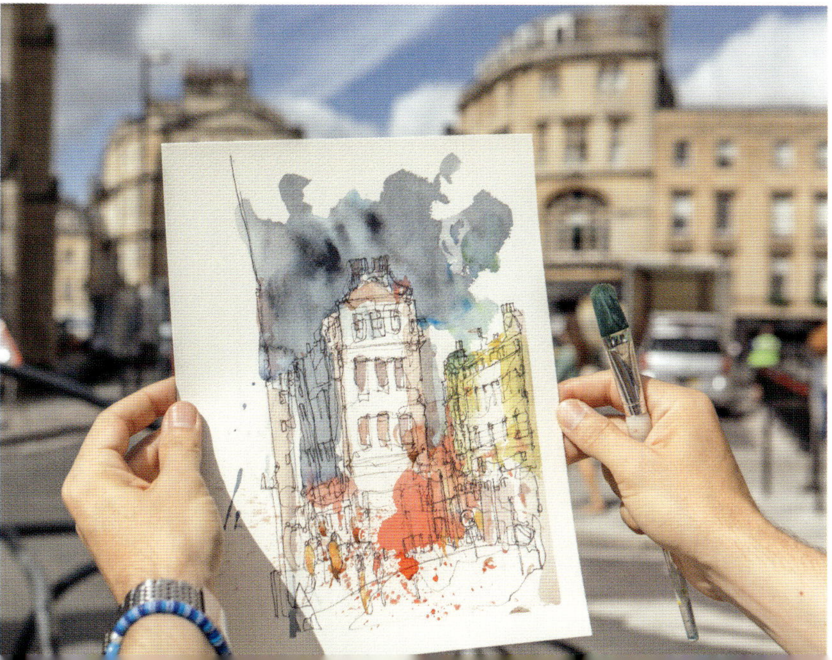

The shape of the sky is nicely isolated in all three of the scenes shown here. Accurately capturing the shape of the sky gives us the outline for two structures on either side.

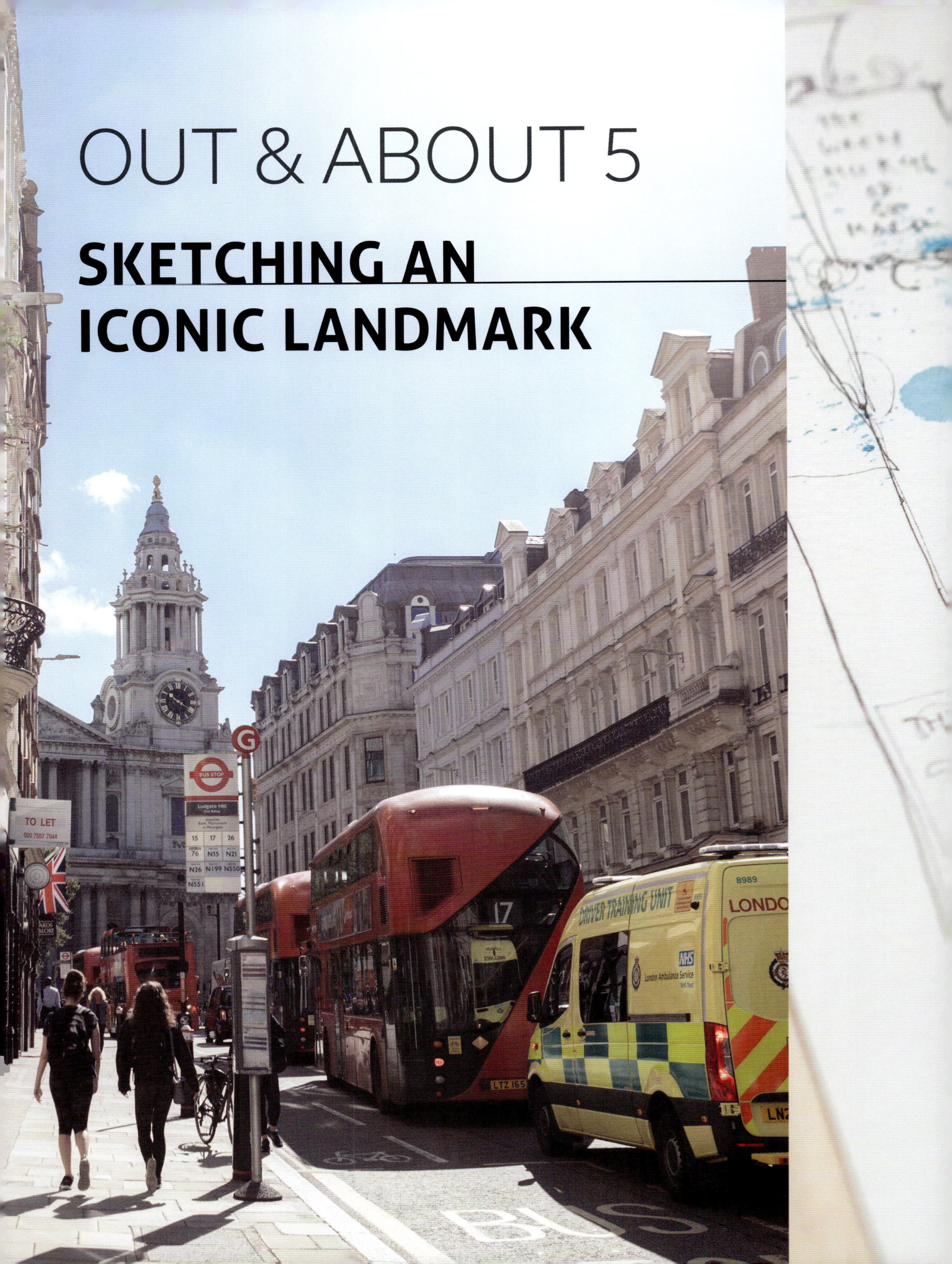

OUT & ABOUT 5
SKETCHING AN
ICONIC LANDMARK

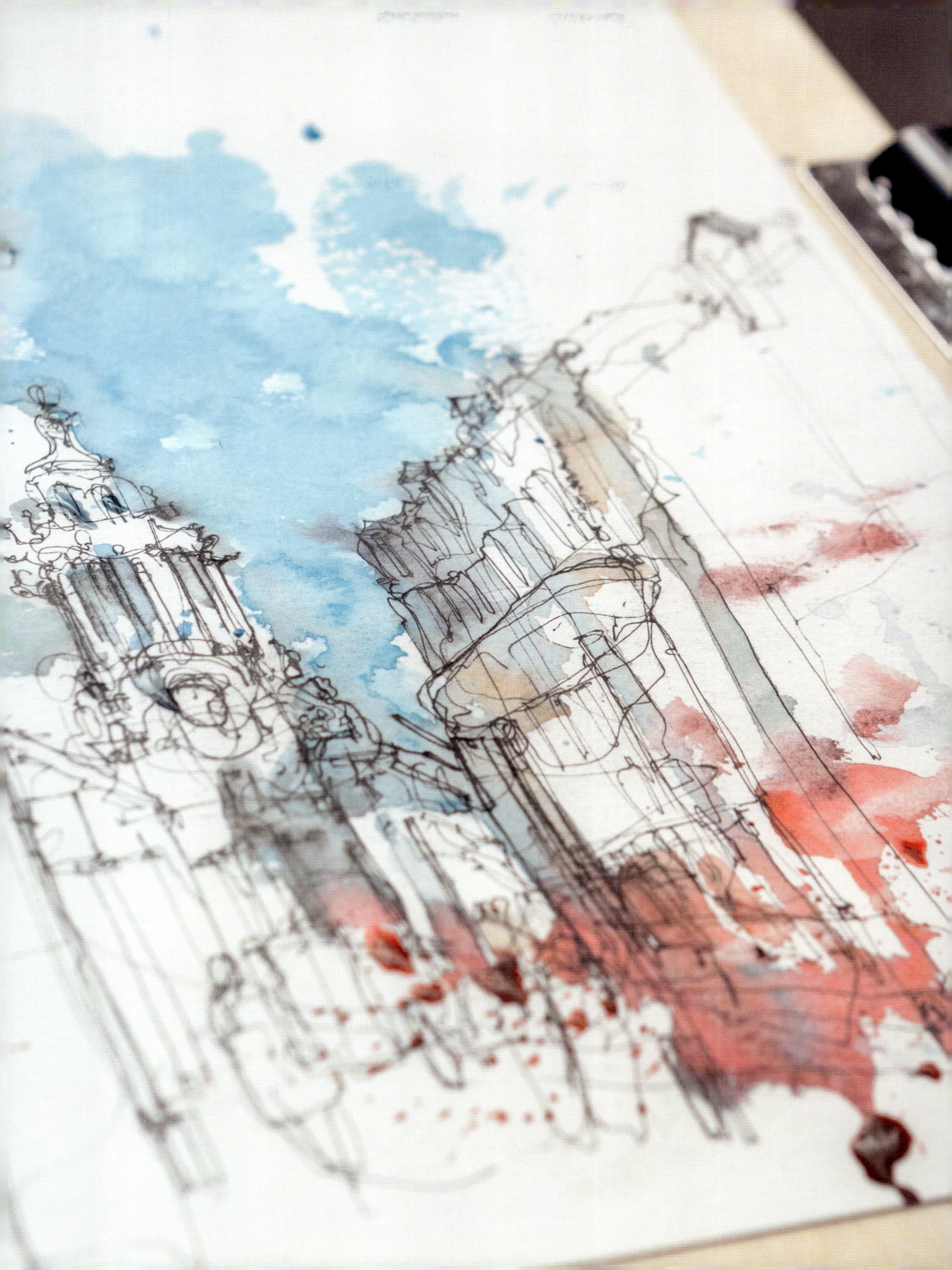

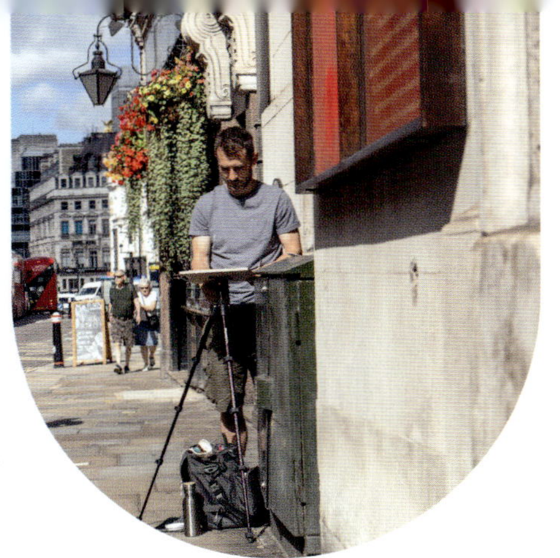

Find your favourite places

A church spire and domed roof is always a favourite focal point for city sketching, and this tight city view lent itself well to a line and wash sketch. I set up the easel in what shade I could find, and set to work straight away with a fast line sketch – no pencil this time as I felt sufficiently warmed up after a few sketches earlier in the day.

As before, I made sure to offset the view, so the feature aspect of the sketch occupied the left-hand third of the page. The vanishing point was also in the same zone but behind the main focus. Starting at the top of the spire, I made sure to keep the line work loose and avoid anything too rigid.

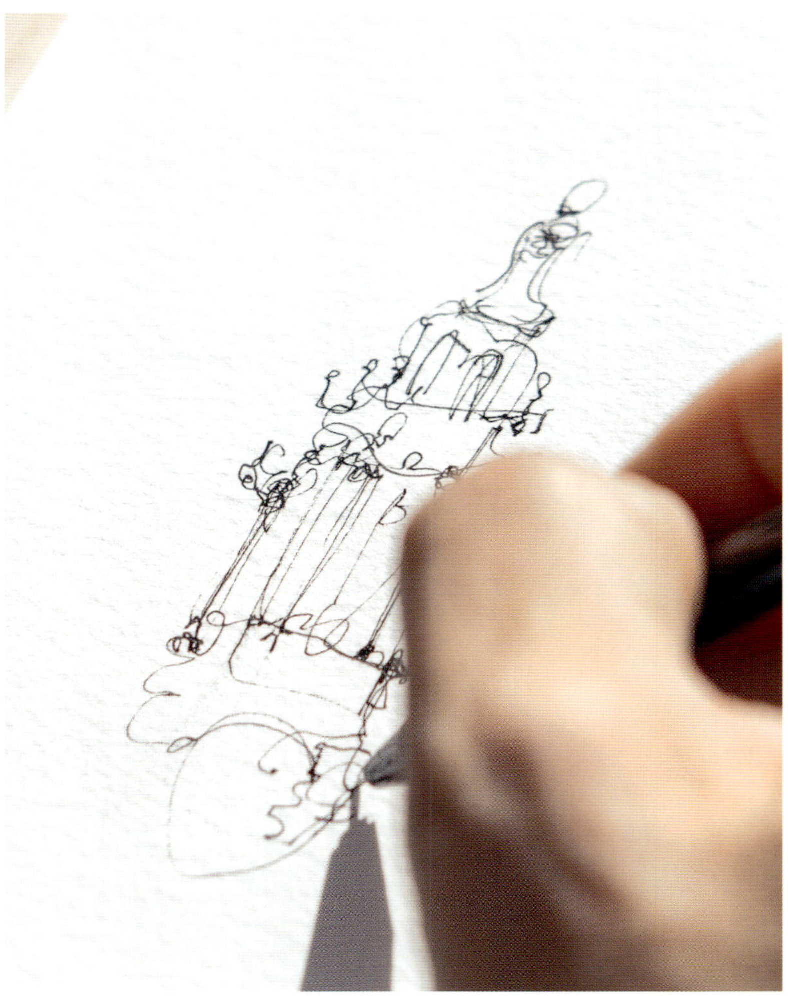

◀ Measurement in practice – is the top spire section the same height as the next section below? Using my pen to measure, I made sure that the height and width of the structure were proportional. At this early stage it's very easy to draw the structure too wide. Keep looking for natural references – how does the area of sky to the left compare to the width of the building? Using this technique, I could see that the sky to the left was slightly smaller in comparison. This relative scale made it a natural move to plot the left-hand vertical building – just like in Out & About 3 (page 72), this dominant vertical would serve well as a natural frame and top contender to remain untouched once the painting started.

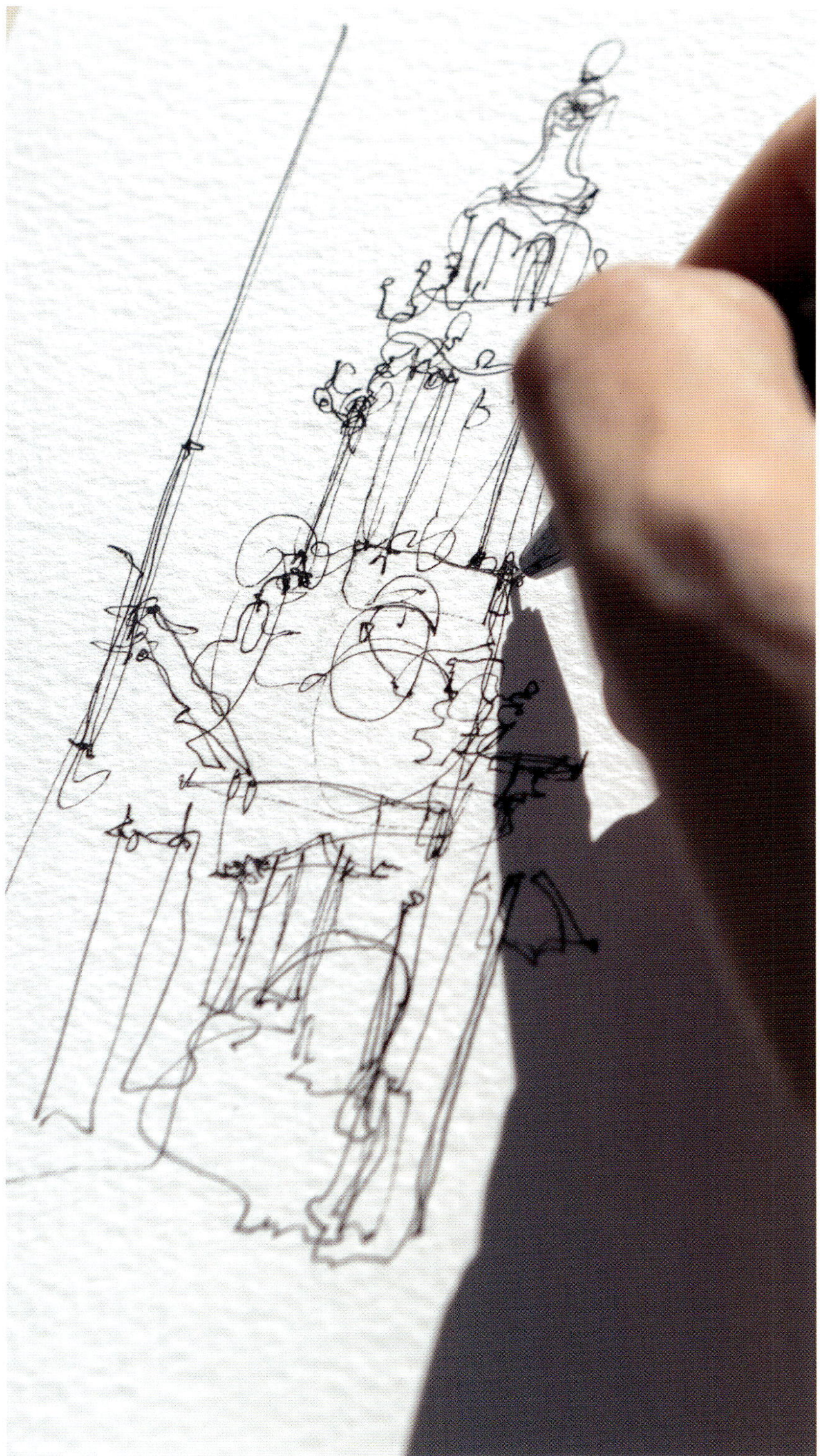

◀ The details on the spire, the clock face, the pillars and all the elaborate architectural forms would be impossible to capture working from this distance and at this scale. I used the pen to pick out the recognizable shapes – circular lines around the clock face and rectangles for the structural blocks. The circles are deliberately loose because these features are so far away. There was a collection of pillars that demanded simplification with the speed of the sketch. I really made sure to vary the line weight here – some areas were in shadow and some picking up reflected light, so varying the line weight was ideal to create some depth.

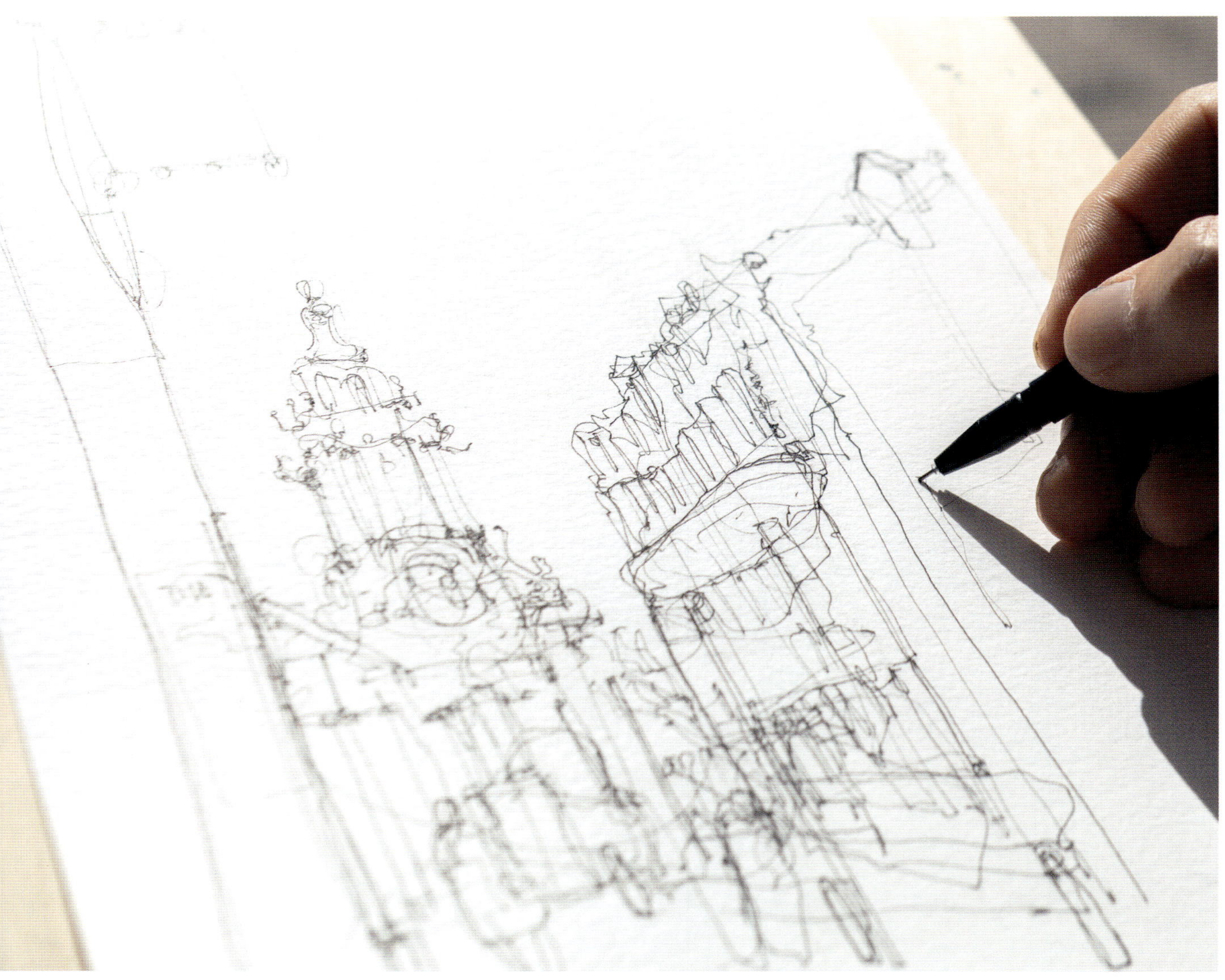

▲ With the cathedral detail sketched and the left-hand vertical section defined, I started to sketch the right-hand side. As a right-handed artist I naturally work left to right – it stops the palm smudging the page, and pulling the pen rather than pushing it offers a little more control.

At this point it's easy to fall into the trap of filling the whole page and making the sketch too wide. I kept my focus on the scene – using the cathedral as a measuring tool, I was able to compare the widths of the larger areas of the scene. Holding my pen up, I regularly looked to mimic the angle to the vanishing point. This helped line up the relative angle of the windows.

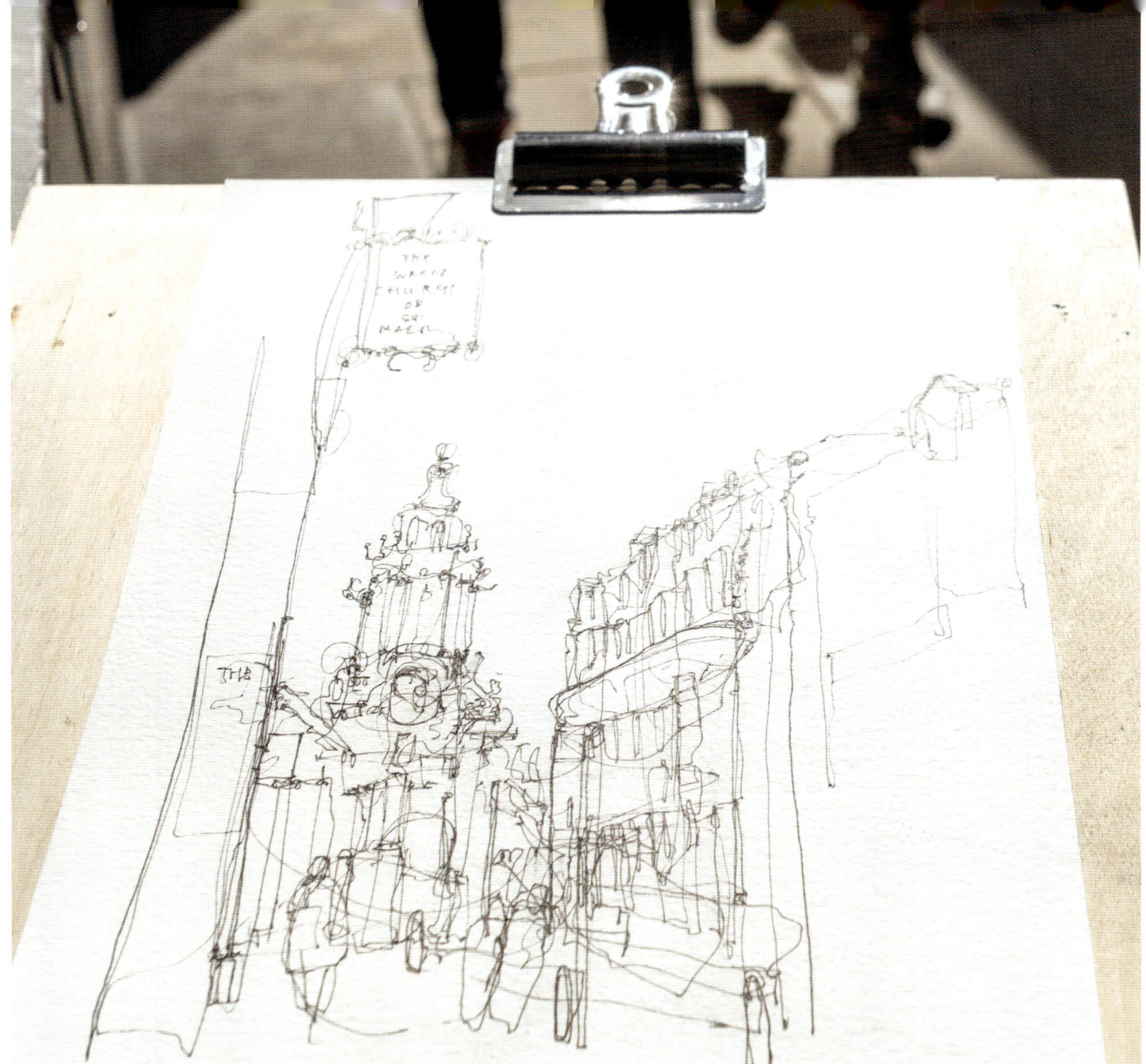

▲ The right-hand side of this sketch is all about drawing the viewer to the action area of the scene. There are probably some windows missing in the final sketch but I've made sure that the horizontal lines help guide the direction of travel. The vertical lines on the right are loose in comparison to the strong vertical on the left – this helps push them into the distance.

The foreground sketch again illustrates just how busy the scene was: the mass of single lines suggest the contours of the passing cars, buses and people. What I did have in the scene, however, were a few static people. I concentrated on capturing the angle of the body and the general shape.

TIP

You'll rarely see me draw feet and hands (or even arms) in this kind of sketch. To capture this detail so exactly is likely to throw some conflict into the scale of the drawing. I did make sure, however, to bring the figures some obvious presence by using a strong line weight. Look back to pages 48–49 for more on drawing people.

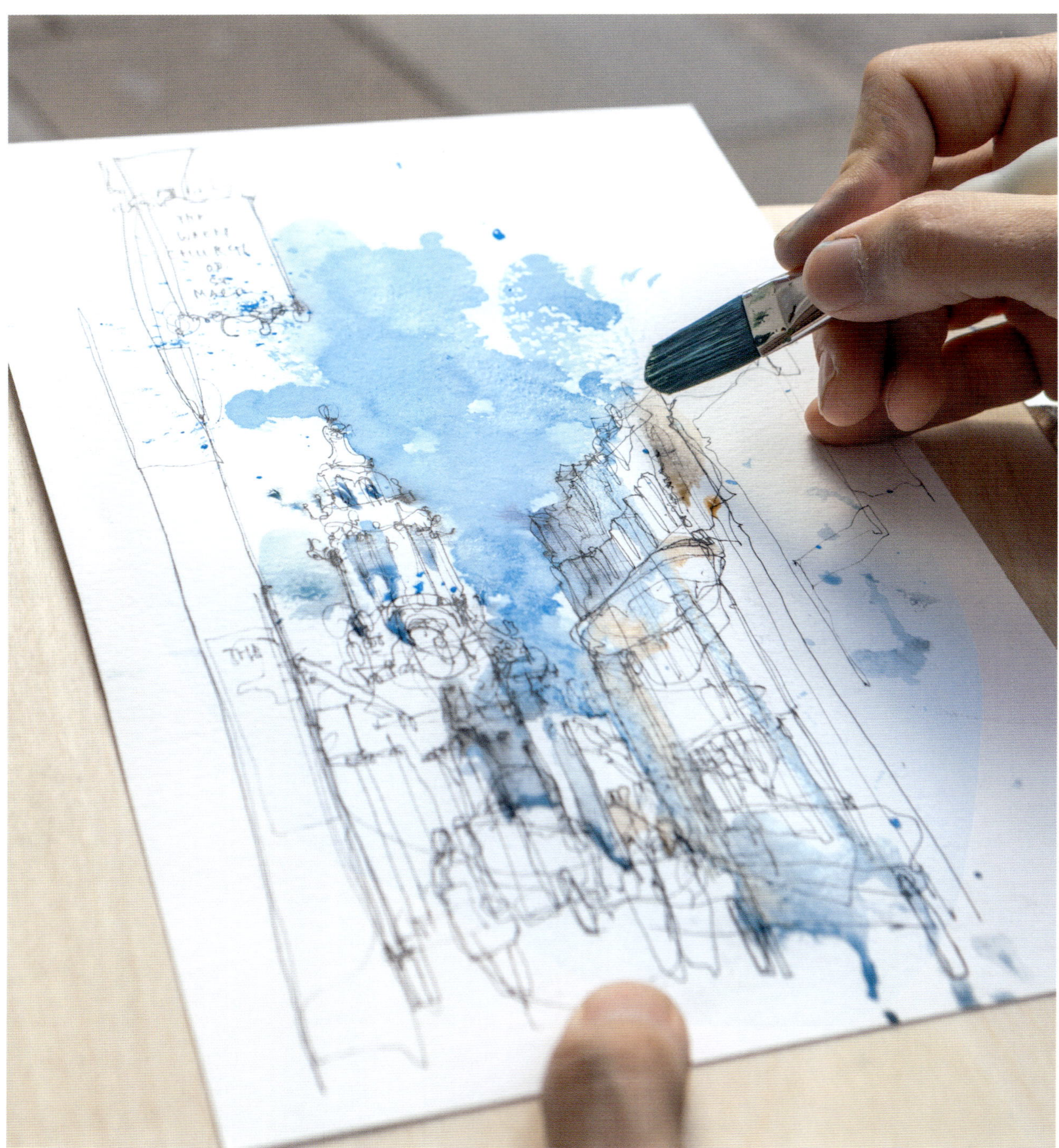

▲ The heat of the day was intense and it was a natural move to use a warm cerulean blue for the sky. This would provide a strong contrast to the focal point if left unpainted. Using my chunky filbert brush, I helped guide the blue down to the horizon line with a generous amount of water.

◄ To encourage a few drips, I picked up the paper and purposely knocked it down onto my easel.

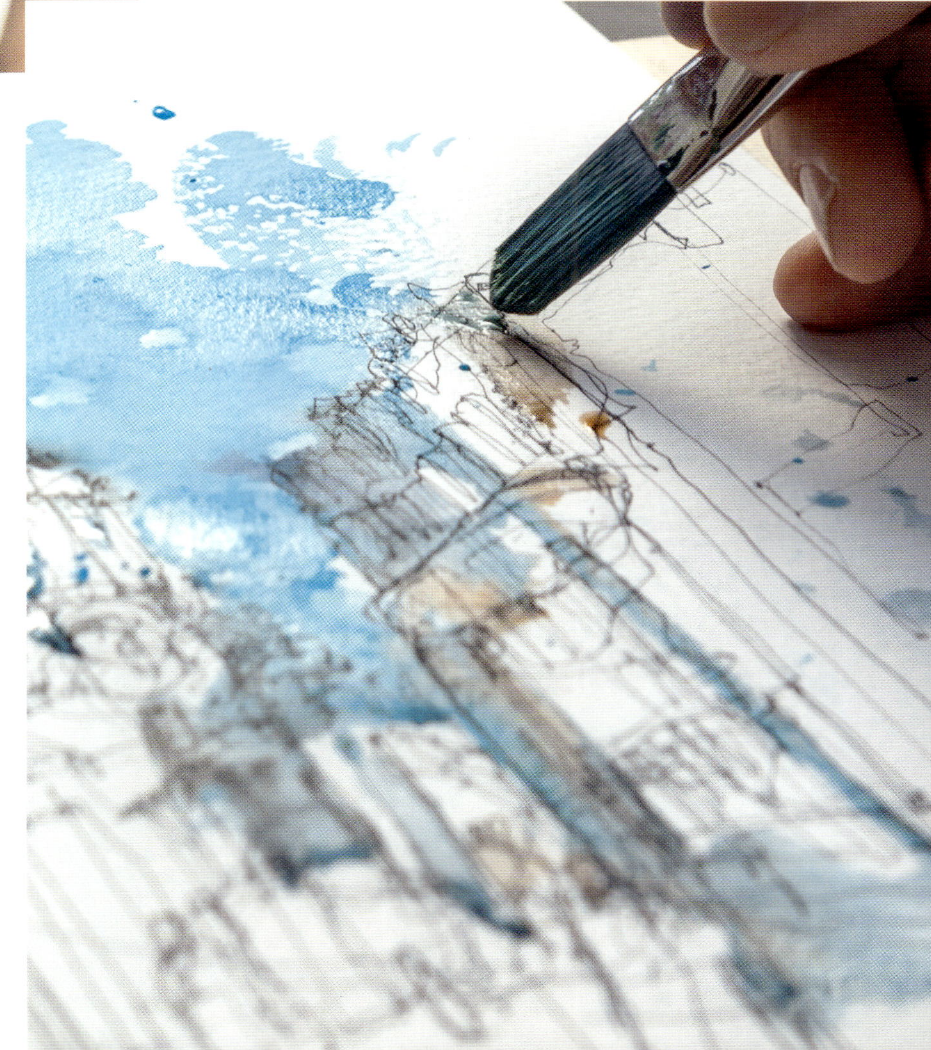

▶ I was keen to give a hint of shadows in the pillars and let a little Payne's grey melt into the blue. I deliberately made sure that some of the vertical pillars remained perfectly white to bring out this strong contrasting feature. This grey tone was extended to the areas of the right side of the sketch, but this mass of windows wasn't particularly exciting and therefore, as I normally do, I filtered it out and allowed the white of the paper to remain dominant.

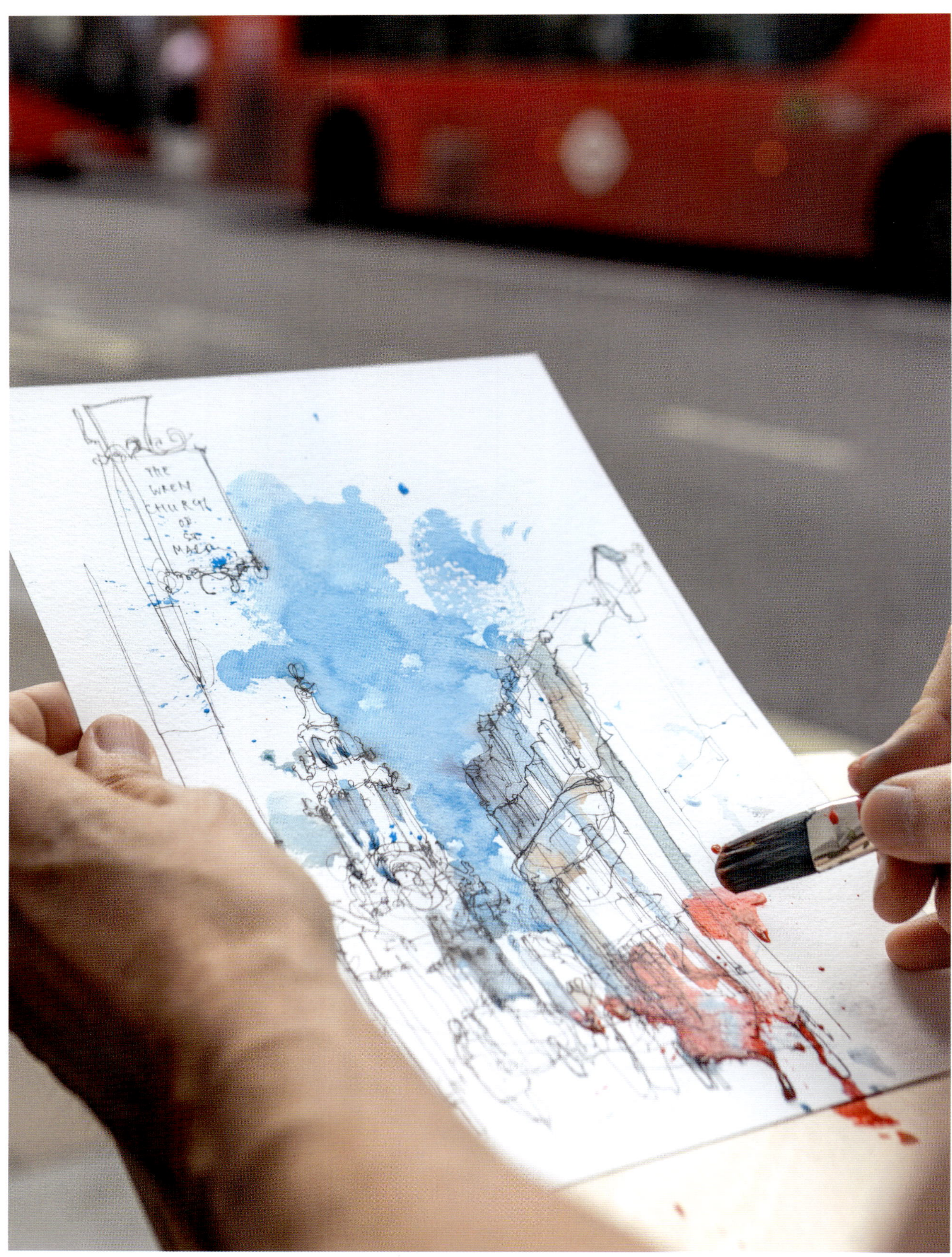

THE
WREN
CHURCH
OF
ST MARY

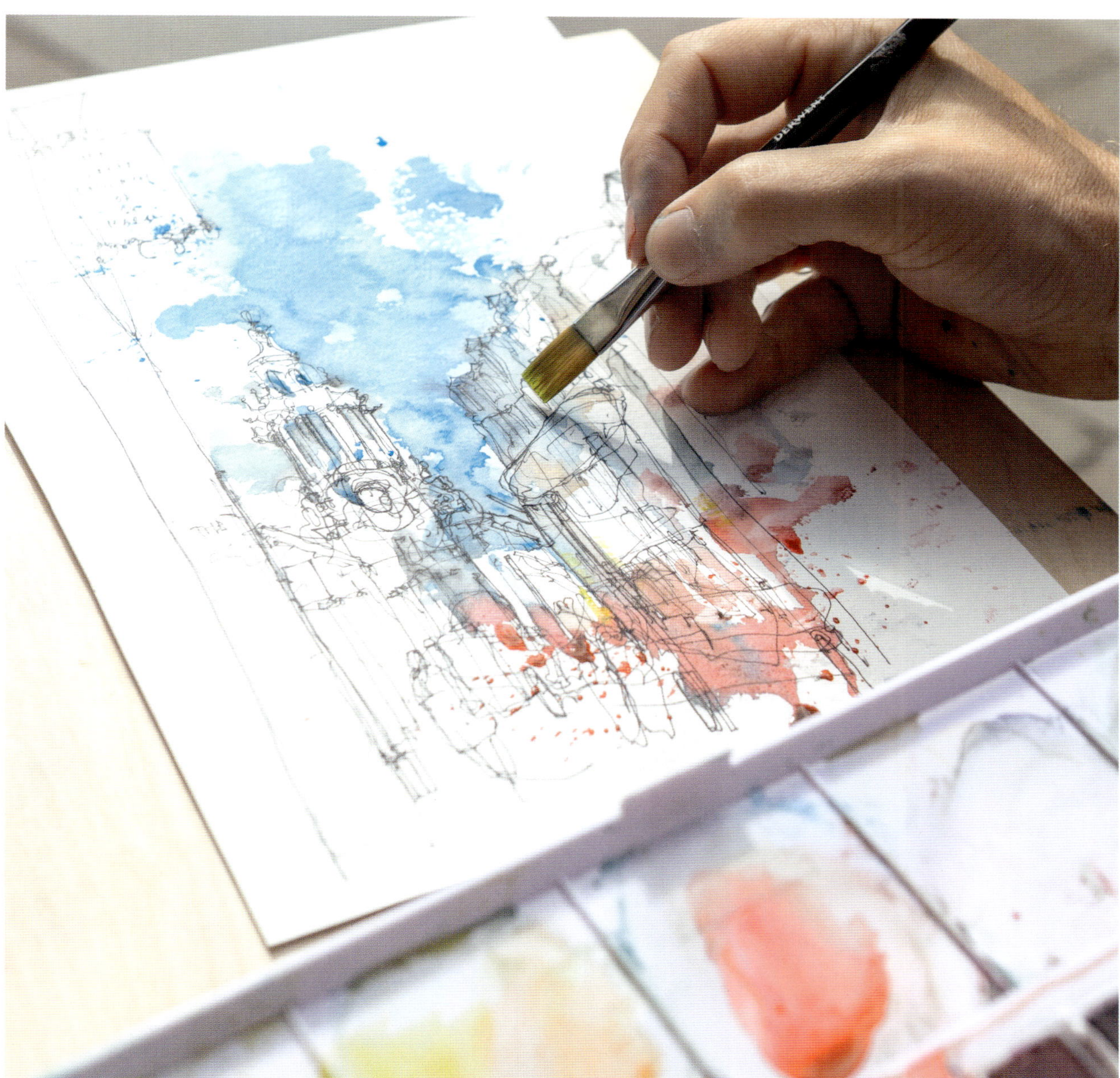

◄ Again, the colours around me were a big influence – the traffic, the red sign and the people. The busy street was ever-changing, so in the same manner as the sketch, I added colour to natural shapes between my lines, and to define or exclude areas that would help establish the scale. For instance the three foreground people are either white or fully painted.

▲ I switched brush here to a more squared-off version to get more edge detail, making sure to paint vertically, almost like an italic style of writing.

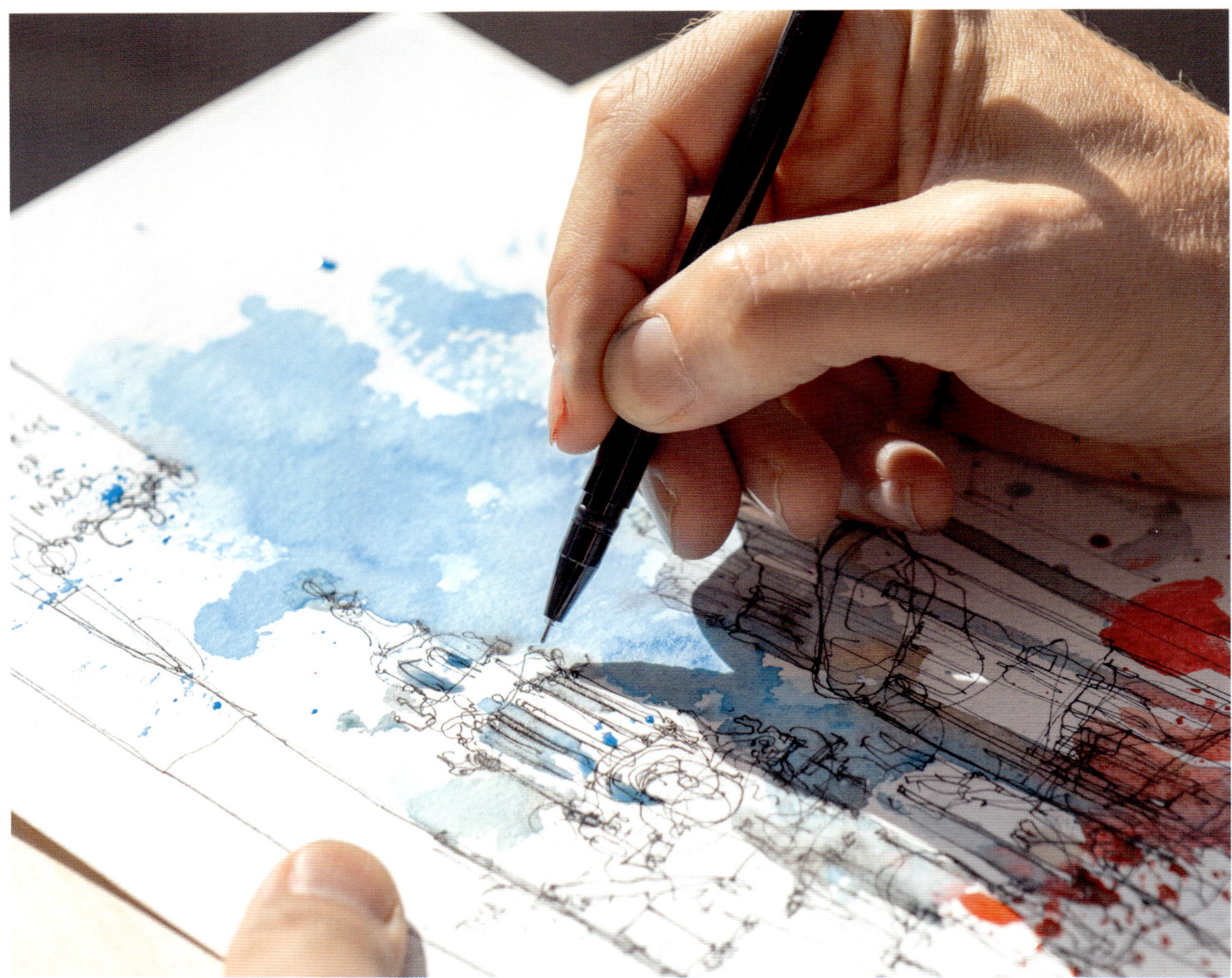

▲ The final thing to do, as usual, was to rework some of my darker lines, again with the paper still damp. The moisture made the darks pop and really brought out the dark tones.

Opposite: There was a definite temptation to paint all of the figures in the foreground, but leaving the figure to the left unpainted helped give the piece that customary 'unfinished/finished' tension that I love.

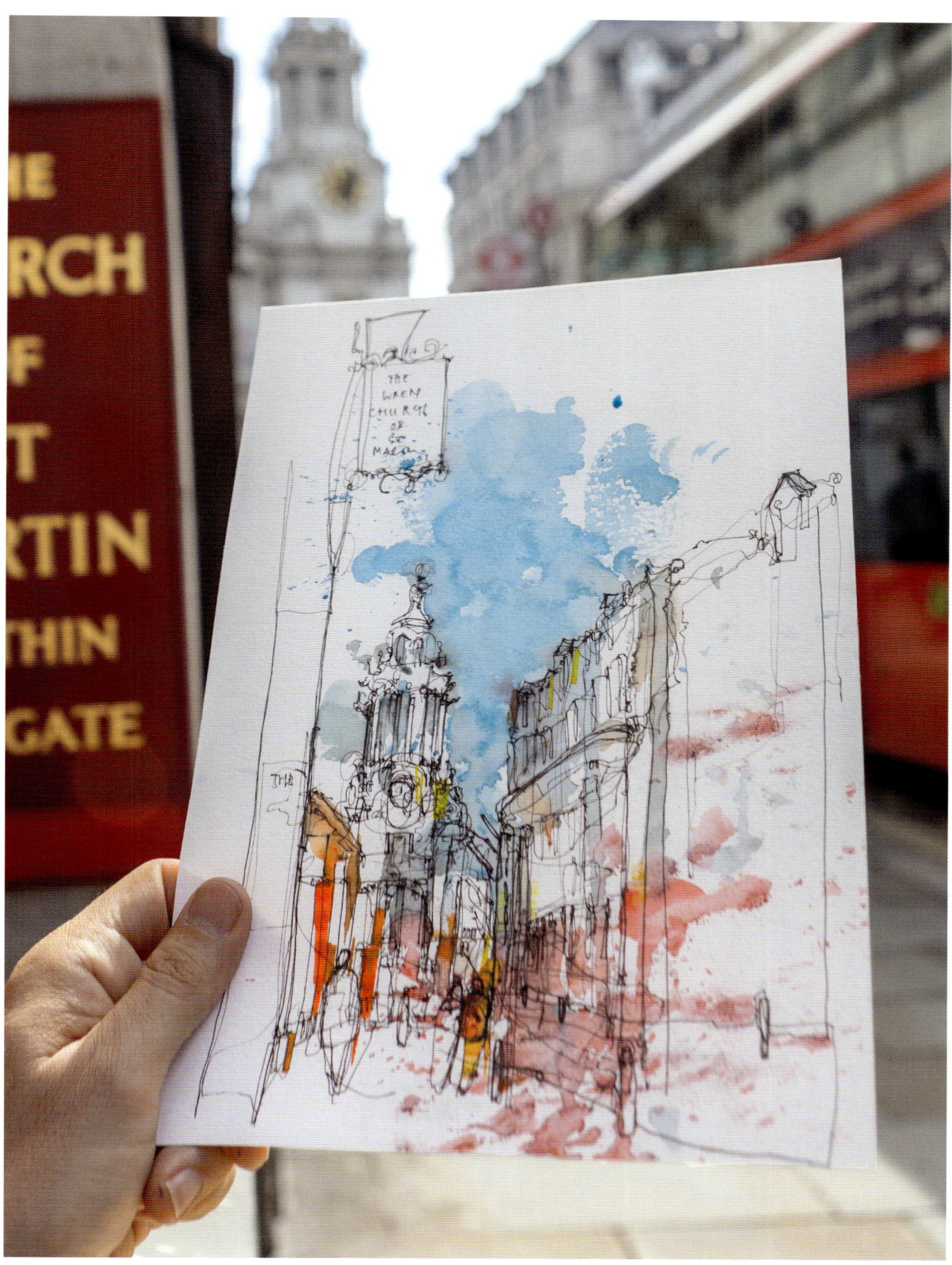
RCH
F
T
RTIN
THIN
GATE
THE
WREN
CHURCH
OF
ST
MALA

Making the sky come alive

I love a big expressive sky. Vibrant and concentrated colours can help create drama, capture attention and bring striking vibrancy to a modest or rather mundane scene. There is a range of things to consider when adding the sky wash, but just like the sketching exercises, these can become second nature with practice.

Vertical brushwork
Working vertically helps add height to the overall artwork. This is not to say that there's no place for creating the sky wash horizontally, but I really like to encourage the sky to bleed into the foreground.

Contrast and depth
Look to boost the impact of the sky by creating contrast and depth. Introduce areas of light and shadow with plenty of water to create a smooth gradient of colour. Contrast warm and cool tones to add interest and visual tension to the composition.

Dynamic compositions
As discussed in earlier chapters, there is scope to experiment with different compositions to create dynamic and engaging skies. This is done by making a conscious decision to set the horizon line low in the painting to emphasize the depth of the sky, or use dramatic angles and perspectives to draw the viewer's eye upward.

The splatters
No sky is without a splatter! Just as these splashes of colour add movement to the main painting, they can help to bring the sky alive. This splattering technique can really help add texture and interest to the sky, suggesting rain, atmospheric effects, birds and light reflections.

Emotional rescue
I would encourage you to infuse your skies with a sense of emotion and mood that complements the urban scene. Use the colours of the day, the colours of your mood or simply the colours you have with you. Sculpting the atmosphere with your expressive skies can help add a real personal edge to your work and make it less about building accuracy and move towards real artistic interpretation.

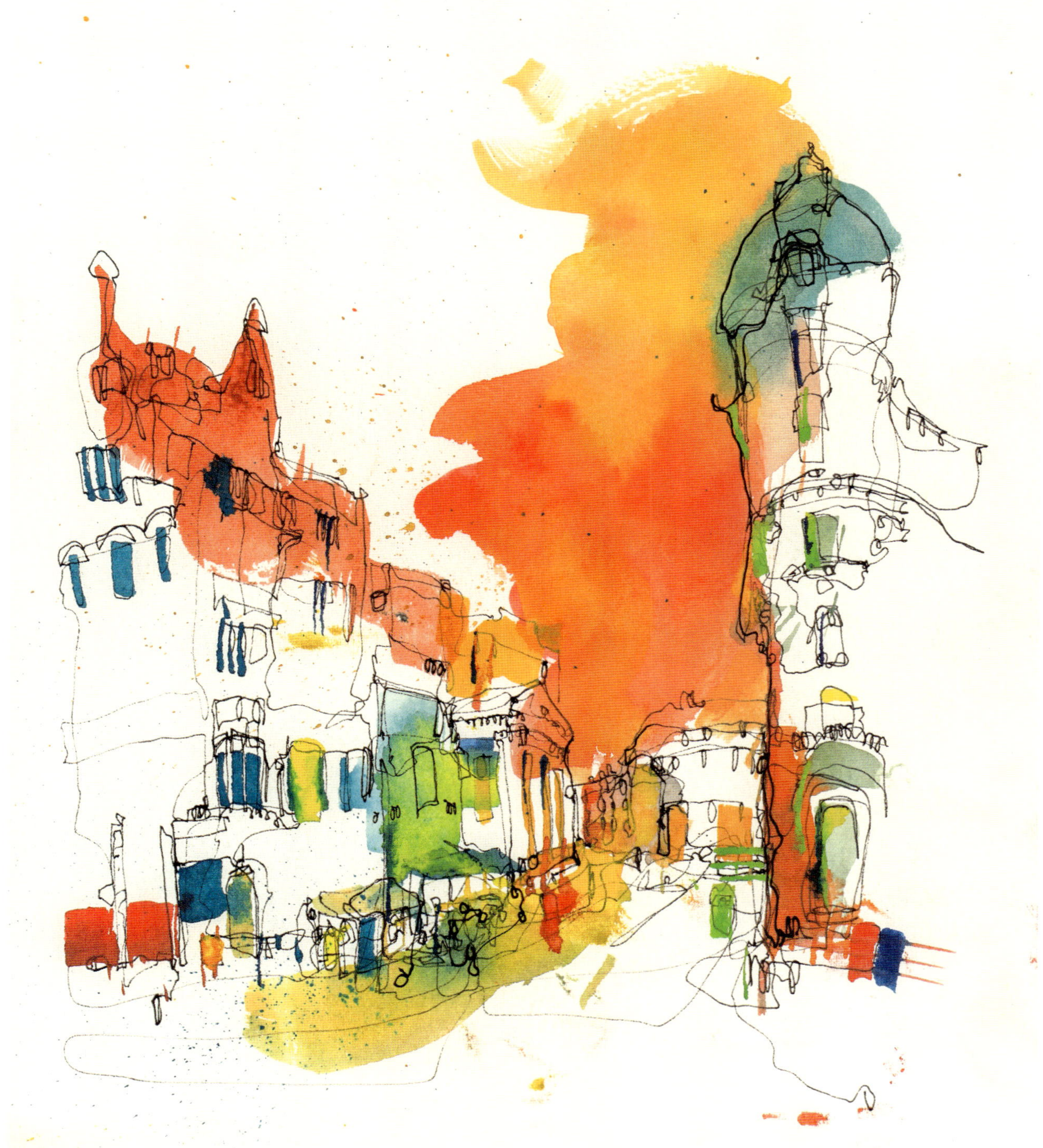

The heat of summer

A sky that might be mistaken for fire on the horizon, this one followed a technique of using just three base colours. The red gradient travels down and merges into the distant background. The tall building on the right is left white to boost the sky contrast.

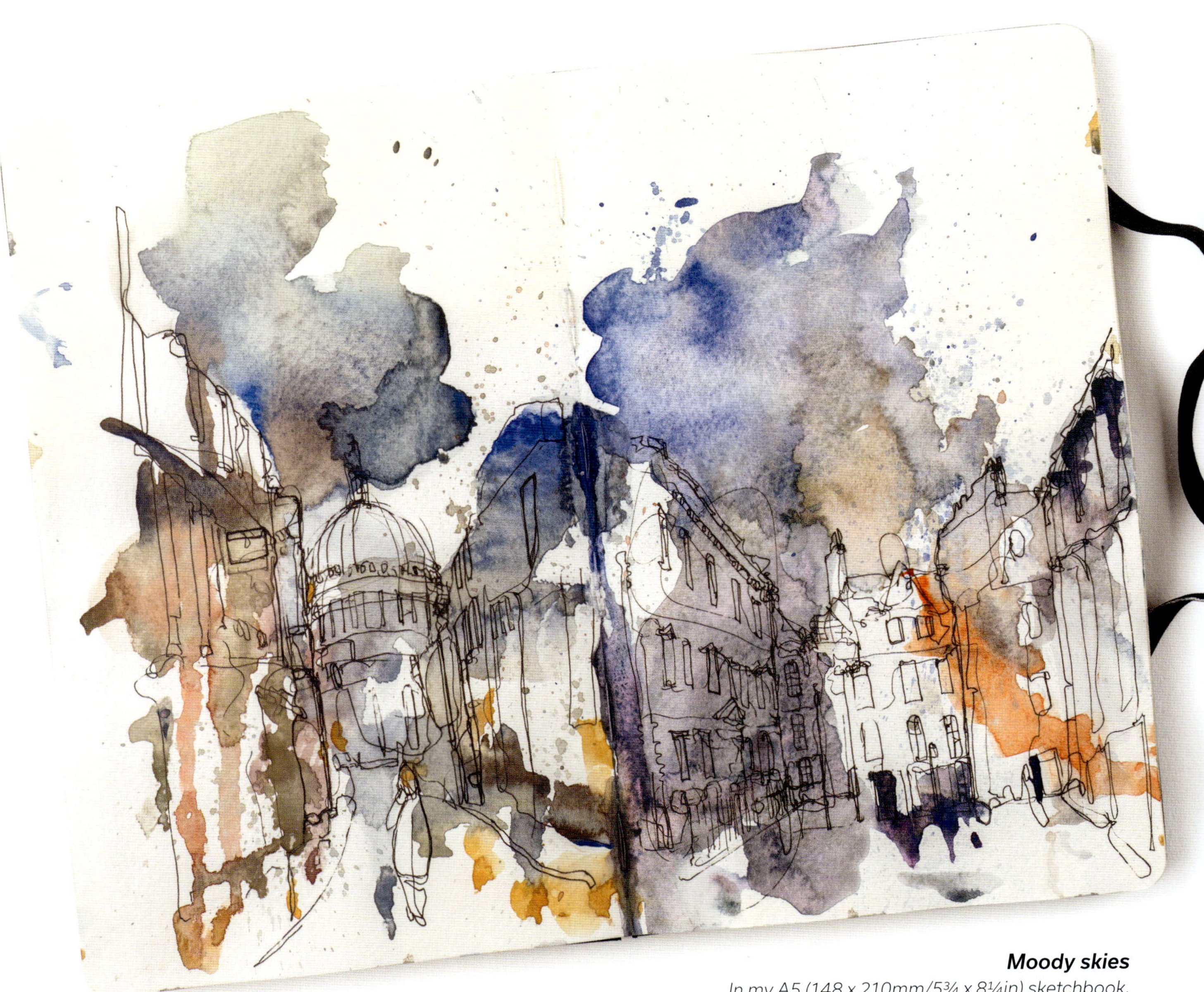

Moody skies

In my A5 (148 x 210mm/5¾ x 8¼in) sketchbook,
using a combination of blues and dark tones, the
brush was pushed into the page and the watercolour
flowed as the brush head was slowly rotated. A slight
tilt of the easel encouraged the pools of water to
slowly seep downwards.

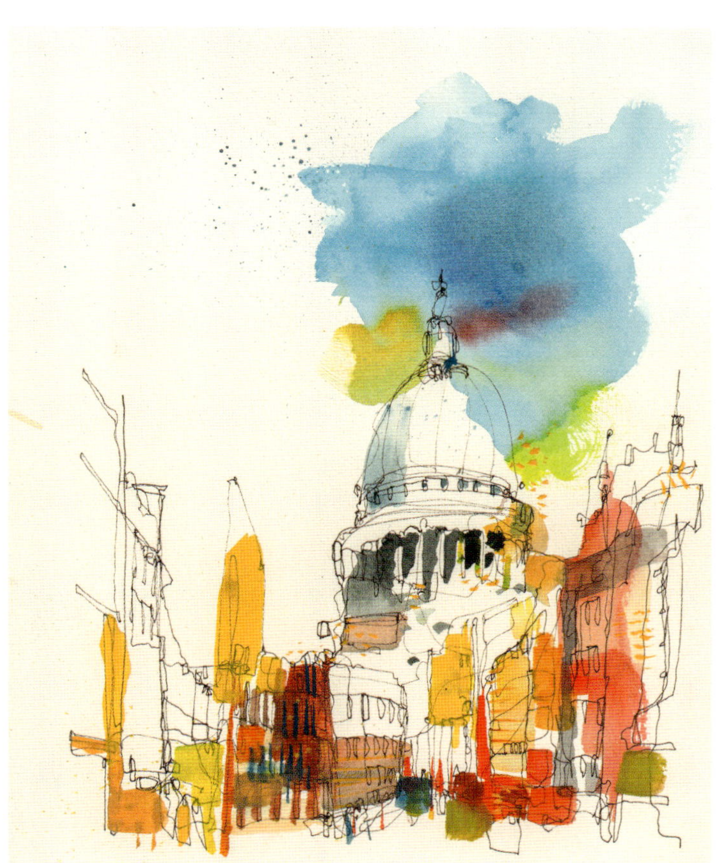

The bold blue

A signature sky for me! Sketching in the sunshine is the best and I cannot wait to break out the phthalo or cerulean blue. As before, the dominant structure avoids being completely washed, but it's not a rigid process – there's still some sky on the domed roof. The sky almost acts as the glue between every part.

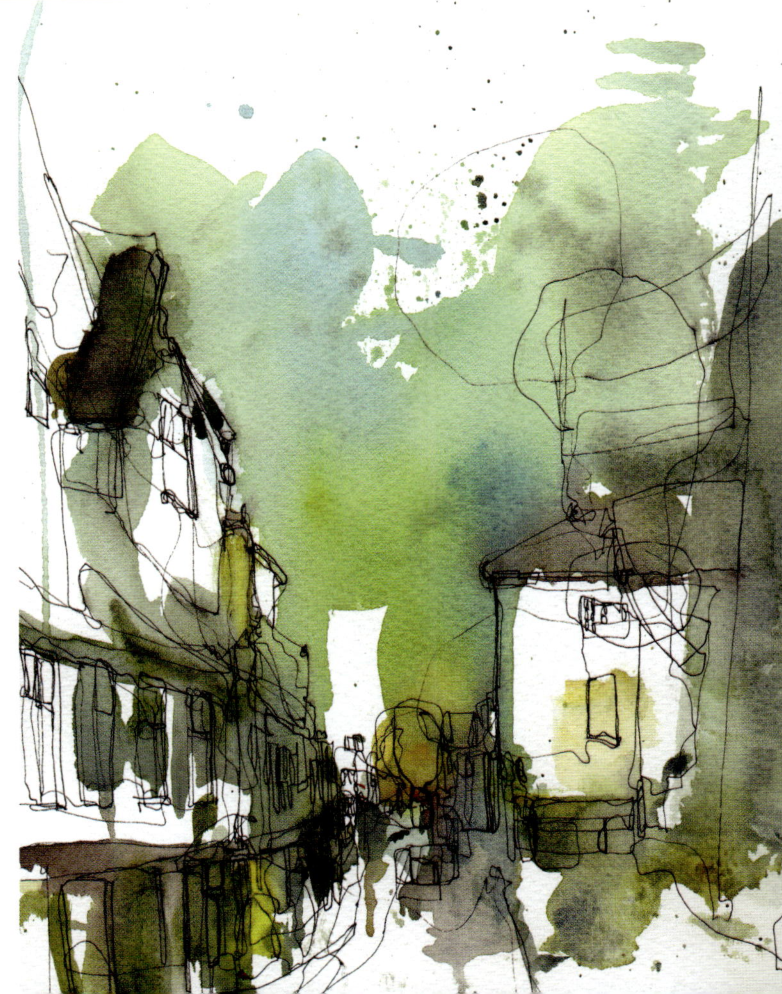

Sometimes the sky can be green!

Inspired by the early summer sunshine, the vibrant greens of the trees were so rich and inspiring that I let them dominate the foreground and the sky, helping it become a very original piece.

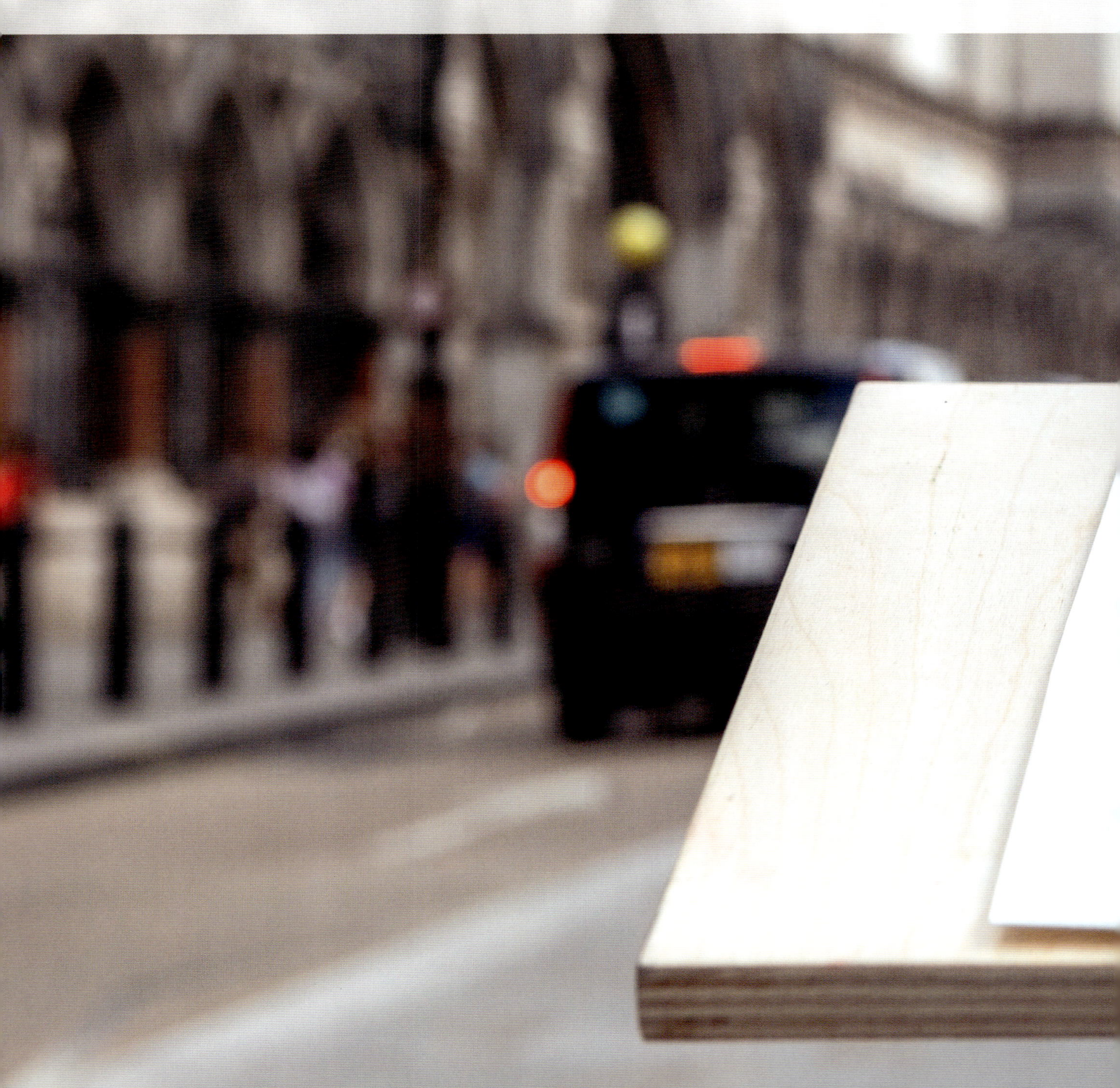

OUT & ABOUT 6

SKETCHING A COMPLEX SCENE

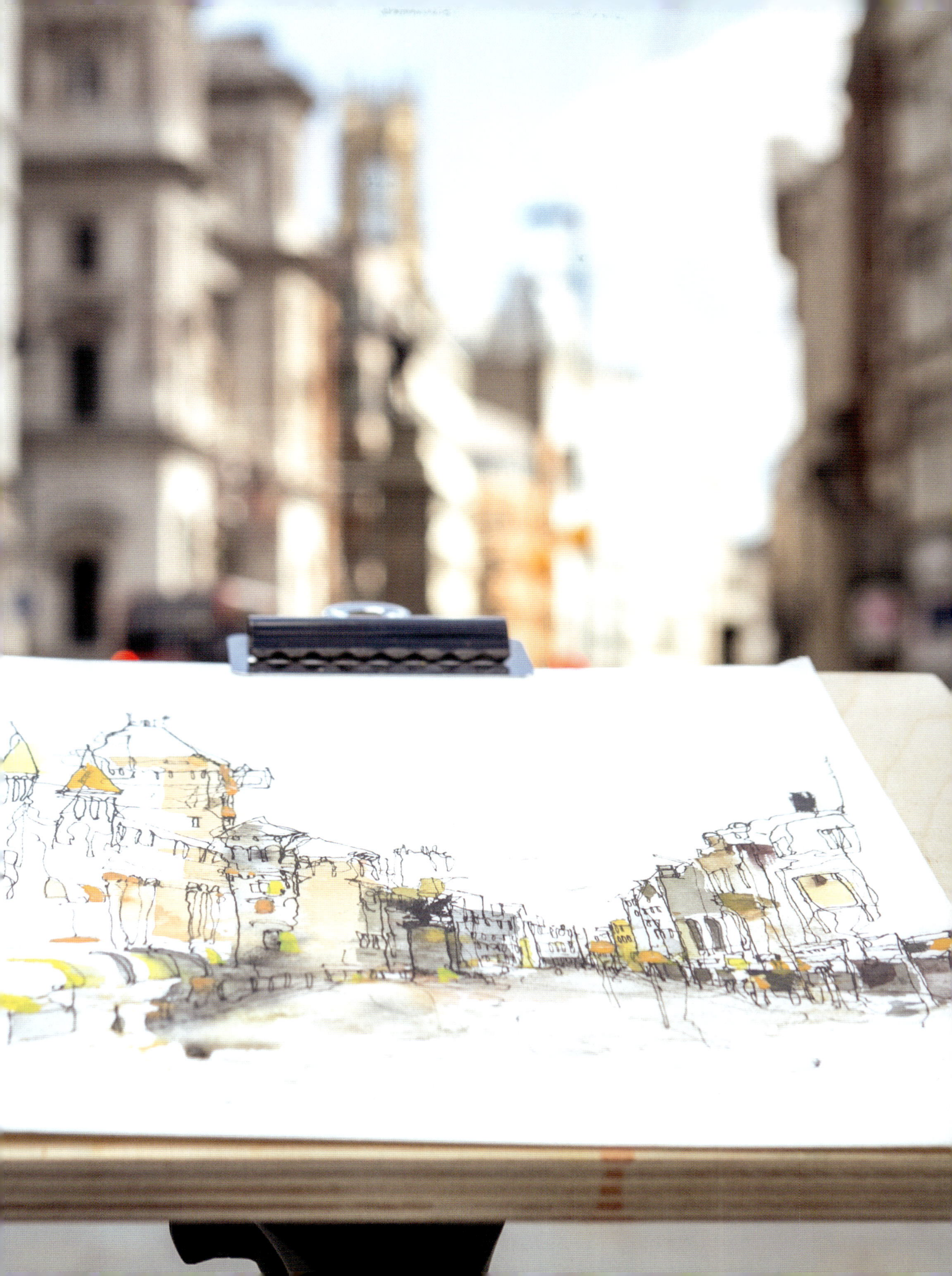

Simplify, simplify, simplify

The really complex – years ago I would have instantly thought this view was too challenging to sketch, as it's barely possible to make out the intricacies of every shop front, spire, doorway and window – but this is where the opportunity to simplify and look for shapes is at its finest, and this is what I look for now. Complex aspects will help fill the page and open up so much opportunity for fluid line work.

My viewpoint was on a central island in the road – mostly free from tourists and passers by, which gave me some time to study the scene in depth and make some decisions about my approach before putting pen to paper.

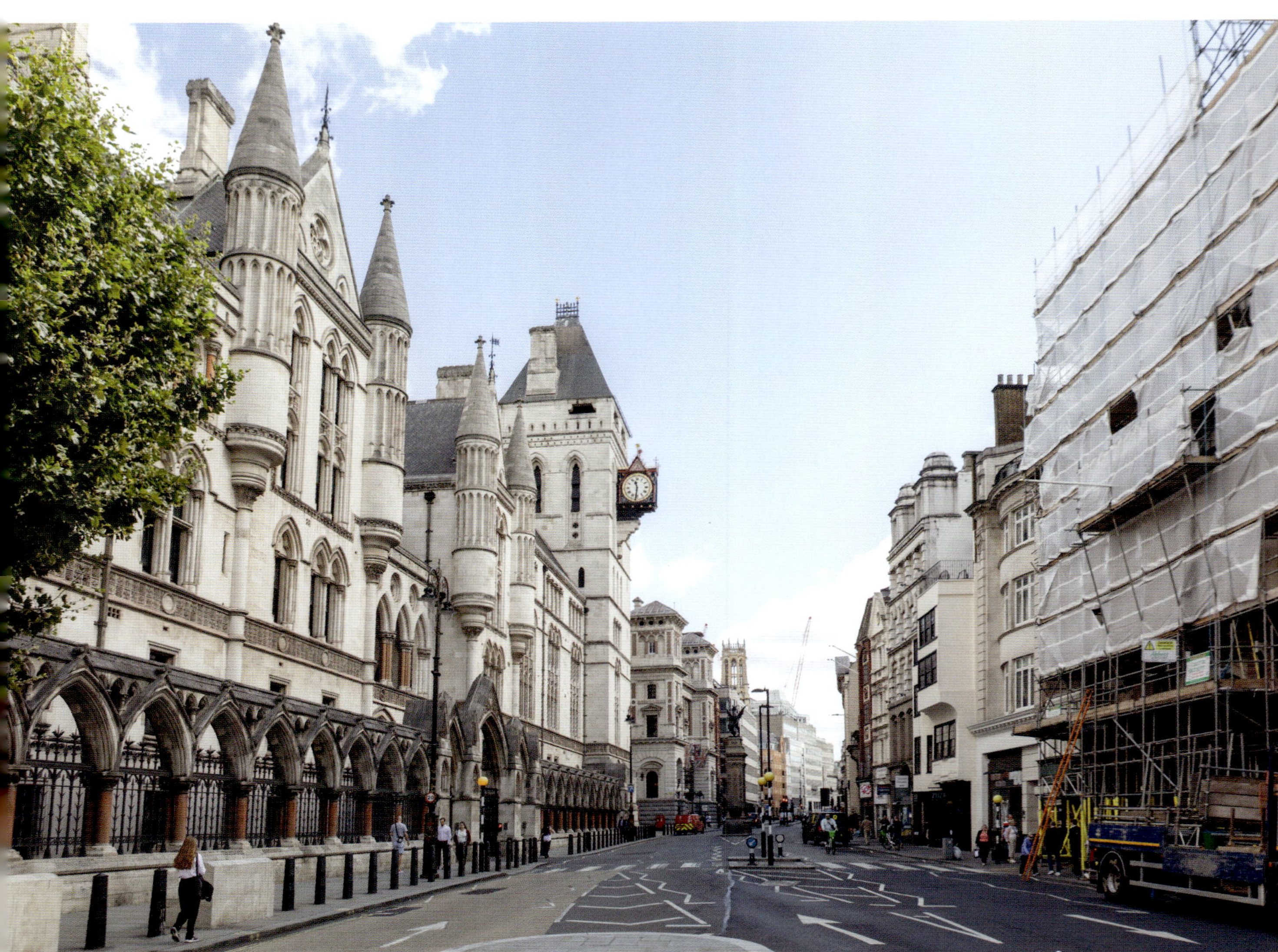

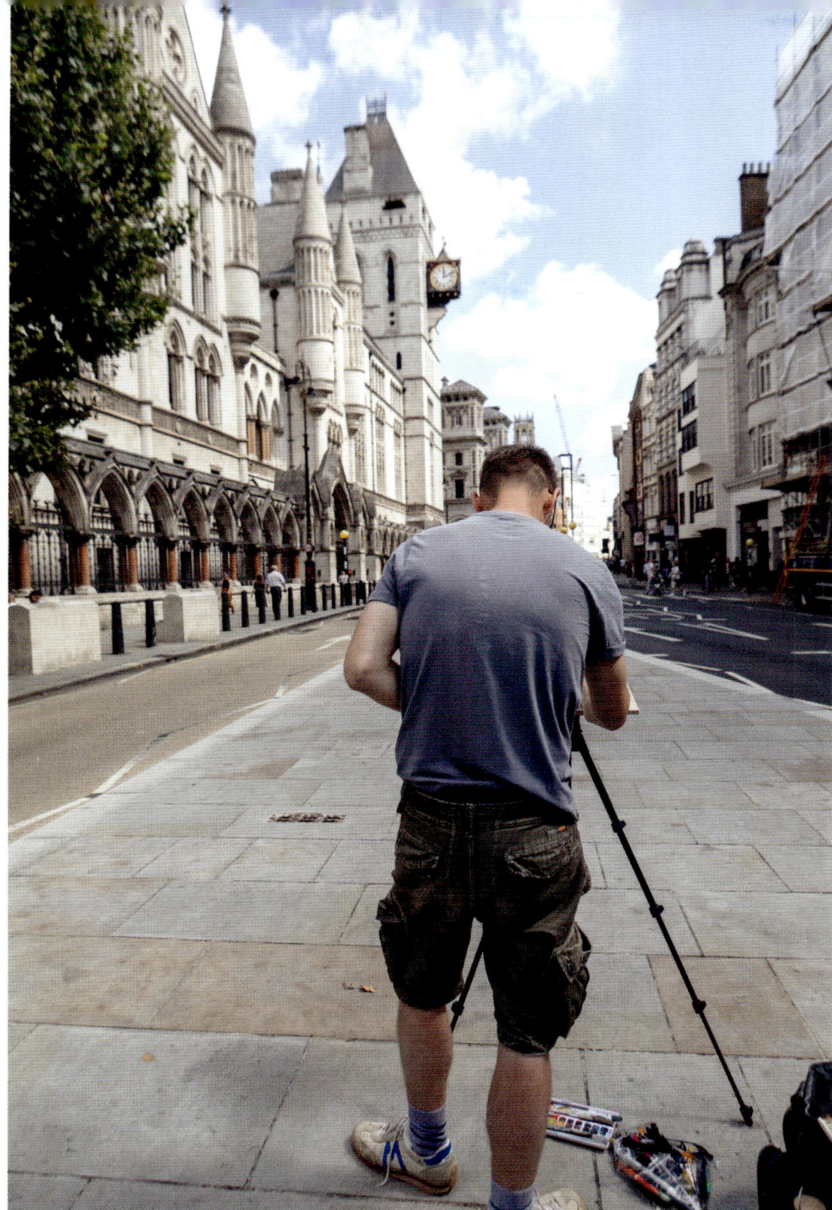

◄ First up, the crop. With so much on view I kept to my standard one-point perspective arrangement and focused on keeping the vanishing point off-centre. I first plotted the boundaries of my view with light pencil marks, effectively masking a good amount of the scene from my page.

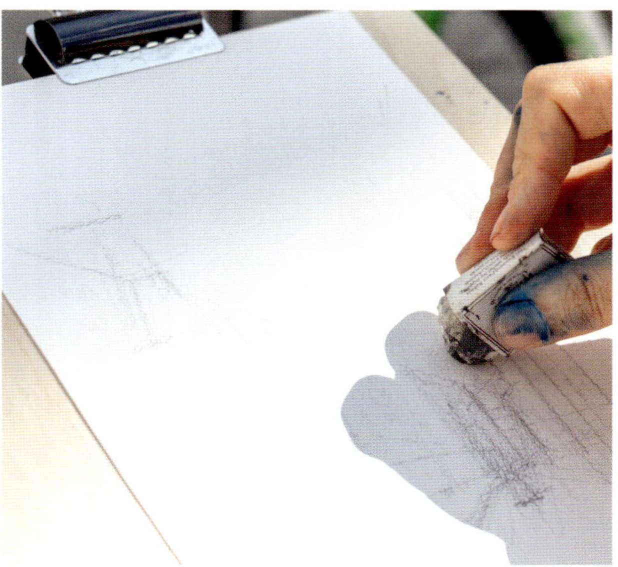

◄ The pencil process is a good option if you're working at a larger scale than normal but it's important not to get into too much detail. I concentrate on marking out relative heights and key window sizes as a guide to the pen sketch which will follow.

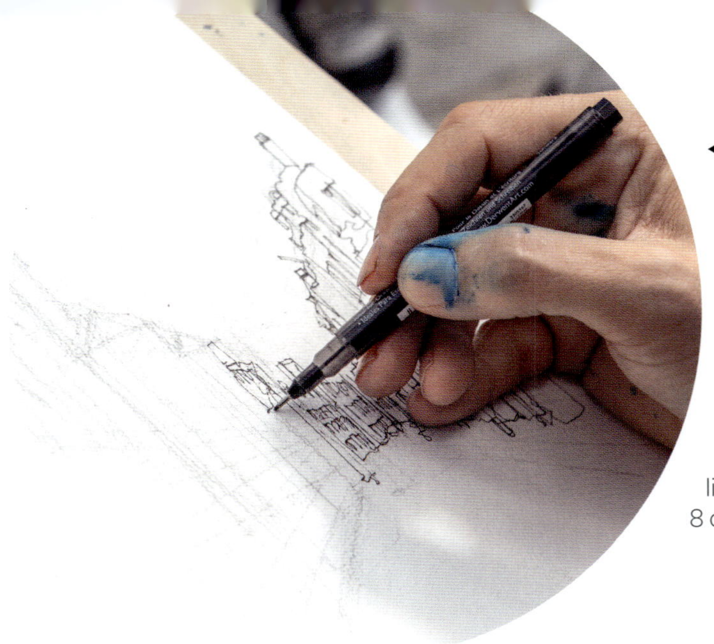

▼ The detail on the right was very complex, so I set about simplifying the shapes of the buildings and used the window angles and shapes to show the direction of travel to the vanishing point. I suggested a hint of detail at best and the tiniest of window outlines, emphasizing the shop front archways, shop signs and the distant outline of people and movement. Windows were mere slits and simple rectangles. Never aiming for perfection and certainly not using a ruler, I worked the right-hand side, keeping the lines solid and not offering up any cross hatching. The buildings featured all manner of detail and decoration under the eaves and in the brick work and this detail just invites a flow of shapes.

The next step was to focus on the very distant detail – a process I really enjoy as the relative size of background details really starts to make the scale and depth appear. The distant skyline was varied by roof peaks and chimneys which always helps add character to a cityscape and avoids a flat roof that can so easily be drawn too rigid and look out of place. I made sure the keep the pen flowing back and forth from foreground to background by simply loosening the pressure to indicate the pavement. These lighter, back-and-forth lines, act almost like a capillary for my ink and the eye to travel around the scene. Keeping them light and frequent offered just enough evidence for the pavement to appear.

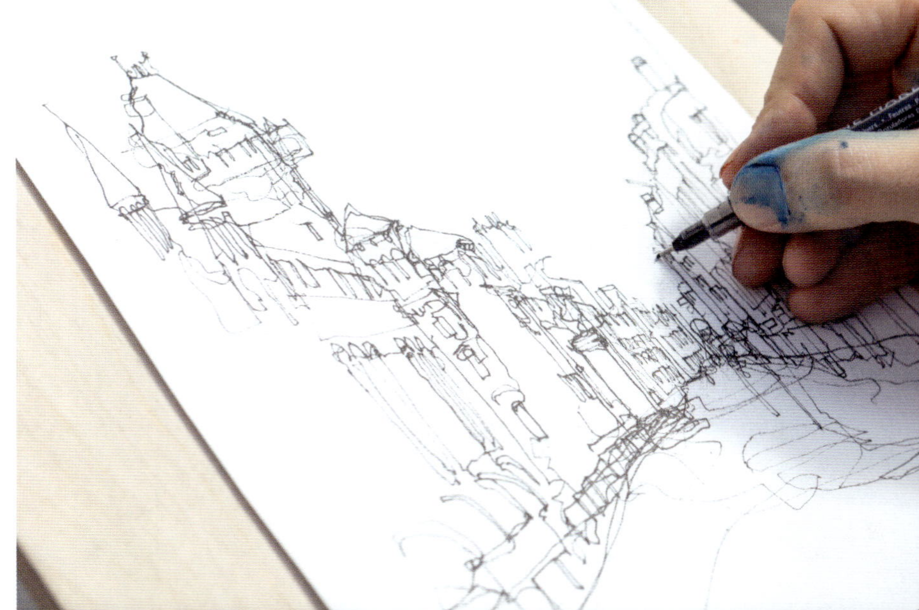

▼ The next task was to focus on the more dominant left-hand side with
the very prominent tower, tall windows, various spires and archways.
To tackle this I elected to try and work a little faster. I had the core sizes
down in pencil but I was very wary of getting caught in the immense
complexity on show. Line quality stayed loose across the spires and
tower roof. The lower archways and posts on the pavement help give
more guides to the height. I wasn't concerned about what I didn't draw.
There's plenty not included, but as a pen sketch I was very happy with
where it was. It was at this point that I made the decision to leave the
sky out – not my usual method. The sky was in effect going to be my
dominant negative space.

The buildings had a similar shade but in the moving sunshine, the
resulting shadows created quite a varying range of tones. It was on this
that I wanted to focus my paint – picking out the darks and bright colours
being enhanced by the sun.

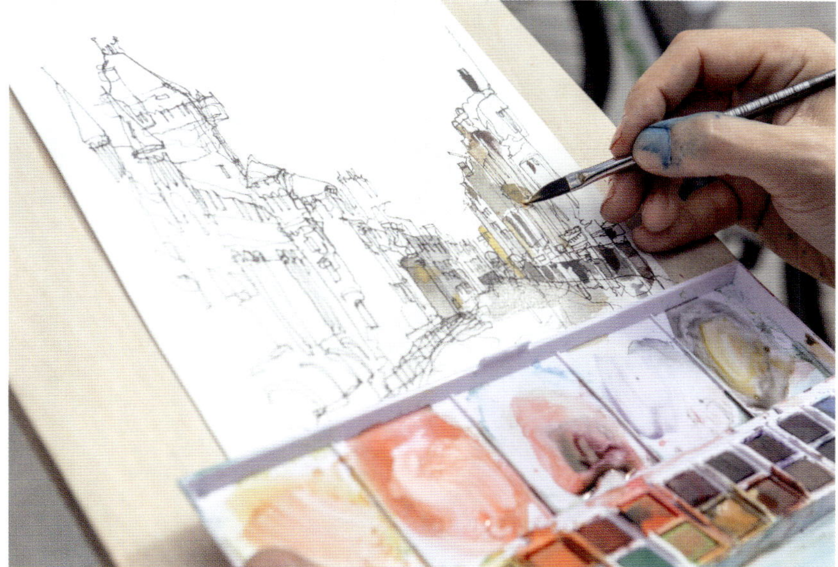

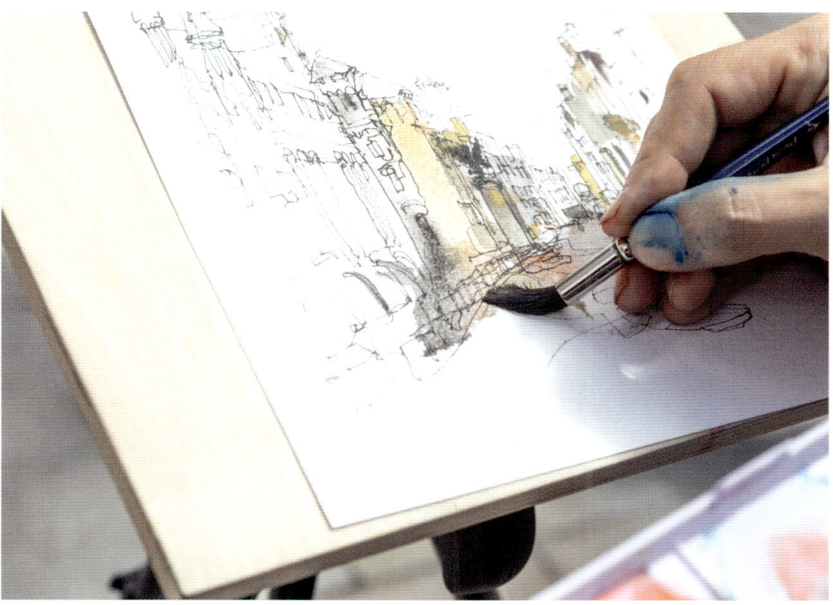

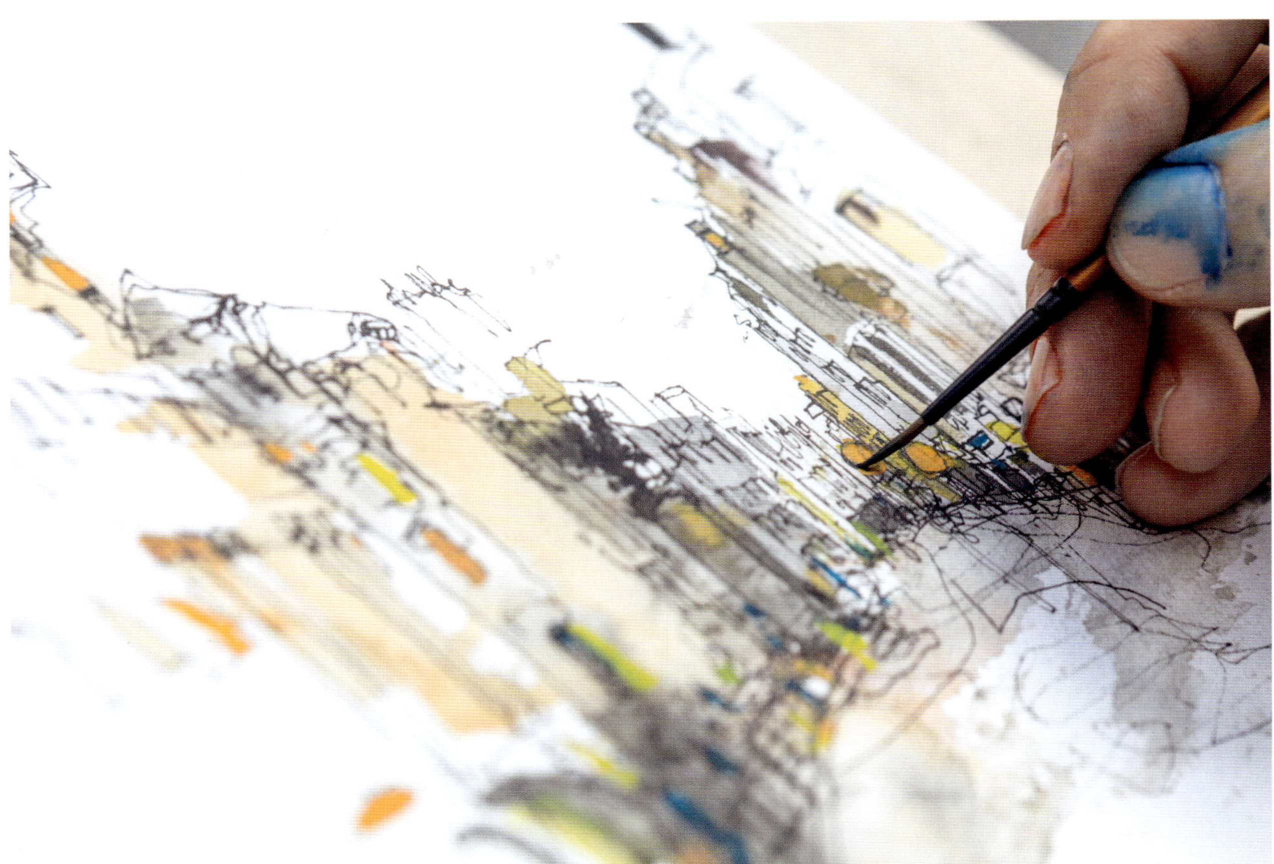

▲ The orange of the street signs, the gold decoration in the clock, the varying browns and reds in the brick work and the road surface all set my palette. Using a combination of brushes including a detailing brush, I made a start, simply colouring some key building shapes with my chosen colour range. The larger brush helped me offer a graduated wash to the road surface. Once almost dry, I made sure to rework some of the lines and bring up some key contrasts on some of the foreground detail. Another splash of yellow and orange was added to highlight certain aspects of the scene.

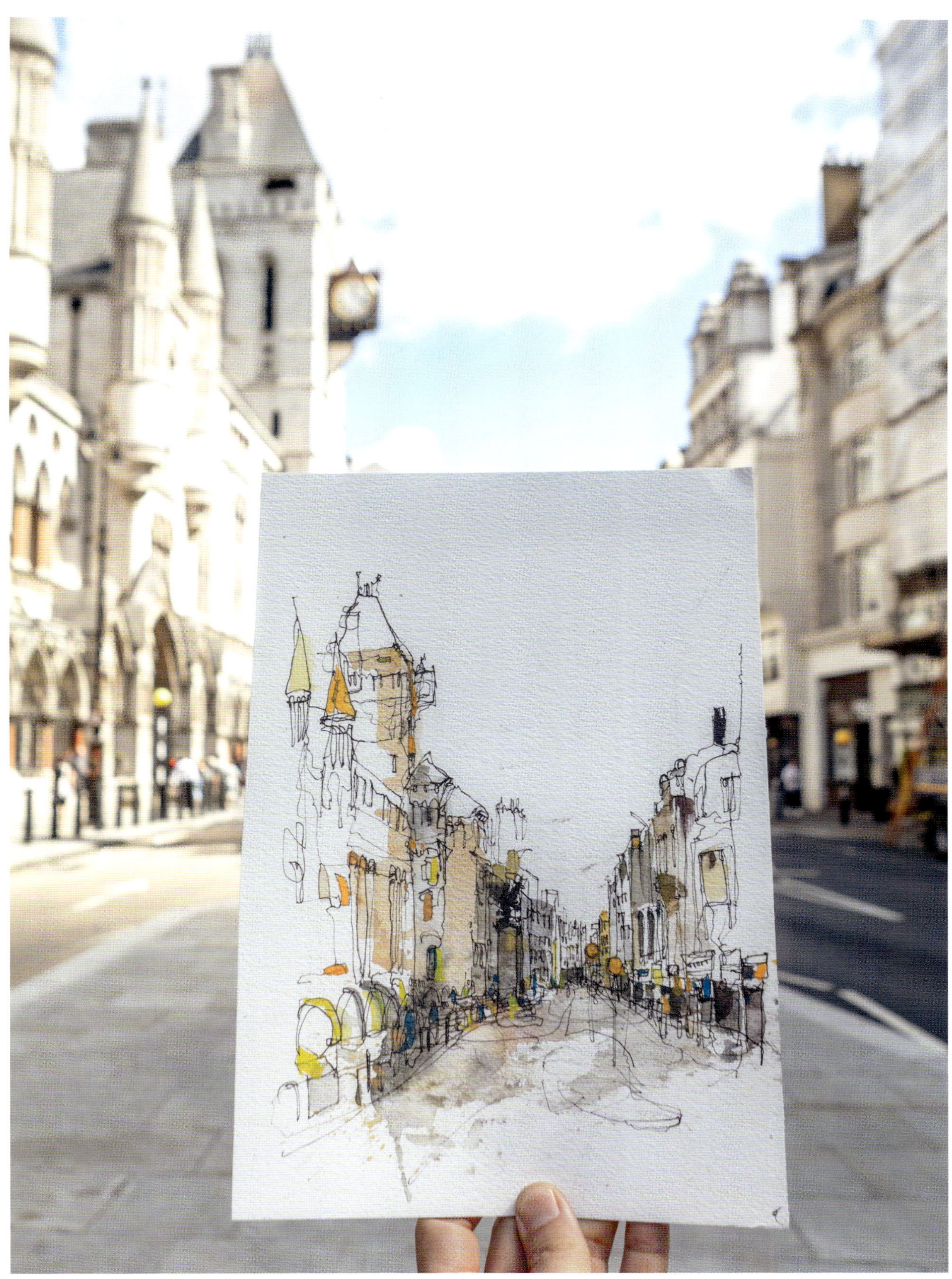

Going further

It doesn't need to stop at your travel sketchbook.

Levelling up to A4 (210 x 297mm/8¼ x 11½in), A3 (297 x 420mm/11¾ x 16½in) and even A2 (420 x 594mm/16½ x 23½in) is entirely possible, and the more I work in line and wash, the more I find I have become better at working larger. Of course, a larger scale demands thicker pens, bigger brushes and more paint. Portability will also become a challenge, but there's something deeply satisfying about framing a large work.

What urban landscape sketching can give you is the springboard to work on more considered studio works. The mighty sketchbook is a collection of ideas, observation and experiments that can fuel the next stage in your development. Don't be afraid to see it as simply the beginning. I have been fortunate to exhibit at galleries and exhibitions and almost all my large studio pieces began life with me stood on a street with a palette in one hand and my sketchpad perched on the wall.

As you progress as an artist and gain confidence in your ability, I encourage you to experiment, challenge what books tell you and find what works best for you. Sketching should be fun; it should capture the scene but leave room for creativity. Follow artists you admire on social media (I know I did, and still do), ask them questions, get yourself to shows, and support artists where you can.

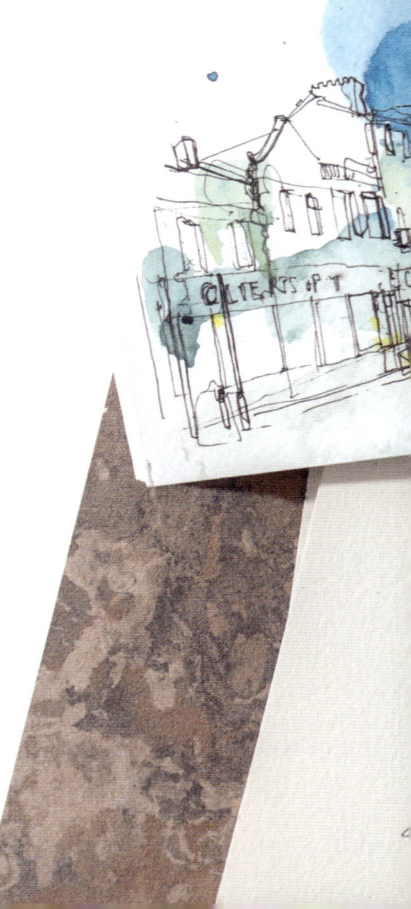

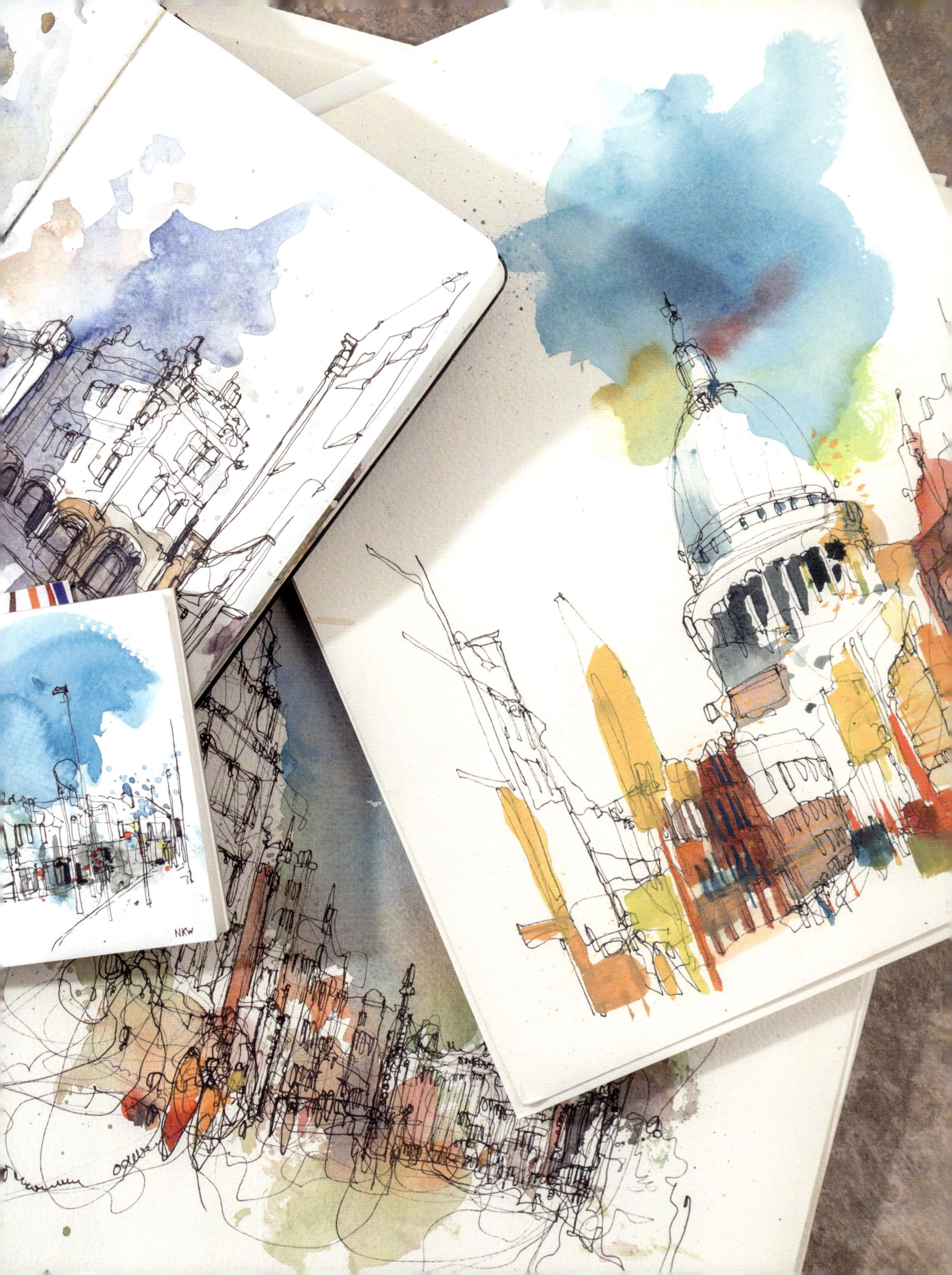
NKW

Index